19/95

The Process of
QUESTION ANSWERING
A Computer Simulation of Cognition

WENDY G. LEHNERT
Yale University

 LAWRENCE ERLBAUM ASSOCIATES, PUBLISHERS
1978   Hillsdale, New Jersey

DISTRIBUTED BY THE HALSTED PRESS DIVISION OF
JOHN WILEY & SONS
New York   Toronto   London   Sydney

To my mother,
Grace Lehnert

QA
76.9
Q4
L43

Lawrence Erlbaum Associates, Inc., Publishers
62 Maria Drive
Hillsdale, New Jersey 07642

Distributed solely by Halsted Press Division

Library of Congress Cataloging in Publication Data
Lehnert Wendy G.
  The process of question answering.

  Includes bibliographical references and index.
  1. Question-answering systems.   I. Title.
QA76.9.Q4L43   001.53'9   78-14743
ISBN 0-470-26485-3

Printed in the United States of America

Contents

Preface

The functions of the human mind may well be the most impenetrable frontiers challenging science today. Neurophysiology, cybernetics, cognitive psychology, and various schools of behavioral psychology are all fields of inquiry that have attempted to investigate how the mind works. It is significant that none of these disciplines have produced a theory of human question answering. The process of answering questions seems to exist at a level of description that is either too high (for neurophysiology and cybernetics) or too low (for most of psychology). Yet the process of question answering is a phenomenon that relies on many realms of human cognition: language comprehension, memory retrieval, and language generation. A theory of human question answering must necessarily entail a theory of human memory organization and theories of the cognitive processes that access and manipulate information in memory.

Most people would not feel deeply disturbed by the phrase, "the art of question answering." If story telling and teaching can be arts, why not question answering as well? But the phrase, "the science of question answering," seems to jostle our sensibilities much more violently. There is no scientific discipline devoted to the study of question answering. Furthermore, it is difficult to imagine how such a phenomenon could be studied scientifically or to imagine what the resulting body of knowledge would tell us.

Question answering can be viewed as one particular task in human information processing. The idea of human information processing is itself fairly recent and is consequently not recognized as the object of any established scientific discipline. Theories of general information processing are traditionally mathematical theories motivated by problems in computer science. But a growing number of researchers in computer science and psychology are now finding it useful to study people in terms of their information processing abilities. It is from this perspective that we can systematically investigate phenomena in question answering.

When we study question answering as a problem in information processing, we are seeking answers to problems often studied by psychologists, but we are using methods from computer science. Most importantly, we have borrowed from computer science the notion of a rigorous process model. Our theories must be specified with sufficient detail so that they can be implemented by computer programs. This level of detailed specification distinguishes theoretical models proposed by artificial intelligence from theoretical models in psychology. The difference is analogous to instructing someone to multiply two numbers together, versus instructing someone to multiply two numbers by means of a particular algorithm. By forcing ourselves to be concerned with the precise form of information in memory, and the precise operations manipulating that information, we can uncover significant problems that would otherwise be overlooked.

This book describes question answering as a particular task in information processing. The theoretical models described here have been built on a foundation of general theories in natural language processing: theories about language that were developed without the specific problem of question answering in mind. Wherever this previous research is exploited, introductory material has been supplied for the uninitiated. It is hoped that enough background and motivating explanations have been provided so that readers from a variety of disciplines can understand the process models described without additional reading or previous preparation. There are references for those who wish to enhance their understanding but these are supplementary materials rather than suggested prerequisites. It is probable that most readers will be drawn from the fields of psychology, linguistics, and computer science, but it is not necessary for the reader to have had any specific training in any one of these fields.

Although the work presented here was ultimately motivated by an interest in human thought processes, its initial motivation was somewhat more pragmatic. I was originally involved in a research project devoted to computerized story-understanding systems: Computer programs were being designed to read paragraphs of text and generate memory representations for what was read. When people understand stories, they can demonstrate their understanding by answering questions about the story. Because questions can be devised to query any aspect of text comprehension, the ability to answer questions is the strongest possible demonstration of understanding. Question answering can therefore be thought of as a task criterion for evaluating reading skills.

If a computer is said to understand a story, we must demand of the computer the same demonstrations of understanding that we require of people. Until such demands are met, we have no way of evaluating text-understanding programs. Any computer programmer can write a program that inputs text. If the programmer assures us that the program "understands" text, it is a bit like being reassured by a used car dealer about a suspiciously low speedometer reading. Only when we can ask a program to answer questions about what it reads will we be in a position to assess that program's comprehension.

The research described here was conducted over a 2-year period while I was a graduate student in the Department of Computer Science at Yale University and a member of the Yale Artificial Intelligence Project. During that time, a number of people contributed in various ways to the work behind this book. Roger Schank, my thesis advisor, introduced me to the joys of natural language processing and has remained a constant source of guiding light. I am also grateful to Robert Abelson, Christopher Riesbeck, and Robert Wilensky for many hours of stimulating conversation and spirited arguments. And special thanks must go to all my New Haven friends, from Yale and elsewhere, for diverting me so thoroughly and pleasantly at those crucial times when little else matters.

Finally, I would also like to acknowledge the cordial efforts of Daniel Bobrow, who invited me to spend a summer at Xerox PARC while he and Terry Winograd worked on a new programming language, KRL. One of the computer programs described here (COIL) was written in an experimental implementation of KRL during my stay at Xerox.

The research reported here was supported by the Advanced Research Projects Agency of the Department of Defense and was monitored by the Office of Naval Research under contract No. N00014-75-C-1111.

WENDY G. LEHNERT

1
Problems, Previews, and Programs

1.0 INTRODUCTION

Question answering is a process. If we wish to program a computer to answer questions, we need some sense of what that process looks like. Human question answering is not merely lexical manipulation; the cognitive mechanisms used in question answering operate on concepts underlying language. The processes of question answering must therefore be characterized as manipulations of conceptual information. This thesis presents a process model of question answering as a theory of conceptual information processing.

The difficulties involved in natural language question answering (Q/A) are not obvious. People are largely unconscious of the cognitive processes involved in answering a question, and are consequently insensitive to the complexities of those processes. It is therefore necessary to become acquainted with the variety and scope of the difficulties involved; the problems intrinsic to question answering must be made visible. There is no way to consciously monitor how questions are understood, how memory is searched for an answer, or how that answer is expressed in language. A question is heard, and an answer surfaces. It is very hard to appreciate the complexity of a process that is effortless and unconscious. But if we examine some examples of questions and answers, we can begin to realize how much is involved in the fundamental and "simple" human ability to answer questions.

1.1 WHAT IS HARD ABOUT ANSWERING QUESTIONS?

Before a question can be answered, it must be understood. The processes used in understanding questions operate on various levels. To see how many kinds of interpretive processes are involved, we will look at some of the ways that ques-

1

tions can fail to make sense. From there we examine problems related to memory retrieval and the processes that operate on memory in order to form an answer.

1.1-1 Conceptual Analysis

Imagine that as you are walking down the street, a well-dressed stranger comes up to you and says:

Q: Pardon me, but do you kronfid grodding slib?

Chances are you will not understand this question. Your failure to understand it occurs at the lowest possible level — lexical processing. The first step of interpretive processing maps the lexical question to a conceptual structure; combinations of words are given meaning. This conceptual analysis is the only interpretive process involved in question answering that is language dependent. If I know only English, I cannot understand questions in other languages. Once a question has been successfully mapped from its lexical expression to a conceptualization, the subsequent interpretive processes are all language independent. If I am learning Russian, I must learn a vocabulary and grammar in order to understand questions stated in Russian, but I do not need to acquire new cognitive processes for understanding a question in Russian once I know its conceptual meaning.

Principle #1:
The Memory Processes of Question Answering
Are Independent of Language

The analytic mechanisms that map words into concepts when a question is understood are language dependent. Similarly, the generational mechanisms that express concepts in words are also language dependent. But the cognitive mechanisms of memory that make inferences about questions and search memory for an answer operate on a conceptual level independent of language.

1.1-2 Reference Recognition

In the course of obtaining a conceptual interpretation, various memory processes operate to see whether all nominal references in the question are understood. For example, if I ask you:

Q: Which is bigger, a basenji or a komondor?

the question makes some sense conceptually, even if the words *basenji* and *komondor* are totally alien. We can understand the question as asking for a size comparison between two things. But if the question refers to something completely unheard of, the question is not fully understood on the level of reference recognition.

Principle #2:
Questions Are Understood on Many Different Levels

Full reference recognition does not guarantee that a question can be answered, but a lack of reference recognition does guarantee that a question cannot be answered (at least knowledgeably). If it is known that basenjis and komondors are two breeds of dog, and nothing more is known about either breed, reference recognition will have been achieved, although the question will still be unanswerable. But if a conceptual reference for either basenjis or komondors is missing, the question cannot possibly be answered.

1.1-3 Conceptual Categorization

If a question has been understood conceptually, it is ready to be classified conceptually. A conceptual categorization of a question determines which memory processes will be invoked to attempt further interpretation. Suppose two people want to have dinner together, but neither of them has any money and there is no food at home. In this context, consider the following exchange:

Q: How are we going to eat tonight?
A: With silverware.

This answer indicates that the question was not interpreted correctly. It was placed in the wrong conceptual category. The answer indicates that the question was understood to be asking about the instruments required in eating. But in the context given, the question should have been understood to be asking about the enabling conditions for eating. The question should be conceptually equivalent to asking, "What are we going to do in order to eat tonight? How are we going to solve this problem?"

Principle #3:
Understanding Questions Requires
Conceptual Categorization

In this thesis we propose 13 conceptual categories for questions. Two of these distinguish between questions that ask about enabling conditions and those that ask about instrumentality. When a question is properly interpreted, it will be assigned to only one conceptual category. All answers to questions are produced by assuming only one conceptual categorization. When a question is conceptually ambiguous (can be assigned to more than one conceptual category), the person being addressed must either clarify the question before attempting to answer it or guess to which category it should be assigned and answer it on that basis. Conceptual categorization guides the subsequent processing of a question by dictating which interpretive mechanisms and memory-retrieval strategies are to be executed.

1.1-4   Understanding Within Context

The proper conceptual categorization of questions is dependent on the context in which the question occurs. Suppose I had been fixing dinner for you at my house and that just as I was about to set the table, I remembered that I had lent all my silverware to a friend. If I explain this to you and then ask:

   Q: How are we going to eat tonight?

it would be quite reasonable for you to respond:

   A: With our hands.

Your answer is reasonable in the sense that it addresses the instrumentality of eating. Instrumentality is clearly what the question should be interpreted as asking about in this context. But when the same question was asked in the context of having neither food nor money, an answer that responded to instrumental interpretation was inappropriate.

Principle #4:
Context Affects Conceptual Categorization

The processes which assign the proper conceptual category to a question must be sensitive to the context in which that question is asked. Questions cannot be correctly understood by processes that do not consider contextual factors.

1.1-5   Conversational Interpretation

In human question-answering dialogues, rules of conversational continuity are often invoked during the interpretative processing of questions:

   John: Did Bill go to class?
   Mary: No, he didn't.
   John: Why not?
   Mary: He was sick.

   John: Did Bill go to class?
   Mary: I don't know.
   John: Why not?
   Mary: I wasn't there.

In both these dialogues, John asks Mary "Why not?" In the first dialogue, he means, "Why didn't Bill go to class?" In the second he means, "Why don't you know whether Bill went to class?" Rules of conversational continuity are needed in cases like this to complete a partial question correctly.

Principle #5:
Rules of Conversational Continuity
Are Needed to Understand Some Questions

The mechanism that operates in cases like these is really very simple: When Mary has to interpret a question of John's in terms of previous dialogue, she needs to know only the last concept communicated to John. In the first dialogue, Mary told John that Bill did not go to class. When John asks "Why not?" she combines his partial question with the last concept communicated to him to get the question, "Why didn't Bill go to class?" In the second dialogue, Mary told John that she does not know whether Bill went to class. When John asks "Why not?" she combines his partial question with the last concept communicated to get, "Why don't you know whether Bill went to class?"

1.1-6 Inferences

Many questions rely on the listener's ability to infer something implicit in the question in order to correctly interpret that question:

Q: Do you drink?
A: Of course. All humans drink.

Q: Who wasn't in class yesterday?
A: George Washington and Moby Dick.

Q: Would you like to dance?
A: Sure. You know anyone who wants to?

Although the answers given to these questions may be technically correct, they seem to have missed the point. One suspects that "Do you drink?" is intended to mean "Do you drink liquor?" and that "Who wasn't in class yesterday?" must have meant "Who wasn't in class yesterday who should have been there?" Finally, "Would you like to dance?" should have been understood to mean "Would you like to dance with me?" If these inferences are not made, answers that are literally correct but totally inappropriate will be given.

Principle #6:
A Good Answer Is More Than a Correct Answer:
Appropriateness Also Counts

When a question relies on the listener's ability to make inferences, missing information may be derived from the conversational context of the question:

John: Hello, Mary! Thanks for inviting me over.
Mary: I'm glad you could come. Sit down.
John: You certainly have a cheerful kitchen.

Mary: It was just painted. Some coffee?
John: No thanks, I don't drink coffee.

In this conversation, "Some coffee?" is an offer. Mary is asking John whether he would like a cup of coffee. To interpret this question as an offer, we must infer that Mary is in a setting in which she has access to coffee (she is not on a subway), that Mary must have a cordial relationship with John (he is not a rapist), and that they must be together (the question makes no sense over the phone).

John: Hello, Mary! Thanks for inviting me over.
Mary: Would you like something to drink?
John: Some coffee?
Mary: Sure.

Now "Some coffee?" is a polite response to an offer already made. John is saying he would like some coffee if she has any. Conversational context is a determining factor in the correct interpretation of these questions.

1.1-7   Knowledge-Based Interpretation

Very often we interpret questions correctly because we have knowledge about the world, things people do, and why they do such things. For example, suppose Mary hears that her friend John roller-skated to McDonald's last night. She may very well ask:

Q: Why did John roller-skate to McDonald's last night?

If someone answers her question:

A: Because he was hungry.

she will be justifiably impatient; she was not told what she wanted to know. Chances are she really wanted to know:

Q: Why did John roller-skate instead of walk or drive or use some other reasonable means of transportation?

She was asking about the act of roller-skating, not the destination. A cooperative and reasonable respondent would have interpreted her question as asking about the roller-skating. But what tells us which part of her question should be addressed? How do we know that the act of roller-skating should receive attention, rather than the destination? This is a problem in knowledge-based focus establishment.

Principle #7:
Shifts in Interpretive Focus
Alter Meaning

Some questions are not fully understood until their focus has been determined. In many cases, the focus of a question can be established only by knowing how the world works and which things are more interesting than which other things.

In the example just given, the focus of our question is "obvious," because adults frequently go to drive-in restaurants but they do not normally roller-skate. For most adults, going roller-skating is more unusual than going to McDonald's; it requires explanation. But if everyone knew that John was an eccentric health-food nut who roller-skates every where he goes, the question:

Q: Why did John roller-skate to McDonald's?

would reasonably be interpreted as asking about McDonald's, not the roller-skating. Our knowledge about John and what constitutes strange behavior for him would override our general knowledge about what people normally do and don't do.

Principle #8 :
Focus Directs Attention to
Variations on Expectations

Interpretation of a question may force the listener's attention to favor some conceptual component of the question. Attention is generally drawn to those things that are unusual or that violate expectations.

In spoken dialogues, intonation patterns in speech very often establish the focus of a question. If *McDonald's* is stressed, the speaker is clearly interested in that particular component of the question. But in written questions, no such clues exist (unless we have italicized words). When no verbal (or visual) stress marks the focus of a question, heuristics must be involved to determine which elements of the question are most deserving of attention. Attention naturally centers on the unexpected, neglecting those things that are predictable.

1.1-8 Memory-Based Interpretation

Sometimes a question does not have any conceptual components that are inherently deserving of focus on the basis of general world knowledge or specific knowledge of individual behavior. If I were to ask you:

Q: Why did John ask Mary to mail the card?

you cannot establish the focus of this question by looking for what seems to be the most interesting thing in the question. The whole question looks rather commonplace. People often ask each other to do things, and there is nothing very interesting about mailing a card.

The focus of a question like this one relies solely on specific knowledge of the episode to which the question refers. Depending on the situation, this question could be answered:

A: Because Susan wasn't there.
A: Because he couldn't afford a personal delivery service.
A: Because he had no right to order her.

The answer "Because Susan wasn't there" could be a response to two possible interpretations of the question. The question ("Why did John ask Mary to mail the card?") could be asking either about John as the actor or about Mary as the recipient of John's request. The answer could therefore mean either that John asked Mary because Susan was not there to ask Mary, or that John asked Mary because Susan was not there to be asked. If the question occurred in a real context (e.g., in reference to a story) there would be no ambiguity to the answer, for only one would make sense in the context. "Because he couldn't afford a personal delivery service" is an answer that can be produced only if the question is interpreted as asking about the act of mailing. And "Because he had no right to order her" comes about by interpreting the question as asking about the act of asking. It would be easy to make up stories for which each of these three answers makes sense.

Principle #9:
Ambiguity of Focus
Rarely Occurs in Context

When a question like this one is answered in the context of a story, focus is immediately established on the basis of what is in our memory. If we heard a story in which John was going to ask Susan to mail a card for him, but ended up asking Mary because Susan was busy, then the question will immediately be understood to be asking about Mary vs. Susan. Other possible interpretations that would have resulted from different focus establishment are never considered.

1.1-9   Selecting the Best Answer

Once a question has been fully interpreted, it is time to look for an answer. The memory search to be conducted is guided by the conceptual category of the question at hand. An immediate problem arises when the memory search turns up more than one reasonable answer to a question. For example, consider the following story:

> John took a bus to New York. Then he took a subway to Leone's. But on the subway his pocket was picked. He went into Leone's and had some lasagna. When the check came, he realized he could not pay the check. He had to wash dishes.

If asked:

Q: Why did John wash dishes at Leone's?

we would have many reasonable answers to this question:

A: Because he couldn't pay the check.

A: Because he had no money.

A: Because he had his pocket picked.

All of these answers are perfectly correct, but the last one seems the best according to the information conveyed. Knowing that John had his pocket picked, one can infer that he had no money and therefore could not pay the check. But if we were told that he could not pay the check or that he had no money, there is still a missing causality: Why couldn't he pay the check? Why didn't he have any money? In fact, the first two answers are poor because not being able to pay a check can be inferred from washing dishes in a restaurant, and not having (enough) money can be inferred from not being able to pay the check. An answer that provides the questioner with new information is preferable to one that tells the questioner something he could have inferred for himself.

Principle # 10:
The More Inferences an Answer Carries,
the Better the Answer

When the memory search seeks an answer, it must take into account what the questioner can be expected to know on the basis of the question asked. The total information conveyed by an answer is not contained by the explicit answer alone. Inferences made by the questioner upon hearing the answer augment the explicit answer. An answer must be chosen on the basis of the inferences it carries.

1.1-10 State Descriptions

Suppose John is eating in a dining car, and, when the train starts up, his soup spills. Something very interesting happens when people answer the question:

Q: Where was the soup?

In an informal experiment, answers to this question tended to say one of two things: in a bowl or on the table. This is very interesting when considered in view of everything people know about the setting of a dining car and how people eat in dining cars. People can infer that the soup was in a bowl, the bowl was on a plate, the plate probably rested on a placemat or a tablecloth, which in turn was on a table, and that the table was attached to the floor of the dining car, which was part of the train. So with all of this information, why are the bowl and the table singled out to describe the location of the soup?

Some people will answer the question: "In the dining car." But the answer "On the train" is odd, and it is very hard to imagine anyone's answering, "On the plate." There must be some rules of locational specification that are used to single out salient references. But what are these rules? Suppose there were a rule that told us to specify the immediately contingent object of containment or support. This rule would account for the response:

Q: Where was the soup?
A: In a bowl.

But it would not account for:

Q: Where was the soup?
A: On the table.

What rule accounts for this second answer? It is not enough to specify the closest supporting object, because that rule would result in:

Q: Where was the soup?
A: On a plate.

The conceptual rules that guide locational specification must be general enough to work in a variety of settings. In the train example, it appears safe to specify the immediately contingent object of containment or location, because this rule yields an acceptable answer:

Q: Where was the soup?
A: In a bowl.

But suppose John went into the kitchen and poured himself some milk. Now answer the question:

Q: Where did John get the milk?

A natural answer is, "From the refrigerator." But no one imagines the milk to be sitting in a puddle at the bottom of the refrigerator. There is a milk container of some sort, which is the contingent object of containment. Yet very few people will mention a milk container when describing where the milk was. So a rule that specifies the object of immediate containment will not produce natural answers in all contexts.

To answer questions like these as a person normally would, we must have conceptual representations for objects that tell us the link between milk and milk containers is somehow too obvious to mention, whereas the link between soup and bowls is not. The relational notions of containment and support do not seem to inspire rules of retrieval that are both simple and effective in terms of producing good answers. We must use a conceptual representational system for physical objects to develop simple and effective retrieval rules for locational specification. (The foundations for such a representational system are proposed in this volume.)

Principle #11:
A Difficult Retrieval Problem May Point to
Weaknesses in the Memory Representation

Sometimes questions that ask for locational specification must be answered according to who is asking the question and why:

Q: Where is Deerfield, Illinois?
A: 87° 54′longitude, 42° 12′ latitude.
A: Near Lake Michigan, about 20 miles north of Chicago.
A: Next to Highland Park.
A: On the planet Earth.

Each of these answers is correct, but in any given context some of them will be useless. If John lives in Illinois and his neighbor asks him where Deerfield is, he will probably not appreciate an answer specifying the longitudinal and latitudinal descriptors. Chances are he would find "On the planet Earth" a stupid answer. Yet there are contexts in which each of these answers would be appropriate. An airline pilot might prefer the first answer, and a nonearthling character in a novel might find the last answer to be the most meaningful. When people answer questions, they must often assess the knowledge state of the person they are addressing. "Next to Highland Park" is a good answer only if the questioner knows where Highland Park is. "Near Lake Michigan, about 30 miles north of Chicago" is likely to satisfy anyone who has a rough familiarity with the United States. 87° 54′ longitude, 42° 12′ latitude" is a good answer only when a technical global specification is required. "On the planet Earth" is a poor answer to anyone who lives on earth.

Principle #12:
Good Answers Can Involve
Knowledge-State Assessment

This problem of finding a suitable description when answering questions of locational specification was described by Donald Norman (1972) as the Empire State Building problem (Where is the Empire State Building?). Locational-specification questions illustrate very clearly how answers must strive to fill in the gaps of the questioner's knowledge state.

1.1-11 Content Specification

Somewhere in the question-answering process, a decision must be made about how much information will be put into the answer. For that matter, the system must be able to decide whether the question is going to be answered honestly, deceptively, sarcastically, or in any other of a hundred different ways. For example, suppose questions are asked about the following story:

John went to a restaurant and ordered a hot dog. But the waitress said they didn't have any so he had a hamburger instead.

If asked:

Q: Did John eat a hot dog?

There are at least three ways in which this question could reasonably be answered:

A: No.
A: No, John ate a hamburger.
A: No, John ate a hamburger because there were no hot dogs.

Each of these answers is correct, but each provides a different amount of information. Some part of the question-answering process must be sensitive to factors that control the system's disposition toward reliability and relative information content. There must be mechanisms that control memory-retrieval processes and provide instructions about how an answer is to be constructed.

Principle #13:
The Same Question Does Not
Always Get the Same Answer

A question-answering system must be able to instruct its retrieval mechanisms how to form answers so that the system does not always return the same answer to the same question. Answers must vary appropriately in response to contextual and motivational factors.

1.1-12 Accessing the Memory

When a story is read, a conceptual structure representing the story is generated in memory that encodes events mentioned in the story and inferences made by the reader at the time of understanding (Schank, 1974b, 1975b). This structure is language independent, existing as a purely conceptual record of the story. When answering questions about a story, this story representation is accessed by memory searches. Question answering is therefore concerned with the form of information in memory and the processes which access that information. In designing memory representations for stories, some assumptions must be made about what belongs in a story representation. When a story describes a chronological sequence of events, it is reasonable to assume that the events preserved in the story representation should encode only information about something that happened either as an event mentioned explicitly in the story or as one inferred by the reader. For example, if a story says that John ate a hamburger at a restaurant, the memory representation should contain the inference that John ordered a hamburger, but it should not contain negative information like the fact that John did not order a pizza.

When answering questions about a story, the story representation that was generated at the time of understanding is examined by memory searches. But at times, the story representation alone is not adequate for finding an answer, and more inferences must be made at the time of question answering. For example, if we adhere to the assumption that a story representation should contain information only about what happened (and what we infer must have happened), then how can we go about answering questions about things that did not happen?

John went to a restaurant and ordered a hamburger. But the waitress said they didn't have any, so John left.

If asked:

Q: Why didn't John eat a hamburger?

We can find nothing in our story representation about eating a hamburger (or about eating anything, for that matter). The story representation simply records a chain of events, which includes John going into the restaurant, sitting down, the waitress coming over, John telling her he wants a hamburger, the waitress telling him there are none, and John getting up and leaving. Yet we should be able to answer this question with a response like, "Because they didn't have any."

Principle #14:
Sometimes Inferences Must Be Made
at the Time of Question Answering

Some additional inference mechanisms must be invoked in order to produce this answer. If, in the context of this story, we had been asked, "Why didn't John swim across the lake?" the question would not make sense. The inference mechansims invoked to answer these questions are capable of seeing when a why-not question makes sense by determining whether the act would have occurred had the story taken a different turn. "Why didn't John eat a hamburger?" makes sense because we expected him to eat a hamburger after he ordered, until the waitress told him there were none. But "Why didn't John swim across the lake?" makes no sense in this story, because we never expected him to swim across a lake.

1.1-13   Constructing Information

People are able to answer many questions by deriving information that is not explicitly present in memory for straightforward retrieval.

Q: Who was President when you were entering the sixth grade?

Q: What is 56 times 8?

Q: How far is New York from Boston?

Each of these questions can be answered, though probably not immediately. The first question may require an associative path from the sixth grade, to your age at that time, to the year, to the President. Or perhaps some event concerning that President occurred at about the time you entered the sixth grade, so that you can answer the question by remembering that event. The multiplication question is likely to require an arithmetic calculation. And the distance question may be a matter of simple retrieval if you happen to "know" that fact. Otherwise the answer could be derived by knowing how long it takes to drive or fly between Boston and New York.

Principle #15:
You Can't Always Expect to Find
Exactly What You Had in Mind

People seem to be very flexible in memory retrieval tasks. When faced with a question like:

Q: How many days does July have?

many people resort to a little rhyme: "30 days hath September, April, June, and November, . . ." But if you ask someone this question on the 31st of July, there is a good chance that they will be able to answer without resorting to the rhyme if they are aware of the date. People tend to know that no month has more than 31 days; so if a month has at least 31 days, it must have exactly 31. If we know that July has at least 31 days, this little bit of reasoning is faster than running through the rhyme.

1.1-14   Finding Only What Is Needed

Efficient retrieval requires an ability to recognize when we have seen enough information to answer the question. Suppose you had read the following:

John boarded the train in Boston Monday morning. He slept most of the afternoon and had dinner in the dining car. Then he played cards in the club car and finally went to bed around 2:00. The train got into Chicago after lunch the next day.

Now if asked:

Q: How long was John on the train?

you will try to piece together as accurate an answer as possible. Running back over the time line of the story, you can piece together his boarding in the morning, the overnight events, and the train's arrival after lunch, thereby arriving at his having been on the train a little over a day. But suppose instead you had been asked:

Q: Did John spend a week on the train?

You can answer "no" to this question much faster than you could answer the previous question. This answer is easily derived from the fact that John spent only one night on the train. No further information from your memory of the story is needed to answer the question. More information had to be examined to answer the first question than was needed for the second.

Principle #16:
A Good Search Strategy Knows When It Has the Answer:
Smart Heuristics Know When to Quit

1.2   WHERE WE ARE GOING

The scope of problems involved in designing a question-answering system ranges in a number of directions and covers a tremendous amount of territory. Section 1.1 does not constitute a definitive survey of problems; it was intended only to convey some sense of the issues we are addressing.

The problems in designing a question-answering system do not exist in isolation from one another; solutions in one area often contribute to solutions elsewhere. It is therefore more productive to view the issues from a vantage point that provides a sense of the entire question-answering process. It would be very difficult to devote a chapter to each problem and still describe a cohesive picture of question answering. For this reason, a process model for question answering is described by following a question from the initial understanding of its words through the final lexical expression of an answer. After this fundamental process model is presented, specific areas of difficulty are identified and discussed in detail.

Within this organization, the problems of the preceding section are distributed throughout as follows:

Chapter 2. *Motivation and Background*   This chapter sets a background for all that follows. We present a brief overview of theories in information processing, including descriptions of Conceptual Dependency, causal chains, scripts, and plans. The notion of process models as theories of human cognition is discussed in both the context of artificial intelligence and cognitive psychology.

Part I. *Interpretation: Understanding Questions*   This overview introduces the processes underlying Principles #1–6. It contains an outline of the interpretive-process model that describes how the issues of conceptual analysis, reference recognition, conceptual categories, understanding within context, conversational interpretation, and inference all fit together in processing a question.

Chapter 3. *Conceptual Categories for Questions*   Chapter 3 elaborates Principle #3 and discusses conceptual categorization. It presents 13 conceptual categories and describes the analysis mechanism that assigns a category to a question.

Chapter 4. *Recategorizing Questions by Inferential Analysis*   Chapter 4 is concerned with Principles #4, 5, and 6. Understanding within context, conversational interpretation, and inferences are all topics in inferential analysis.

Part II. *Memory Searches: Finding an Answer*   This overview of the memory search introduces the processes underlying Principles #7, 8, 9, and 13. Content specification and the memory-search strategies needed to produce an answer are outlined here.

Chapter 5. *Content Specification*   Chapter 5 elaborates Principle #13 and explains how content specification controls the amount of information that goes into an answer.

Chapter 6. *Searching Memory*   Chapter 6 describes search heuristics for finding an answer.

Chapter 7. *Focus Establishment*   Chapter 7 is concerned with Principles #7, 8, and 9. We explore knowledge-based and memory-based interpretation.

Chapter 8. *Understanding What did Not Happen*   Chapter 8 presents an example of Principle #14 by describing a technique for accessing memory.

Chapter 9. *Finding the Best Answer*   Chapter 9 explores Principles #10 and 12. This chapter is primarily concerned with selecting the best answer to a question.

Chapter 10. *Conceptual Primitives for Physical Objects*   Chapter 10 illustrates Principle #11 while exploring problems in state descriptions. We propose a system for representing physical objects by decomposition into primitives.

Chapter 11. *More Problems*   Chapter 11 presents additional aspects of question answering that have not been adequately handled by our current theory.

Chapter 12. *Perspective and Conclusions*   Chapter 12 compares our theory of question answering to other research efforts in computational question answering.

1.2-1 How to Survive the Trip

Whenever one confronts a 12-course dinner, there is always the danger of getting glutted before dessert or maybe even before the main courses. It sometimes helps to know what you are up against before you start.

Throughout the text, many of the illustrations are Conceptual Dependency graphs. A brief overview of Conceptual Dependency is presented in Chapter 2 for unfamiliar readers. This introduction should provide adequate background; however, more thorough introductions can be found in Chapter 3 of *Conceptual Information Processing* (Schank, 1975a) and Chapter 5 of *Computer Models of Thought and Language* (Schank & Colby, 1973).

Chapter 2 also outlines the theory of scripts and plans and their use in story understanding. Further explication of scripts and plans is found in *Scripts, Plans, Goals and Understanding* (Schank & Abelson, 1977). Other introductory references include: Schank & Abelson, 1975; Schank & the Yale A.I. Project, 1975; Cullingford, 1975; Wilensky, 1976; and Lehnert, 1977.

If the reader wants a minimal overview of QUALM, it would be sufficient to read the prefatory chapters of Parts I and II, which serve as introductions to the chapters that describe the basic process model. Part I summarizes Chapters 3 and 4. Part II summarizes Chapters 5 and 6.

The basic process model is described in Chapters 3 through 6. A reader who wants only a basic introduction to the problem could stop after Chapter 6. But anyone interested in the real difficulties will find the more challenging issues discussed in Chapters 7 through 11.

1.3 QUALM

QUALM is a computational model of question answering. As such, there is a computer program that is an implementation of QUALM. This program runs in conjunction with two larger systems, SAM and PAM. Both SAM and PAM are comprehensive story-understanding systems that input stories in English and generate internal memory representations for what they read. These story representations can then be accessed by processes designed to paraphrase, summarize, and answer questions about the stories read. QUALM is responsible for the question-answering capacities of SAM and PAM. Both systems are modularized so that parsers and generators can be attached for different input and output languages. At the moment, SAM and PAM operate with English input and produce paraphrase output in English, Spanish, Russian, Dutch, and Chinese. All of the question answering done by SAM and PAM has been in English. QUALM itself is language independent. No changes would have to be made to QUALM in order for SAM and PAM to understand and answer questions in different languages.

Two experimental programs have been designed in addition to QUALM. These are ASP (Answer Selection Program) and COIL (Conceptual Objects for

Inferencing in Language). Both were designed to explore specific issues relevant to the design of QUALM as a system independent of SAM and PAM.

ASP is a small interactive system that inputs a question about a story, along with a set of possible answers. It asks the user to characterize those answers according to instructions given by the program. ASP then picks out what it considers to be the best answer to the question.

COIL is a larger system designed to generate memory representations for stories and to answer a small variety of questions about them on the basis of its memory representation. COIL incorporates a toy parser and generator, because problems in parsing and generation are peripheral to the theoretical issues addressed by COIL. COIL was primarily designed to see how a new representational system for physical objects could be exploited by inference and retrieval mechanisms.

QUALM is an independent system that can be attached to any story-understanding system generating story representations according to the theories of predictive understanding by scripts and plans. Although the computer implementation of QUALM is limited to the context of answering questions about stories, the theoretical model goes beyond this context. As a theoretical model, QUALM describes question answering in its most general form, as a verbal-communication device between people.

1.4 COMPUTER PROGRAMS USING QUALM

The process model for question answering described in this thesis is currently implemented in two computer programs, SAM and PAM. These two programs have been designed to understand stories and to answer questions about what they read. In the following pages are examples of stories that have been processed by these systems, along with questions and answers. The stories and questions were input in English as they appear here, and the answers given here are the actual English-generated responses returned by the computer.

In all cases, the system first reads the story one sentence at a time and generates a memory representation for that story as it reads. When the story has been completed, questions are asked. The questions are processed and answered one at a time.

The last two programs, ASP and COIL, are experimental systems designed to explore issues raised by QUALM.

1.4-1 SAM

SAM was developed by the Artificial Intelligence Project at Yale. It processed its first story in 1975 and has been undergoing continual expansion ever since. The actual programming of SAM has relied on the persistent efforts of many: Richard Cullingford, Gerald DeJong, Leila Habib, James Meehan, Richard Proudfoot, Christopher Riesbeck, Walter Stutzman, and Robert Wilensky.

The following stories and question-answering dialogues represent actual input and output. The stories and questions were read by the system just as they appear here. The answers are the exact English outputs generated by SAM.

John went to a restaurant. The hostess seated John. The hostess gave John a menu. The waiter came to the table. John ordered a lobster. He was served quickly. He left a large tip. He left the restaurant.

Why did John go to the restaurant?
SO JOHN COULD EAT A MEAL.

Did John go to a table?
JOHN WENT TO A TABLE.

Why did John go to a table?
SO JOHN COULD SIT DOWN IN A CHAIR.

Did the waiter give John a menu?
JOHN GOT A MENU FROM THE HOSTESS.

Who gave John a menu?
JOHN GOT A MENU FROM THE HOSTESS.

Why did the hostess give John a menu?
SO JOHN COULD ASK THE WAITER FOR A MEAL.

What happened when the hostess gave John a menu?
JOHN READ THE MENU, THE WAITER SAW THAT JOHN WAS AT THE TABLE, THE WAITER WENT TO THE TABLE.

Did John enjoy the lobster?
I DON'T KNOW.

Did the waiter give John the check?
JOHN GOT THE CHECK FROM THE WAITER.

Why did John leave the waiter a large tip?
PROBABLY JOHN REMEMBERED THE WAITER SERVED JOHN A LOBSTER QUICKLY.

Did John pay the bill?
JOHN PAID THE CHECK.

Why did John pay the check?
SO JOHN COULD LEAVE THE RESTAURANT.

John went to a restaurant. He sat down. He got mad. He left.

Did a waiter come to the table?
NO.

Did John order?
NO.

John went to New York by bus. On the bus he talked to an old lady. When he left the bus, he thanked the driver. He took the subway to Leone's. On the subway his pocket was picked. He got off the train and entered Leone's. He had some lasagna. When the check came, he discovered he couldn't pay. The management told him he would have to wash dishes. When he left, he caught a bus to New Haven.

Who went to New York?
JOHN WENT TO NEW YORK.

Why did John go to New York?
BECAUSE JOHN WANTED TO GO TO LEONE'S.

Why did John go to Leone's?
BECAUSE JOHN WANTED TO HAVE SOME LASAGNA.

How did John get to New York?
JOHN TOOK A BUS TO NEW YORK.

Did a thief pick John's pocket?
A THIEF PICKED JOHN'S POCKET.

Did John order lasanga?
JOHN ORDERED LASAGNA.

Did John eat a steak?
NO, JOHN ATE LASAGNA.

What did John eat?
JOHN ATE LASAGNA.

Did John order lobster?
NO, JOHN ORDERED LASAGNA.

Did John eat lasagna?
JOHN ATE LASAGNA.

Did John pay the check?
NO, JOHN DIDN'T HAVE ANY MONEY.

Did John leave the waitress a tip?
NO, JOHN DIDN'T HAVE ANY MONEY.

Did John leave Leone's?
JOHN LEFT LEONE'S.

Why did John take the subway from Leone's?
SO JOHN COULD TAKE A BUS TO NEW HAVEN.

How could John take the subway from Leone's?
PROBABLY JOHN HAD A TOKEN.

How did John get to Leone's?
JOHN TOOK A BUS TO NEW YORK AND THEN HE TOOK THE SUBWAY TO LEONE'S.

Did anything unusual happen on the bus?
I DON'T REMEMBER ANYTHING.

Did anything unusual happen on the subway?
A THIEF PICKED JOHN'S POCKET.

What did John order?
JOHN ORDERED LASAGNA.

Who gave John a menu?
THE WAITRESS GAVE JOHN A MENU.

Did anything unusual happen at the restaurant?
JOHN DISCOVERED THAT HE COULDN'T PAY THE CHECK AND SO HE HAD TO WASH DISHES.

Why couldn't John pay the check?
BECAUSE JOHN DID NOT HAVE ANY MONEY.

Why didn't John have any money?
BECAUSE A THIEF PICKED JOHN'S POCKET.

How did John get back to New Haven?
JOHN WENT FROM LEONE'S BY SUBWAY AND THEN HE WENT TO NEW HAVEN BY BUS.

How was John able to take the bus to New Haven?
PROBABLY JOHN HAD A TICKET.

John went to a restaurant and the hostess gave him a menu. When he ordered a hot dog the waitress said that they didn't have any. So John ordered a hamburger instead. But when the hamburger came, it was so burnt that John left.

Did the waitress give John a menu?
NO, THE HOSTESS GAVE JOHN A MENU.

Did John order a hot dog?
YES.

Did John eat a hot dog?
NO, THE WAITRESS TOLD JOHN THEY DIDN'T HAVE ANY HOT DOGS.

What did the waitress serve John?
THE WAITRESS SERVED JOHN A HAMBURGER.

Why didn't John eat the hamburger?
BECAUSE THE HAMBURGER WAS BURNT.

Was John angry?
PROBABLY.

Why didn't John pay the check?
JOHN WAS ANGRY BECAUSE THE HAMBURGER WAS BURNT AND SO HE LEFT.

Why didn't John eat the hot dog?
BECAUSE THE WAITRESS TOLD JOHN THEY DID NOT HAVE ANY HOT DOGS.

What happened when John ordered the hamburger?
THE WAITRESS GAVE THE ORDER TO THE COOK, THE COOK PREPARED THE HAMBURGER, THE COOK GAVE THE HAMBURGER TO THE WAITRESS, THE WAITRESS SERVED JOHN THE HAMBURGER.

What happened when John ordered the hot dog?
THE WAITRESS TOLD JOHN THEY DIDN'T HAVE ANY HOT DOGS.

Friday evening a car swerved off Route 69. The vehicle struck a tree. The passenger, a New Jersey man, was killed. David Hall, 27, was pronounced dead at the scene by Dr. Dana Blauchard, medical examiner. Frank Miller, 32, of 593 Foxon Rd., the driver, was taken to Milford Hospital by Flanagan Ambulance. He was treated and released. The passenger was extricated from the vehicle by the Branford Fire Department. No charges were made. Patrolman Robert Onofrio investigated the accident.

Was anyone killed?
YES, DAVID HALL DIED.

Was anyone hurt?
YES, FRANK MILLER WAS SLIGHTLY INJURED.

Why was Frank Miller hurt?
BECAUSE THE AUTOMOBILE HIT THE TREE.

Did Miller go to the hospital?
YES, HE WAS IN THE MILFORD HOSPITAL.

How did Miller get to the hospital?
THE FLANAGAN AMBULANCE COMPANY TOOK HIM TO THE MILFORD HOSPITAL.

1.4-2 PAM

PAM was developed by the Yale Artificial Intelligence Project in 1976. The actual programming of PAM has been primarily the work of Robert Wilensky. Supporting programs for PAM have been handled by Gerald DeJong, Christopher Riesbeck, and Walter Stutzman.

The following stories and question-answering dialogues represent verbatim input and output.

John loved Mary but she didn't want to marry him. One day, a dragon stole Mary from the castle. John got on top of his horse and killed the dragon. Mary agreed to marry him. They lived happily ever after.

Why did John get on his horse?
BECAUSE HE WANTED TO BE NEAR MARY.

Why did Mary agree to marry John?
BECAUSE SHE WAS INDEBTED TO HIM.

Why did John kill the dragon?
BECAUSE HE WANTED MARY TO NOT DIE.

John disliked his job as the bank janitor. One day, a thief tried to rob the bank. John jumped on the thief and knocked him out. The bank president made John the bank guard. John enjoyed his new job.

Why did John knock the thief out?
BECAUSE HE WANTED THE THIEF NOT TO HAVE THE BANK'S MONEY.

Why did the bank president make John the bank guard?
BECAUSE THE BANK WAS INDEBTED TO JOHN.

1.4-3 ASP

Designed in 1975, ASP is a small program for investigating theories concerned with finding the best answer to a question. Its implementation required no efforts outside of my own. ASP is given a set of answers to a question about a story and tries to select the best one. The program makes it decision by asking the user to respond "yes" or "no" to a sequence of questions about the answers provided.

ASP has no memory representation for the story and no understanding of the question or answers given. It chooses an answer on the basis of selection rules that respond to the user's "yes" or "no" answers.

The following dialogue represents an interactive session with ASP. The answers given to ASP are stored in memory as lists, so that it can ask questions about pairs of answers by combining those questions with fixed connectives.

Story Context: One morning John noticed that his dog was having trouble walking. That afternoon he took it to the vet.

    Q: Why did John take his dog to the vet?
    A1: It was sick or injured.
    A2: It was having trouble walking.
    A3: He wanted to make it well.

Here is an interactive session with ASP. For this execution, ASP has been given the lexical answers *A1, A2,* and *A3* as initial input to the program.

Interactive Session Begins:

    ASP: GIVEN THE CONTEXT OF THE STORY, CAN EITHER *He wanted to make it well* OR *It was sick or injured* BE INFERRED FROM ONE ANOTHER?

    User: YES

    ASP: DOES IT MAKE SENSE TO SAY *He wanted to make it well* BECAUSE *It was having trouble walking?*

    User: YES

    ASP: DOES IT MAKE SENSE TO SAY *He wanted to make it well* AND HE KNEW THAT *It was having trouble walking?*

    User: YES

    ASP: THE BEST ANSWER IS BECAUSE *It was having trouble walking*

1.4-4   COIL

COIL was developed at the Xerox Palo Alto Research Center during the summer of 1976. It was written in an experimental implementation of KRL (Knowledge Representation Language), which was developed by Daniel Bobrow and Terry Winograd (1977).

Unlike SAM and PAM, which answered all of their questions after reading an entire story, COIL interrupts the input story to answer questions.

John picked up a newspaper. He went from the hall into the kitchen and got some milk.

Where did John come from?
THE HALL.

Where did the milk come from?
THE REFRIGERATOR.

But the milkcarton was empty so he threw it out.

Where did the milkcarton go to?
THE GARBAGE BAG.

Why did John throw the milkcarton into the garbage bag?
BECAUSE THE MILKCARTON WAS EMPTY.

He turned on the light and radio. Then he listened to music and read.

Where did the music come from?
THE RADIO.

What did John read?
THE NEWSPAPER.

Why did John turn on the light?
SO HE COULD READ THE NEWSPAPER.

Why did John turn on the radio?
SO HE COULD HEAR THE MUSIC.

2 Motivation and Background

Question answering is a fundamental human ability. When people speak to each other, a substantial amount of communication is achieved by asking and answering questions. It would be very difficult to function normally for a day without asking or answering any questions. We also use question answering as a basis for all kinds of judgmental evaluations. Intelligence and learning are assessed by asking questions on tests. From the first grade to our first job interview, we are judged and evaluated by our ability to answer questions. Because question answering is such a pervasive means of conveying information, it is ironic that we know so little about it as a cognitive process.

Other forms of communication have received attention and analysis. Writing is studied in terms of rhetorical composition. Serious art forms, such as painting and theater, receive critical analysis. Even the notion of body language has recently been recognized as a major communication device. It is easy to find books on composition, art appreciation, drama, and body language. But how many books exist on the subject of question answering?

There is a very simple reason for our ignorance of question answering. Until very recently, we were able to study only those communication phenomenon that were somehow amenable to conscious analysis. One can learn to be conscious of a novelist's style or a painter's techniques. One can even become conscious of unspoken signals in other person's posture and voice. But question answering is so fundamental and basic that it is impossible to be conscious of how we understand a question or how we arrive at an answer. There are, of course, times when a question is problematic in some way. Then we may be conscious of wording the question very carefully or with avoiding ambiguous interpretations. But for the vast majority of questions we ask and answer, it is impossible to introspect and perceive the cognition involved.

Question answering, like other communication forms, relies on a cognitive process. The simple fact is, we know very little about cognitive processes. Although we can understand the paintings of Rembrandt in terms of art, we cannot understand them in terms of the cognitive processes that produced them. If someone had such an understanding, he would be able to produce paintings artistically indistinguishable from original Rembrants. To the extent that we can be conscious of question-answering phenomena, we can speak of question answering as an art. But this kind of awareness is usually on the level of speaking styles (the "art" of conversation). We have no awareness of the lower, purely cognitive mechanisms. For example, we cannot talk very intelligently about exactly how one distinguishes nonsensical answers from acceptable ones; we take it for granted that people know an answer when they hear one.

A cognitive process can be described on many levels. On a physical level, it can be described in terms of neurophysiology. On this level we can study the electrical and chemical activity of neurons in the brain. We can also map regions in the cerebral cortex associated with various perceptual sensations and memory functions. Physically, cognitive processes are brain phenomena, and can therefore be characterized in terms of physiology. But even if we had a complete description of cognitive processes on this level, we would still have only a partial understanding.

Suppose a Martian or some alien intelligent being were exposed to a computer for the first time. Given knowledge of electricity and the appropriate testing equipment, our Martian could derive a complete circuit diagram of the computer. But how could he move from the circuit diagram to understanding the computer's operating system or stored programs? Knowledge of a system's hardware does not constitute complete understanding of that system. It is also necessary to understand a system's symbolic manipulations.

Cognitive processes performed by the human brain must also be understood in terms of symbolic manipulation. The brain must be considered an encoding device that preserves information. A cognitive process is a manipulation that acts on this information. But how can these processes be studied? We cannot see a cognitive process by studying the physical brain, any more than we can see a computer program by watching the computer's display of blinking lights. There is no way to directly observe a cognitive process. At best, we can only make guesses about what a cognitive process might look like, and then try to test our hypotheses. At this point, computers become a critical key in the study of cognition. They provide a means for hypothesis testing.

Many people who are acquainted with the field of artificial intelligence are amused by the general direction of inquiry the field has taken. In its early years artificial intelligence was dominated by an interest in behaviors that were ostensibly intelligent: theorem proving, chess playing, and general problem solving were strong areas of research activity. These tasks are no longer in the mainstream of artificial intelligence. Research is currently dominated by such "fundamental" problems as visual scene analysis and natural-language processing. Research in artificial intelligence seems to have regressed from activities that are impressively "adult" to those that are mastered by 3-year-olds. It would be a tremendous step forward if we could produce a computer program that conversed at the level of a 3-year-old child.

Those processes that are the most basic and fundamental for people tend to be the most challenging for a computer. This is partially so because the more fundamental a process is, the less we know about the cognition behind it. When an activity requires conscious thought (like chess or theorem proving), we are able to say something about the cognition involved. We can study the process by introspection and protocol analysis. But when a process is so low level (recognizing the letter "A" or remembering your middle name) that there is no conscious awareness of how it is achieved, it is very hard to know where to begin.

Question answering falls squarely into this category of tasks that seem to be as difficult for computers as they are trivial for people. It is therefore no surprise that initial research in computational question answering has not been characterized by major breakthroughs or advances. If a computer is to answer questions in a manner that is natural for human interaction, it must have knowledge of how people ask questions and what kinds of answers are expected in return. That is, a computer program designed to answer questions must implement a theory of human question answering. Early work in question answering was not grounded in any such theory.

The theory of question answering we will propose here (QUALM) was not developed by considering the task of question answering per se. It evolved from considering question answering as one aspect of natural-language processing. Because of this perspective, it was possible to formulate a theory of question answering that built upon theoretical notions for general natural-language processing. When question answering is viewed as a process, we can see that it involves many different processes. First, a question must first be understood; then memory processes attempt to retrieve relevant information from the memory; finally the information found in the memory must be translated into an English answer. So the process of question answering can be described in terms of three distinct cognitive processes: parsing, retrieval, and generation. QUALM is an extension of memory-processing theories that originated with the study of parsing (Riesbeck, 1975) and generation (Goldman, 1975).

2.1 CONCEPTUAL DEPENDENCY

The primary idea underlying QUALM is a theory of memory representation called *Conceptual Dependency*. Conceptual Dependency is a representational system that encodes the meaning of sentences by decomposition into a small set of primitive actions. When two sentences are identical in meaning, the Conceptual-Dependency representations for those sentences are identical. For example, "John kicked the ball" and "John hit the ball with his foot" will have identical Conceptual-Dependency representations.

Cognitive memory processes operate on the meaning of sentences, not on the lexical expression of that meaning. It follows that simulations of human cognition must rely on conceptual representations of information. Conceptual Dependency facilitates necessary recognition processes on this level of conceptual representation. For example, if memory contains an encoding for "John bought a book from Mary," then the processes that access memory should be able to answer "Did Mary sell John a book?" on the basis of that encoding. This sort of recognition is trivial when "John bought a book from Mary" and "Mary sold John a book" have similar conceptual representations.

The Conceptual-Dependency theory is not dependent on the particular set of primitives chosen, or the number of primitives used (although the strength of a given representational system is lost if the set of primitives is too large). The following acts define one set of primitives that have proved to be effective in the knowledge domain of general world knowledge.

ATRANS *The transfer of possession, ownership, or control.* ATRANS requires an actor, object, source, and recipient. For example, "John gave Mary the book" is an ATRANS with an actor (John), object (book), source (John), and recipient (Mary). "John took the book" is an ATRANS with an actor (John), object (book), and recipient (John).

PTRANS *The transfer of physical location.* PTRANS requires an actor, object, origin, and destination. For example, "John ran to town" is a PTRANS with an actor (John), object (John), and destination (a town).

PROPEL *The application of a physical force.* If movement takes place because of a PROPEL, then a PTRANS also occurs. PROPEL requires an actor, object, origin, and direction. For example, "push," "pull," "throw," and "kick" are all actions that involve a PROPEL.

MTRANS *The transfer of information.* An MTRANS can occur between animals or between memory locations within a person. Human memory is partitioned into three mental locations: the CP (Conscious Processor), which holds information of which we are consciously aware, the IM (Intermediate Memory), where information from the immediate context is held for potential access by the CP; and the LTM (Long-Term Memory), where information is stored permanently. MTRANS requires an actor, object, source, and recipient. Sources and recipients are either animals or mental locations in a person. For example, "tell" is an MTRANS between people; "see" is an MTRANS from eyes to the CP; "remember" is an MTRANS from the LTM to the CP; and "learn" is an MTRANS to the LTM.

MBUILD   *The thought process that constructs new information from old.* MBUILDS take place within the IM, receiving input from the CP and placing output in the CP. For example, "decide," "conclude," "imagine," and "consider" are all instances of MBUILD.

INGEST   *The internalization of an external object into an animal's system.* INGEST requires an actor, object, origin, and destination. For example, "eat," "drink," "smoke," and "breathe" are common examples of INGEST.

EXPEL   *The act of pushing an object out of the body.* EXPEL requires an actor, object, origin, and destination. Words for excretion and secretion are described by EXPEL. For example, "sweat," "spit," and "cry" are EXPELS.

Many acts require an instrumental action on the part of the actor. The following primitive acts are used primarily as instrumental conceptualizations. Each of these acts requires an actor and object. MOVE requires an origin and destination as well.

MOVE   *The movement of an animal involving some body part.* MOVE is instrumental to actions like "kick," "hand," and "throw." It can also occur non-instrumentally, as in "kiss" and "scratch."

SPEAK   *Any vocal act.* Humans usually perform speaking actions as instruments of MTRANSing.

ATTEND   *The act of focusing a sense organ toward some stimulus.* ATTEND is almost always instrumental to MTRANS. For example, "see" is an MTRANS from the eyes to the CP with an instrumental ATTEND of the eyes to an object.

GRASP   *The act of securing contact with an object.* For example, "grab," "let go," and "throw" each involve a GRASP or the termination of a GRASP.

2.2   CAUSAL CHAIN CONSTRUCTIONS

When people conceptualize a series of events, they connect individual events together with causal links. For example, suppose John walks over to Mary, John hits Mary, Mary falls, Mary breaks her arm, and Mary goes to the hospital. This series of events is remembered with causal connections linking them together. John moved into Mary's physical proximity, enabling him to propel his hand against her, resulting in John's hand applying force to Mary, resulting in gravity propelling Mary to the ground, resulting in a negative state change to Mary's arm, which initiated a decision process that led to Mary's going to the hospital.

Causal-chain constructions connect individual conceptualizations through causal relationships. A fully expanded causal chain alternates events and states; events result in states, and states enable events. In Conceptual Dependency there are six basic causal links.

RESULT (r)   An event "results" in a state. This causal link can be used with any state other than mental states.

REASON (R)   Mental activity (MBUILD) can be the "reason" for performing an action. This link joins mental events with nonmental actions.

INITIATE (I)   A state or event can "initiate" a thought process (MBUILD).

ENABLE (E)   A state "enables" an event to occur.

LEADTO (L)   This causal link is used to connect two events in a causal chain representation that is not fully expanded. That is, the LEADTO link is used to indicate that a causal chain expansion exists between two events that is not being explicitly spelled out.

CANCAUSE (C)   This link is a modification of the LEADTO link. The CANCAUSE indicates that an unspecified causal chain expansion has been left out of the causal chain representation. The difference between a CANCAUSE link and a LEADTO link is that the events and states joined by a CANCAUSE link are hypothetical.

ABBREVIATED LINKS   In the same way that the LEADTO link is used to indicate a missing expansion, various causal links can be combined to indicate specific contractions. For example, an "initiate—reason" (I/R) link is used to describe a state that leads to an action by means of a mental process. This link indicates that an MBUILD is implicit in the causal chain representation.

2.3 UNDERSTANDING STORIES

The process of story understanding is largely one of translating a series of sentences into a causal chain of conceptualizations. This process normally involves inference generation. For example, if we hear that Mary went to the hospital after John hit her, we construct a causal chain representation that includes a negative state change in Mary's health; we infer that Mary was hurt. This information did not need to be explicitly stated. We were able to infer it from knowing that John hit Mary and Mary went to the hospital. Causal chain construction usually involves filling in missing information of this sort. People are constantly making inferences about what must have happened, in addition to making use of those things explicitly stated.

Many major problems in story understanding are therefore concerned with inference generation. Where do inferences come from? How are they made? Exactly which inferences are made? When? Although we do not have all the answers to these questions, progress has been made in characterizing certain classes of inferences (Schank & Abelson, 1977). To begin with, inferences are made on the basis of knowledge about the world. If we hear that Mary called her lawyer when John threatened her, we can infer that Mary is concerned about her legal rights and is probably planning to protect herself or initiate retaliatory actions. If we hear that Mary called her psychiatrist when John threatened her, we can infer that Mary is looking for emotional support. These inferences are made on the basis of our knowledge about the professional roles of lawyers and psychiatrists. We are also using knowledge about how people react to being threatened. It would make less sense to hear that Mary called her lawyer when her pen ran out of ink, because there is no discernible connection between lawyers and running out of ink.

In order for a system to make the kinds of inferences that people make, it must have access to the same kind of knowledge people use when making inferences. In particular, if we expect a computer to generate inferences, it must have knowledge structures in its memory comparable to those found in human memory. Schank and Abelson (1977) have developed a theory of human knowledge structures that has been used as the basis for a number of story-understanding systems (Cullingford, 1978; DeJong, 1977; Wilensky, 1976). We briefly outline two of these memory structures, scripts and plans.

2.4   SCRIPTS AND PLANS

Scripts and plans are theoretical structures in human memory that have been proposed as models of human memory organization. A vast amount of our mundane world knowledge appears to be encoded in the form of scripts and plans. These same constructs are being exploited as a means of organizing world knowledge in a computer. Scripts are memory units containing information about frequently encountered situations or activities. They describe the expectations involved in extremely mundane situations, such as going to a restaurant, shopping in a grocery store, or stopping at a gas station. People acquire most scripts through experience and use them both operationally (as in actually going to a restaurant) and cognitively (as in understanding stories about restaurants). When you go to a restaurant, you have certain expectations about finding a table, ordering, being served, eating, getting a check, paying the check, and so on. These are so ingrained that you probably do not have to spend much conscious processing time on them. Most likely you only think about them when they fail or deviate from your expectations. If you hear that John went to a restaurant and ordered a hamburger, you will infer that he ate a hamburger unless you hear something to the contrary. You were not told that he ate a hamburger; you used your scriptal knowledge of restaurants to make the inference. Although scriptal knowledge must vary from person to person according to variations of experience, quite a few standard scripts will be held in common as a cultural norm. Most people have the same restaurant script, because restaurants are highly standardized.

The important scripts for natural language processing are those that a large population holds in common. Whenever a script is shared by people, it can be referenced very efficiently. "I went to a restaurant last night" conveys the entire restaurant script to anyone who has that script.

Plans are used when scripts do not apply or fail to contain sufficient information. Although scripts are tightly bound to well-specified situations, the same plan can be invoked in a variety of settings. For example, suppose you are trying to find a friend's house in San Francisco. You have the address, but you've never been there. Clearly, there is no script for this situation (assuming it is novel); nevertheless, you know what sorts of things to do. You might invoke a plan that says to wander randomly until you reach the right street, but a better plan would entail knowledge acquisition. You need to find out where the street is. So you consult appropriate knowledge sources. If you have a map you look at it. If you don't have a map you might go about finding one, or you may opt for another knowledge source and try asking people whether they can tell you. If you have asked 10 people to no avail, you might give up trying to find it yourself and call your friend for help. The principles involved in this process are very general. The same planning structures could be used for finding a particular office in the Pentagon or finding a book in the library (without the possibility of the book's helping you). Plans are extremely general procedures that are adaptable to a number of situations and are used when there is no standard routine to follow.

Plans and scripts are related in that plans may give birth to scripts. If I invoke the same plans for getting stores to cash my checks, and these plans are always successful, I will have a script after a while. Should my script fail at some time, I will have to revert back to planning mode. But as long as the Park Avenue address and the AMA membership card work, I will try them first. What originated as an inform/reason plan evolved into a script, thanks to repeated successes. For a more complete discussion of scripts and plans, see Schank and Abelson (1977).

2.4-1 Terminology

A SCRIPT is a knowledge structure used as a predictive-inference mechanism during understanding. Scripts contain knowledge about highly stereotypic situations. The important scripts for natural language processing are those that describe situations familiar to a large population.

SCRIPT APPLICATION is the process that accesses a script at the time of understanding in order to make predictions about what is apt to happen next. As subsequent text is processed, old predictions may be incorporated into the memory representation as inferences about things that must have occurred even if they were not explicitly stated.

SCRIPT INSTANTIATION is the generation of a memory representation for a specific event. The script applier instantiates scripts when it generates story representations.

DEFAULT ASSIGNMENTS are inferences made by the script applier about role bindings within a script that have not been explicitly described by the input.

SCRIPT EXECUTION is the actual performance of a script activity.

A PLAN is a knowledge structure used as a predictive-inference mechanism at the time of understanding.

PLAN APPLICATION accesses plans at the time of understanding in order to make predictions about what is likely to happen next.

PLANNING STRUCTURES are those constructions in a memory representation that were generated by plans.

2.5 STORY REPRESENTATIONS

Once a story has been read, a memory representation is generated, encoding events explicitly mentioned along with those that were inferred. Part of this representation is a causal chain of individual conceptualizations connected by causal links. But a complete story representation involves levels of understanding that are not expressed by causal chains. In this overview we describe the story representations generated by SAM and PAM. But we do not attempt to describe how these representations are created during the understanding process. For a discussion of SAM's understanding processes, see Cullingford (1978), and for a description of the PAM system, see Wilensky (1976). In general we can say that both systems are based on predictive mechanisms, which make many inferences at the time of understanding. All substantiated inferences made during understanding are incorporated into the story representation; and once the story representation has been created, there is no record of which conceptualizations were explicitly stated in the story and which were inferred. Most of the questions that can be answered about a story are answerable on the basis of the story representation alone, without additional inferencing or reasoning. For a theoretical discussion of memory and inferencing in story understanding, see Schank and Abelson (1977).

2.5-1 Causal Chains

The causal chain level of representation encodes a chronology of events and states that describes everything that happened in the course of the story. The individual conceptualizations in this chain are joined by causal links according to the syntax of causal chains (Schank, 1973a). Basically, a causal chain is a string of alternating states and acts, with the causal links ENABLE, RESULT, REASON, INITIATE, CANCAUSE, and LEADTO joining them. Causal chains tend to be fairly linear, but at times a single conceptualization has multiple antecedents or consequents.

One way to think about a causal chain representation is to imagine a movie of the story and to record each event as it occurs. For example, in a story describing John's going to a restaurant, John is involved in numerous events between the time he enters the restaurant and the time he leaves. Each of these events enters the causal chain. If there is more than one character in a story, a point of view is adopted for the causal chain representation. If John goes to a restaurant, the causal chain will be dominated by events that involve John directly. We want to keep the camera on John for the most part.

To give you some concrete sense of causal-chain representations, we look at a story that SAM has understood:

John went to New York by bus. On the bus he talked to an old lady. When he left the bus he thanked the driver. He took the subway to Leone's. On the subway his pocket was picked. He got off the train and entered Leone's. He had some lasagna. When the check came he discovered he couldn't pay. The management told him he would have to wash dishes.

The following paraphrase for this story was generated by SAM by translating into English all of the conceptual acts found in the causal-chain representation for this story (Schank & Yale A. I. Project, 1975). The actual causal chain has states between consecutive acts, but these were not included in the paraphrase. Notice how single sentences from the original story are broken down into sequences of conceptual acts. Also notice how conceptualizations have been inferred from the story in order to form complete causal chains between two input conceptualizations:

John went to a bus stop. He waited at it a few minutes. He entered a bus. The driver got the ticket from John. He went to a seat. He sat down on it. While John was on the bus an old lady and John talked. The driver took John to New York. He went to the driver. When getting off the bus John thanked the driver. He got off it. He entered a station. He put a token in the turnstile. He went to the platform. He waited at it a few minutes. He entered a subway car. A thief went to John. He picked John's pocket. He went. John went to a seat. He sat down in it. The driver took John to Leone's. He left the subway car. He left the station. He entered Leone's. He looked around inside it. He saw he could go to a table. He went to it. He sat down in a seat. He ordered some lasagna. The waiter indicated to the chef John would like him to prepare something. The chef prepared the lasagna. The waiter got it from the chef. The waiter went to the table. He served the lasagna to John. He ate it. He became full. He asked the waiter for the check. He got it from the waiter. John read the check. John discovered he was unable to pay the check. He indicated to the waiter he was unable to pay the check. The management told John he would have to wash dishes. He entered the kitchen. He washed dishes. He left Leone's.

Some of the inferences made here could be wrong. For example, there is no way of knowing whether John had his pocket picked before or after he sat down on the subway. For that matter, we do not really know that John sat down on the subway. In the causal chain representation, some inferred conceptualizations are tagged according to their relative certainty (Cullingford, 1978). But the basic notion behind the causal chain level of representation is a chronology of states and acts describing everything that must have happened.

2.5-2 Script Structures

Script structures constitute a higher level of representation. They encode a rough bird's-eye view of the story. This level of representation is most important when more than one script is referenced in the course of a story. Script structures describe how various scripts relate to each other. For example, a general trip script contains various travel scripts (nested or sequentially ordered) as well as scriptal descriptions of the destination activities. Scripts are generally related sequentially or by nesting, and some scripts (like the trip script) predict scriptal relations within themselves. The scriptal structure for the Leone's story looks like:

$$
\text{\$TRIP1} \begin{cases} \text{GOING} & \text{\$BUS1 \$SUBWAY1 (\$PICKPOCKET1)} \\ \text{DESTINATION} & \text{\$RESTAURANT1} \\ \text{RETURNING} & \text{NIL} \end{cases}
$$

Each pointer in a script structure points to a particular instantiation of a script. $BUS1 in the going part of $TRIP1 refers to that part of the story that involved a bus ride to New York. This instantiation of the bus script binds John as the main actor and includes him thanking the driver and talking to an old lady. Had the story included John going back home by bus, a second instantiation of the bus script would appear under the returning part of $TRIP1. Although most of the scripts that appear in the Leone's story are sequentially related, some are nested within others. All scripts in the Leone's story are part of the trip script, and the pick-pocketing episode is nested within the subway ride.

Script structures allow access to script-related information, which is stored independent of the causal chain representation. Each pointer in a script structure allows access to the conceptualization summarizing that script instantiation, any events that occurred during that script instantiation that were recognized as being particularly unusual or interesting, and any role bindings for that particular script instantiation. This ability to extract the most important aspects of a script instantiation is crucial in many retrieval tasks.

2.5-3   Planning Structures

In order to understand some stories, knowledge is needed about human goals and strategies for achieving these goals. Suppose John saves Mary from a dragon and she marries him. This makes sense as a unified story only because we infer that the dragon intended to harm Mary, John didn't want Mary to get hurt, and Mary was grateful to John after he rescued her. Suppose instead that Mary married John after he fed her beloved pet poddle to a lion. This story is much harder to understand because it violates rules about human behavior and mental states. For Mary to marry John we expect that Mary loves or likes John. But if John destroyed a pet that she liked, we expect Mary to dislike John. If Mary marries John after his cruel behavior, we are forced to assume either that we are missing some critical piece of information (although it is hard to imagine what), or that Mary and John are into some sort of strange sadist/masochist relationship. The causality between John turning Mary's pet poodle into cat food and Mary marrying John is very difficult to account for.

To understand stories on this level of human motivation and behavior, we invoke plans to assist the understanding process. The story representation generated must incorporate plan-related information. PAM creates story representations that include both a causal chain level of representation and a planning-structure representation. To see what kinds of plan-related inferences are made at the time of understanding, consider the following story:

> John loved Mary but she didn't want to marry him. One day, a dragon stole Mary from the castle. John got on top of his horse and killed the dragon. Mary agreed to marry him. They lived happily ever after.

In the course of understanding this story, PAM makes the following inferences:

> John wanted to marry Mary.
> Mary was endangered by the dragon.
> John learned that the dragon had kidnapped Mary.
> John wanted to save Mary from the dragon.
> John rode his horse to where Mary was.
> Mary became grateful to John for rescuing her.
> John and Mary got married.

These inferences are interrelated by plan-related causal links. For example, the story representation encodes the fact that Mary married John because she felt grateful to him (for rescuing her); that John got on his horse to get to where Mary was; that being where Mary was enabled John to rescue her, that John's knowing that the dragon had kidnapped Mary initiated a thought process in

John ending in his decision to save Mary. The causalities connecting these conceptualizations go beyond the chronological causality found in causal chains.
These relational links are concerned more with why people do what they do
than with the physical chain of events in the course of a story.

In addition to plan-related inferences, PAM generates a causal-chain representation that encodes the events of the story as they occur. To get a sense of the
causal chain representation generated by PAM, we look at a paraphrase based on
the causal chain for the dragon story. This paraphrase was generated in the same
way that the long paraphrase for the Leone's story was created by SAM. Each
conceptual act in the causal chain has been translated into English, leaving out
all of the intervening states with the exception of emotional ones:

> John was in love with Mary. She did not want to marry him. A dragon
> took her from the castle. He learned that the dragon had taken her from
> the castle. He mounted a horse. It took him to her. He killed the dragon.
> She was indebted to him. She told him she was going to marry him. He
> married her. He and she were happy thereafter.

This paraphrase gives some sense of how the story is understood on the causal
chain level alone. The inferences about goals and plans, with the causal relationships connecting them, exist outside the causal-chain representation but are
connected to conceptualizations in the chain. The planning-structure level exists
in story representations as a sort of overlay atop the causal-chain representation.
For a description of how PAM generates causal chains and script structures
during understanding, see Wilkensky (1976).

2.6 ARTIFICIAL INTELLIGENCE AND
COGNITIVE PSYCHOLOGY

Let us return for a moment to our original problem of how we study cognitive
processes. The science of cognition is not a well-established discipline like physics
or genetics. It is a very new area of inquiry and, as such, is subject to paradigmatic
disputes. Among scientists interested in cognition, there is no general agreement
on how it can best be studied. Cognitive science is therefore characterized as an
interdisciplinary area, to which contributions may be made by either computer
scientists or psychologists. This may seem surprising at first, since computer
science and psychology are not commonly considered strongly related fields of
interest. Once one understands exactly how a computer scientist and a psychologist go about studying cognitive phenomenon, however, the connection is
less mysterious.

Suppose that a psychologist is interested in some cognitive process (e.g., the
generation of inferences) and that he wants to account for the mechanisms of

human memory at work. If he works within the experimental paradigm of psychology, he will:

1. Propose a theory describing what he thinks is going on.
2. Design an experiment to test his theory.
3. Run the experiment.
4. Analyze the results to see in what ways his theory is substantiated or contradicted.

Now suppose that a researcher in artificial intelligence confronts the same problem and would also like to account for the memory mechanisms operating. Working from within an artificial-intelligence paradigm, he will:

1. Propose a theory to describe what he thinks is going on.
2. Write a computer program that implements this theory.
3. Run the computer program.
4. See whether the program does what it was intended to do, and analyze the ways it fails.

In both paradigms, the investigators are concerned with a theory of memory processes. A psychologist uses experiments to develop his theories, while an artificial-intelligence researcher uses computer programs. In both paradigms, theories undergo continual revision and expansion. One experiment usually leads to another. And, in fact, the point of writing a computer program in artificial intelligence is very often simply to find out how to write a better one next time. The four steps of both research paradigms describe a cyclic process: After the step 4 we go back to step 1 to incorporate what we have learned in a revised, extended, or totally new theory.

Does this mean that the only difference between the two paradigms is that one uses experiments and the other uses computers? Yes and no. Some problems lend themselves to experimental investigation, and some do not. The experimental paradigm imposes a restriction on the kind of phenomena that can profitably be investigated. If experiments cannot be designed to isolate the variable factors of a proposed theory, the psychologist can go no further. Problems concerning human cognitive processes are difficult to study within the paradigm of experimental psychology for precisely this reason. An analogy has often been made between trying to design an experiment to shed light on human memory processes and trying to perform brain surgery with a hammer and chisel. What experiment can be designed to help us understand how people are able to answer simple questions like "What's your name?" Natural language processing is a prime example of a cognitive process that slips through the net of empirical experimentation.

Natural language processing can be productively studied within the artificial-intelligence paradigm. If we construct a process model designed to account for a particular language task (e.g., question answering, summarization, translation, etc.), then we can write a computer program to implement that model. By running the program, we can see where the model is weak, where it breaks down, and where it appears competent. A program that does not run may not be working because of technical programming errors. These can always be fixed. The interesting failures are those that occur because the process model underlying the program failed to recognize some critical problem or failed to handle some problem adequately.

When a program fails for theoretical reasons, we learn something we did not know before. When an artificial-intelligence researcher wants to investigate human cognitive processes, he uses the computer as an investigative tool that can help him see what would otherwise be overlooked. Computers can help us study cognitive processes in much the same way that microscopes help us study cell biology. Without a computer we can only guess at what is there; with a computer we are still guessing, but we at least know when we are wrong.

I INTERPRETATION: UNDERSTANDING QUESTIONS

INTRODUCTION

QUALM can be split up into roughly two fundamental processes: understanding the question and finding an answer. In Chapters 2 and 3 we describe the processes of QUALM that are devoted to understanding questions. Questions are understood on different levels, and complete interpretation on preliminary levels must occur before the more comprehensive interpretation of subsequent levels can be attempted.

FOUR LEVELS OF UNDERSTANDING

All questions must pass through four levels of interpretive analysis before a memory search can begin to look for an answer. Interpretation on one level must be completed before interpretation on the next can begin. The four successive levels are:

1. Conceptual parse
2. Memory internalization
3. Conceptual categorization
4. Inferential analysis.

The first interpretive process, parsing, is the only one that is language dependent. Internalization, conceptual categorization, and inferential analysis all operate within Conceptual Dependency, a language-independent meaning representation (Schank, 1975a). This means that questions in any language can be processed by changing only the parser. English questions require an English parser, Russian questions require a Russian parser; and so forth. But the other interpretive modules that perform internalization — conceptual categorization and inferential analysis — do not have to be changed to accommodate questions in different languages. If an English parser were replaced by a Russian one, the other interpretive modules would require no adjustment to function with the new parser.

Of the four interpretive processes, only the last two, conceptual categorization and inferential analysis, are concerned solely with questions. The conceptual parser and internalization programs are general language-processing mechanisms, designed to deal with declarative statements as well as questions. These first two levels of interpretation are actually a front end for QUALM; they are not, strictly speaking, a part of QUALM. In fact, these analysis programs were independently developed long before anyone considered applying them to the task of question answering. Christopher Riesbeck has been refining his conceptual parser (ELI) since its original implementation in 1974 (Riesbeck, 1975; Riesbeck & Schank, 1976). Versions of the internalization program (MEMTOK, TOK) have been operating since 1975 as a part of the SAM system (Cullingford, 1978).

To understand the interpretive processes within QUALM, what they do and how they do it, we need not know how the parser and internalization programs work. But for the sake of an overall picture, we take a moment to explain what they do (and do not do) so that the reader has some sense of the entire understanding process that begins with a string of words ending in a question mark.

THE CONCEPTUAL PARSE

When a question passes through the parser, it is translated into a conceptual-meaning representation, Conceptual Dependency. Once the Conceptual Dependency representation for a question has been produced, that is all the system needs to work with from that point on. None of the subsequent processes require knowledge of what words or syntactic constructions were in the original lexical question.

The Conceptual Dependency representation of a question generated by the parser constitutes one level of question interpretation. Understanding of the question on this level is generally a literal or naive understanding. For example, the parser will understand:

Q1: Can you tell me where John is?

to mean "Are you capable of telling me where John is?" If the interpretation ended here, we would have no way of knowing that this is probably a request for information about John's location. The person asking Q1 wants to know where John is. He will probably not be satisfied to find out that the person he is addressing is merely capable of saying where John is. But the parser cannot know that this question is a request for information. As far as the parser is concerned, *Q1* is a simple inquiry about whether the listener is capable of telling the questioner John's whereabouts. Higher memory processes within the interpreter must be summoned to complete the interpretation of this question in order to arrive at the intended meaning of *Q1*.

This does not mean that the parser is oblivious to general world knowledge, context, or higher memory processes. On the contrary, parsing strategies often interact with other memory processes to arrive at the correct interpretation of verbs and nouns (Riesbeck & Schank, 1976). For example, if the parser is processing the sentence "John walked into a restaurant and ordered a hamburger," it will receive from the Script Applier a preferred word sense for the verb "to order" predicting that "ordered" in this sentence means to communicate a request for a meal (instead of issuing a command or establishing a sequential arrangement of some sort). This preferred sense of the verb is established before the parser even gets to the object of the verb, the hamburger.

The parser interacts with contextual-memory processes primarily to anticipate correct word senses. Suppose that two people meet on the street and one asks the other:

Q2: Do you have a light?

The parser would understand that this question is equivalent to asking:

Q3: Do you have in your immediate possession an object that is capable of producing a flame?

If *Q2* had been asked in the context of two auto mechanics working on an engine in a garage, the parser would be capable of understanding that *Q2* is equivalent to asking:

Q4: Do you have in your immediate possession an object that is capable of producing light?

The parser would pick up a different sense of the word "light" from an auto mechanic script. It still does not understand the request aspect of the question, but it does receive word-sense priorities from script-applier processes that keep track of currently active scripts. The parser is sensitive to context in its conceptual analysis of statements and questions. But it is not capable of total understanding.

Complete understanding of *Q2* recognizes this question to be a request for a lit match or a lighter. This understanding is accompanied by a strong expectation that the questioner wants to light a cigarette. Such a level of predictive understanding can only be achieved by processes that have knowledge about questions and why people ask them. The parser does not have access to such knowledge. A correct parse of a question signifies the first level of understanding, on which all subsequent interpretations are based. The proper conceptual parse of a question may not represent the intended meaning of that question; but when the parser's interpretation is not correct, it is better described as an incomplete interpretation than as a wrong one.

MEMORY INTERNALIZATION

All sentences and questions must pass from an initial parse to an internalized parse. An internalized parse is a rewriting of the initial parse that substitutes pointers to memory tokens for all nominal references in the conceptualization. For example, the initial parse of the sentence "John went to a restaurant" will place in the actor slot the word JOHN. When this conceptualization is internalized, memory is consulted to find out whether previous processing has already established a memory token for a human with the name John. If so, JOHN is replaced by a pointer to the memory token already established (e.g., GN001). If no previous reference to someone called John has occurred, memory will find no token for John and one will have to be created. In either case, the word JOHN will be replaced with a pointer to a memory token. When all nominal references in the initial parse have been so replaced, we have an internalized parse of the sentence.

The internalization process establishes nominal referents and integrates new information into memory-token descriptions of objects and people. For example, newspaper stories often begin:

John Doe of 4616 Lakewood Drive, Bingham, a construction worker, was killed yesterday when. . . .

The internalization program is responsible for creating a memory token and organizing properties within it:

G0001:
    ISA = Human
    First Name = John
    Last Name = Doe
    Sex = Male
    Age = >18 yrs
    Occupation = Construction Worker
    Street Address = 4616 Lakewood Drive
    City Residence = Bingham
    Date of Death = 18 April 1976

If further information were given later in the article (he had a wife and a son), these new facts would have to be added to the memory token for John Doe during internalization. Internalization would also be responsible for recognizing that any references to "the deceased," "Mr. Doe," or "Mrs. Doe's husband" are in fact references to the same memory token.

Sometimes internalization requires accessing knowledge structures. If after hearing "John went to a restaurant," the next sentence is "He ordered a hamburger," the initial parse will fill the Actor slot with HUM0 where HUM0 has the properties of being human and male. When this parse is internalized, the restaurant script activated by the first sentence is accessed to see whether any of the conceptualizations predicted by the script applier match the current input. In this case a match would be found, and it tells us that the actor of the current concept must be bound to the role of the patron in the restaurant script. If someone orders food in a restaurant, we expect him to be acting in the role of a restaurant patron. During the processing of the first sentence, the memory token for John was bound to the patron role. In this way the pronominal referent in the second sentence is determined to be John. HUM0 from the initial parse is then replaced with a pointer to the memory token representing John.

Problems in internalization affect question answering whenever references must be correctly recognized. Some question-answering problems related to internalization are discussed in subsection 3.1-3. But for the most part, QUALM is independent of internalization processes. For a description of the Internalization program used by SAM and PAM, see Cullingford (1978).[1]

CONCEPTUAL CATEGORIZATION

Conceptual categorization is performed by the question analyzer. The question analyzer takes the internalized parse of a question and decomposes it into two descriptive components: a question concept and a conceptual question category. For example, the question:

Q5: Did John hit Mary?

has the conceptual question category "Verification" and a question concept representing "John hit Mary." Question concepts are represented in Conceptual Dependency and are derived from the internalized parse of the question according to rules developed for each question category.

There are 13 conceptual categories for questions. The question analyzer recognizes in which category a question belongs by running the question through a series of tests, which function like a simple discrimination net (Feigenbaum, 1963). For example, "Causal Antecedent" questions are recognized by a test that checks for the following features:

1. There is a causal-chain construction.
2. The causal link = LEADTO.
3. All or part of the leading conceptualization is unknown.

---

[1]Throughout this volume, conceptualizations in Conceptual Dependency presented as illustrations are written in graphic form, with components as they would appear after the initial parse, before Internalization takes place. This is done at the expense of technical correctness for the sake of the reader, who I assume feels more at home with JOHN than with G0001.

Conceptual question categories, the rules used to identify the conceptual category of a question, and the rules used to extract question concepts are all described in Chapter 3.

INFERENTIAL ANALYSIS

Very often the correct interpretation of a question involves an understanding of inferences. These inferences may rely on assumptions about the questioner's desires or goals, assumptions about what the questioner does and does not know, and assumptions about what is really being asked. All inferences of this sort are the result of higher-memory processes that examine the question concept and its conceptual categorization in an effort to understand it beyond its literal meaning.

For example, if John is packing for a business trip and asks his wife:

Q6: What haven't I packed?

His question is inferred to mean:

Q7: What haven't I packed that I should have packed?

Without this additional interpretation, *Q6* will admit all sorts of ridiculous and useless answers.

In a similar way, many requests are recognized only after inference processes are invoked. For example:

Q8: Why don't you get Mary a drink?

can easily be meant as a request:

Q9 Would you get Mary a drink?

rather than as an inquiry for reasons behind not getting a drink. On the other hand,

Q10: Why don't you feel angry?

makes little sense as a request:

Q11: Would you (please) feel angry?

Inferential Analysis contains the inferential processes essential to understanding what the questioner really wants to know. Without this understanding, many seemingly simple answers cannot be produced. Without inferential analysis of questions, the following exchange would be impossible:

Q12: Does it snow in Portland?
A12: Maybe once every year or two.

If no inference-based interpretation is allowed, the information given in *A12* would have to be painfully extracted:

Q13: Does it snow in Portland?
A13: Yes.
Q14: How often?
A14: How often what?
Q15: How often does it snow in Portland?
A15: Maybe once every year or two.

If a system had no capacity for the inferential interpretation of questions, question-answering dialogues would progress slowly and deliberately, like the one above. Rules for inferential analysis of questions are described in Chapter 4.

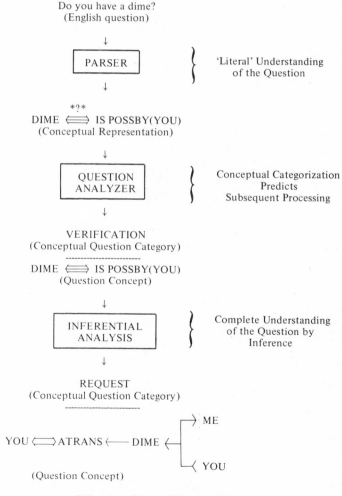

FIG. I.1.   Stages of interpretation.

In Fig. 1.1., the interpretive processes of parsing, conceptual categorization, and inferential analysis are outlined. A sample question ("Do you have a dime?") is parsed into a Conceptual Dependency representation, which is equivalent to the question "Do you have a dime in your immediate possession?" The Question Analyzer (Chapter 3) then categorizes this question as a Verification question and extracts a question concept ("You have a dime in your immediate possession"). Inferential analysis (Chapter 4) then recategorizes the question as a request and reinterprets the question as a request and reinterprets the question to mean "Will you give me a dime?"

3 Conceptual Categories for Questions

This chapter describes the question analyzer within QUALM. The question analyzer examines the conceptual parse of a question and assigns a conceptual category to that question.

Q1: Why did John kill the dragon?

is a "Causal Antecedent" question, which could be answered with either:

A1a: Because the dragon took Mary.
A1b: To save Mary.

But if Q1 were worded a little differently, it would fall into a different conceptual category:

Q2: For what purpose did John kill the dragon?

Q2 is a "Goal Orientation" question. As such, it does not elicit the same kinds of answers as a Causal-Antecedent question. *Q2* can be appropriately answered with A1b, but A1a is no longer a good answer:

Q2: For what purpose did John kill the dragon?
A1a: Because the dragon took Mary.

Conceptual categorization recognizes essential conceptual differences in questions. These differences are ultimately reflected by the types of answers that are appropriate for a given question.

3.0 INTRODUCTION

In grammar-school textbooks, questions are often categorized lexically. There are who-questions, what-questions, where-questions, when-questions, why questions, did-questions, and how-questions. Sometimes questions are categorized according to which grammatical part of speech will provide an answer. Thus, there are nominal questions and adverbial questions. A special case of answer-oriented categories are yes/no questions. These familiar categories do not constitute a comprehensive system and are not motivated by anything greater than a desire to have a few general descriptive devices.

Lexical question categories seem to exist primarily for the purpose of textbook exercises. They are also used to describe parts of speech: for example, an adverb is a word that answers where, when, or how. But lexical question typing has one indisputable advantage: Everyone can understand that a who-question is any question that begins with the word who. The concepts are sufficiently obvious to be universally understood. As long as these categories are intended to function descriptively for a general and nontechnical audience, lexical typing is an effective and adequate system. In fact, throughout this thesis references to lexical categories of questions are found despite the fact that these lexical categories are not recognized by QUALM and are not useful from a processing point of view.

In this chapter, we present a system of 13 conceptual categories for questions. Subsequent references to question types describe questions according to this conceptual category system whenever the technical process model is being discussed. When a nontechnical reference is admissible, lexical categories are used for the sake of readability. If the reader has a passing familiarity with Conceptual Dependency decompositions (Schank, 1972, 1973b, 1974a, 1975a) the relationships between lexical and conceptual question categories should be grasped with little difficulty.

When formulating a process model for question answering, a category system for questions must be descriptive in terms of that process model. If a question falls into a particular category, this should tell us something about the processing that the question must undergo. To see how lexical typing fails in this respect, consider all the different kinds of how-questions:

Quantity.

Q1: How long is this?
    (What is the length of this?)
Q2: How often does this happen?
    (What is the frequency of this occurrence?)

Q1 and *Q2* are quantification questions. Each of these questions asks for a description of quantification requiring a measurement in units. How long is this? — 14 inches. How often does this happen? — Once every week or two. The units of quantification do not always have to be explicitly referenced. If *Q2* is answered "Seldom," this answer must be interpreted against some norm of frequency.

Relative Description.

Q3: How intelligent is John?
(What is the relative intelligence of John?)
Q4: How wet is your coat?
(What is the relative wetness of your coat?)

Q3 and *Q4* are relative-scale questions. These questions ask for a description along some scale (say −10 to 10) where there is a norm dependent on the nature of the property. Although some people might chose to quantify intelligence in terms of IQ points, it is also acceptable to describe relative intelligence with terms like "very bright" or "a little slow," where these descriptions implicitly reference some assumed norm against which a comparison is being made.

Attitude.

Q5: How do you like New York?
(What are your feelings about New York?)

Q5 asks for an attitudinal orientation. This question could be answered by specifying virtually any attitude imaginable: I hate it, I love it, I am totally unaffected by it, I try not to think about it, I wouldn't wish it on a dog, I can't wait to get out, I've found my niche, and so on. Appropriate answers to this question are more flexible than relative-scale specification. "I can't wait to get out" tells us that the answerer expects to leave someday, as well as that he has a negative attitude toward New York.

Emotional/Physical State.

Q6: How do you like your eggs?
(In what physical state do you prefer your eggs?)
Q7: How is John?
(What is the emotional/physical state of John?)

Q6 and *Q7* ask for state descriptions. Eggs can be over-easy, sunny-side-up, poached, fried, or scrambled. John could be just fine, on the critical list, morbidly depressed, euphoric, or he could have a slight cold. Very often, answers to questions like this include causal information: "He is depressed about the stock market," or "He is excited about the new house."

Enablement.

Q8:   How were you able to buy this without money?
(What enabled you to buy this?)

Q9: How did you get here so fast?
(What enabled you to arrive faster than I expected?)
Q10: How could you hear what he said?
(What enabled you to hear him?)

Q8, Q9, and Q10 ask about enabling conditions. Some state or act was a necessary enablement for the acts in question.

Instrumentality.

Q11: How did you get here?
(By what means did you come here?)
Q12: How did you send word to him?
(By what means did you communicate to him?)

Q11 and *Q12* asks about the instrumentality of the acts in question. In *Q11*, some transportational conveyance is sought, and *Q12* asks for a vehicle of communication.

Causal Antecedent.

Q13: How did the glass break?
(What caused the glass to break?)

Q13 is asking for a causal antecedent. Something happened that caused the glass to break (it was dropped, hit, thrown, crushed, etc.)

Instructions.

Q14: How do I get to your house?
(Would you give me instructions to your house?)
Q15: How do you get service around here?
(What do you have to do to get service here?)

Q14 and *Q15* ask for instructions. Answers to these questions often involve describing a chain of actions that must be sequentially executed.

The memory searches that will find answers to these questions vary considerably. Quantification questions require an examination of object properties in terms of a numerical measurement. Relative-scale questions require a description on a comparative scale relative to some norm. Attitudinal orientation and state descriptions may be combinations of relative-state scales and other information. Enablement questions require an examination of events causally related to the conceptual event in question. Instrumental questions ask for descriptive specification of events simultaneous in time with the act in question. Causal-antecedent questions require knowledge of causal responsibility, and procedural specification questions require retrieval of instructional information.

A useful taxonomy of questions would predict the kinds of memory searches needed to answer any given question. It would also be useful if question categories could determine which inference mechanisms have to be invoked for a complete interpretation of the question. A question category should predict the processes needed to understand and answer questions falling in that category.

To be useful as a predictive mechanism that effectively guides processing, categories must be assigned to questions before higher-memory processes are summoned for further interpretation and memory searches. This means that a question category should describe its members in some manner that will allow us to assign the correct category to a question as soon as possible.

The earliest point at which categorization could take place is before the question is parsed, while it exists only as a lexical entity. But we have seen that lexical categories are too misleading for process-model predictions. So we cannot expect to assign question categories before the question has been parsed. This should not be viewed as a loss. The parsing processes for questions rely on the same predictive mechanisms that are applied to declarative statements (Riesbeck, 1975; Riesbeck & Schank, 1976). The parser would not benefit from knowing that the question it was working on fell into one question category or another. But after the parse of a question is completed, the conceptual question is ready for higher interpretive memory processing. A question category should be recognized before the higher-memory processes are invoked. Therefore question categories should be assigned immediately after a question is parsed.

In QUALM, question types are assigned as soon as the parse is completed and a Conceptual Dependency representation for the question has been produced. Categorizing a question is the first task of the interpreter.

QUALM uses 13 conceptual question categories:

1. Causal Antecedent
2. Goal Orientation
3. Enablement
4. Causal Consequent
5. Verification
6. Disjunctive
7. Instrumental/Procedural
8. Concept Completion
9. Expectational
10. Judgmental
11. Quantification
12. Feature Specification
13. Request

These question categories can be recognized by a simple examination of the conceptual question. Salient structural features of the conceptual question are examined by testing procedures that are hierarchically organized in the manner of a discrimination net (Feigenbaum, 1963). The question analyzer that performs this analysis is described in section 3.14. Once a question category has been assigned by the question analyzer, this categorization will be a central factor in subsequent interpretation and memory searches.

In addition to assigning conceptual categories to questions, the question analyzer also establishes question concepts. A question concept is roughly what is left of a question when its interrogative aspect is removed. For example, the question concept for "Why did John go to New York?" is the conceptualization representing "John went to New York." Rules for extracting question concepts are different for each conceptual question category.

Categories for questions are only useful to the extent that they predict which processing strategies will result in a correct interpretation and a successful memory search. If two proposed categories require identical processing strategies, there is no rationale for distinguishing separate categories. Conversely, if a single proposed category requires many different processing strategies to effectively understand and answer all questions in that category, then it will be useful to split that category up into smaller ones that better predict the necessary processing. The conceptual categories proposed here can be thought of as processing categories that are predicted by features of conceptual representation.

The justification for these 13 categories will become more apparent when the processes predicted by them are described. Inferential analysis, content specification, and retrieval heuristics are all processing modules within QUALM that rely on conceptual question categorization.

3.1   CAUSAL ANTECEDENT

Causal Antecedent questions ask about states or events that have in some way caused the concept in question. Many different kinds of causal relationships are covered by Causal Antecedent questions (e.g., some examples are: physical causality and motivating emotional states).

Q1: Why did John go to New York?

Q2: What caused John to go to New York?

Q3: How did the glass break?

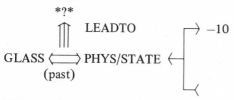

```
      *?*
       ⇑   LEADTO            ⌐→ −10
       ⇑                     │
GLASS ⟺ PHYS/STATE ⟵────────┤
      (past)                 └⟨
```

Q4: What resulted in John's leaving?

```
      *?*
       ⇑   LEADTO                    ⌐→
       ⇑                             │
JOHN ⟺ PTRANS  ⟵─── JOHN ⟵─────────┤
     (past)                          └⟨ UNSPEC
```

Causal Antecedent questions are always represented as causal chain structures (Schank, 1973a, 1974b, 1975b; Section 2.2 of this volume), where the chain antecedent is unknown. Because the precise nature of the causal relationship is also unknown, the causal link between the unknown antecedent and the question concept is a LEADTO link.

Recognizing the category.   All Causal Antecedent questions are recognized by the following features:

1. There is a causal chain of two conceptualizations.
2. The causal link is LEADTO.
3. All or part of the first conceptualization is unknown.

Finding the question concept.   The question concept of a Causal Antecedent question is extracted from the parsed question by deleting the first conceptualization in the causal chain. For example:

```
      *?*
       ⇑   LEADTO                    ⌐→ NEW YORK
       ⇑                             │
JOHN ⟺ PTRANS  ⟵─── JOHN ⟵─────────┤
     (past)                          └⟨
```

has the question concept:

```
                                     ⌐→ NEW YORK
                                     │
JOHN ⟺ PTRANS  ⟵─── JOHN ⟵─────────┤
     (past)                          └⟨
```

3.2 GOAL ORIENTATION

A Goal Orientation question is a special case of what is commonly called a why-question. Questions in this category may be paraphrased as why-questions, but Goal Orientation questions ask about the motives or goals behind an action. This makes them slightly more specific than Causal Antecedent questions. Because a mental goal is being sought as the explanation, the unknown causal antecedent relates to the question concept as a reason for the act in question; therefore the causal link between the unknown antecedent and the act in question is a REASON link. Some examples are:

Q1: For what purpose did John take the book?

Q2: Mary left for what reason?

Appropriate answers to Goal Orientation questions should describe the mental state of the actor within the question concept. This presupposes that the actor of the question concept is a human who acts of his own volition. Goal Orientation questions ask about the mental processes and desires underlying human behavior. It does not make sense to ask "For what purpose did the book fall?", because the conceptual representation for a falling book has gravity PTRANSing the book; however, gravity does not act out of volition but from laws of physics. "For what purpose did John fall?" is similarly nonsensical, because gravity is still acting upon John, and John presumably did not fall on purpose. For this question to make any sense at all, we have to twist our usual understanding of what it means to fall; we assume that John feigned a fall or purposely threw himself off balance. As soon as this element of intentionality is injected, it makes sense to ask what was John's reason for falling.

Some Causal Antecedent questions can be answered in terms of either a Causal Antecedent or a Goal Orientation:

Q3:   Why did Mary drop the book?
A3a: Because John bumped her.
         (causal antecedent)
A3b: To get John's attention.
         (goal orientation)

A3a describes an act that RESULTed in Mary's dropping the book; *A3b* described a REASON Mary had for dropping the book. If the question is understood as a Causal Antecedent question (as would be the case for *Q3*), either answer can be returned. But if the question were worded as a Goal Orientation question ("For what purpose did Mary drop the book?"), the answer would have to describe a reason for the act in question. It does not make sense to answer:

Q4: For what purpose did Mary drop the book?
A3a: Because John bumped her.

In Section 6.2, we see how QUALM looks first for a Goal Oriented answer and then settles for a more general Causal Antecedent answer if the former is not found. The issues of how to answer why-questions when there are many reasonable responses are dealt with at length in Chapter 9.

Recognizing the Category: All Goal Orientation questions are recognized by the following features:

1. There is a causal chain of two conceptualizations.
2. The causal link is REASON.
3. The first conceptualization is unknown.

Finding the Question Concept: The question concept of a Goal Orientation question is extracted from the parsed question by taking the second conceptualization in the causal chain. For example:

has the question concept:

3.3 ENABLEMENT

Enablement questions are similar to Goal Orientation questions insofar as they specify a causal relationship between an unknown conceptualization and the question concept. The causal relationship is an ENABLE, and the concept in question is enabled by the unknown act or state. Some examples are:

Q1: How was John able to eat?

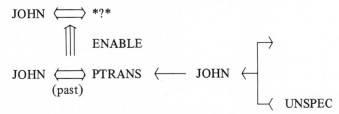

Q2: What did John need to do in order to leave?

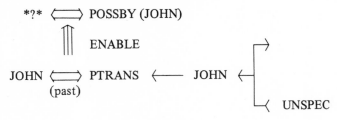

Q3: What did John need in order to leave?

? $\Longleftrightarrow$ POSSBY (JOHN)

‖ ENABLE

JOHN $\Longleftrightarrow$ PTRANS $\longleftarrow$ JOHN
(past)

UNSPEC

Enablement questions may specify some information about the unknown concept. *Q1* describes the unknown enablement as an action; *Q2* describes it as a state of immediate possession. In general, an Enablement question consists of a question concept enabled by another concept, which either is completely unknown or has an unknown component.

The precise nature of the enabling relationship is left unspecified. Enablements can occur in a variety of ways. Eugene Charniak (1975b) has explored different kinds of enabling causation. Two categories are physical enablement (John needed a car to go to New York) and social enablement (John needed money to eat at the restaurant). World knowledge about cars, money, and restaurants is needed to determine when enablements are physical and when they are social. In SAM and PAM there is only one causal link describing enablement: the ENABLE link.

If more than one enablement link were used within these systems, there would have to be a process that relied on such distinctions. If no such process exists, there is no justification for having different causal links. Thus far, SAM and PAM have had no need for different enablement links.

The inference processes that operate on enabling relationships appear to be very knowledge specific. For example, if you go to a restaurant without money, you will be waited on and served without any difficulty until the check comes. Then the consequences of having no money can include having to wash dishes or being arrested. If you go to a restaurant without shoes on, you may very well be turned away at the door. But you will not be arrested or made to wash dishes. Knowing that the enablements violated in these two cases are both social does not in itself help us know the specific consequences of violating those conditions. Only very specific knowledge about restaurants will allow us to predict the consequences of not having money or not wearing shoes.

Recognizing the Category: All enablement questions are recognized by the following features:

1. There is a causal chain of two conceptualizations.
2. The causal link is ENABLE.
3. All or part of the first conceptualization is unknown.

Finding the Question Concept: The question concept of an enablement question is extracted from the parsed question by taking the second conceptualization in the causal chain. For example:

JOHN ⟺ *?*

ENABLE

JOHN ⟺ INGEST
(past)

has the question concept:

JOHN ⟺ INGEST
(past)

3.4 CAUSAL CONSEQUENT

Causal Consequent questions are causal structures in which the question concept in some way causes an unknown concept or causal chain. The general causal link for such questions is the LEADTO link. Some examples are:

Q1: What happened when John left?

JOHN ⟺ PTRANS ⟵ JOHN ⟵
(past)

LEADTO   UNSPEC
?

Q2: What resulted from John's leaving?

JOHN ⟷ PTRANS ⟵ JOHN ⟵ →
    (past)
    ⇑ LEADTO   ⟨ UNSPEC
  ?

Q3: What happened after John left?

JOHN ⟷ PTRANS ⟵ JOHN ⟵ →
    (past)
    ⇑ LEADTO   ⟨ UNSPEC
  ?

Q4: What if I don't leave?

ME ⟷̸ PTRANS ⟵ ME ⟵ →
    (future)
    ⇑ LEADTO   ⟨ UNSPEC
  ?

Q5: What happens if I don't leave?

ME ⟷̸ PTRANS ⟵ ME ⟵ →
    (future)
    ⇑ LEADTO   ⟨ UNSPEC
  ?

Q6: If I don't leave, then what?

ME ⟷̸ PTRANS ⟵ ME ⟵ →
    (future)
    ⇑ LEADTO   ⟨ UNSPEC
  ?

Some Causal Consequent questions have partially known consequents:

Q7: What did John do after Mary left?

MARY $\Longleftrightarrow$ PTRANS $\longleftarrow$ MARY $\longleftarrow$ UNSPEC
(past)

$\Uparrow$ LEADTO

JOHN $\Longleftrightarrow$ *?*
(past)

Recognizing the Category: All causal-consequent questions are recognized by the following features:

1. There is a causal chain of two conceptualizations.
2. The causal link is LEADTO.
3. All or part of the second conceptualization is unknown.

Finding the Question Concept: The question concept of a Causal Consequent question is extracted from the parsed question by taking the first conceptualization in the causal chain. For example:

JOHN $\Longleftrightarrow$ PTRANS $\longleftarrow$ JOHN $\longleftarrow$ UNSPEC
(past)

$\Uparrow$ LEADTO
?

has the question concept:

JOHN $\Longleftrightarrow$ PTRANS $\longleftarrow$ JOHN $\longleftarrow$ UNSPEC
(past)

3.5 VERIFICATION

Verification questions ask about the truth of an event. These questions correspond roughly to those that can be answered yes or no. They are represented as single concepts or as causal-chain constructions with a MODE value = *?*. Some examples are:

Q1: Did John leave?

```
        (*?*)
JOHN  <===>  PTRANS  <——  JOHN  <—┌——>
        (past)                      │
                                    └—< UNSPEC
```

Q2: Did John do anything to keep Mary from leaving?

```
        (*?*)
JOHN  <===>  *DO*
        (past)
          ⇑  RESULT
          ‖
          ‖
MARY  <≠=>  PTRANS  <——  MARY  <—┌——>
        (past)                    │
                                  └—< UNSPEC
```

Q3: Does John think that Mary left?

```
                                        ┌——>                  (*?*)
MARY  <===>  PTRANS  <——  MARY  <——┤              <===>  IS MLOC
        (past)                      │                            (JOHN)
                                    └—< UNSPEC
```

Recognizing the Category: All Verification questions are recognized by one
of the following features:

1. There is a single conceptualization with MODE = *?*.
2. There is a causal-chain construction containing a conceptualization with
MODE value = *?*.

Finding the Question Concept: The question concept of a Verification
question is extracted from the parsed question by removing the MODE value *?*
from the conceptualization. For example:

```
        (*?*)
JOHN  <===>  PTRANS  <——  JOHN  <—┌——>
        (past)                      │
                                    └—< UNSPEC
```

has the question concept:

```
                                              ┌──→
   JOHN ⟺ PTRANS ⟵── JOHN ⟵┤
        (past)                               └─< UNSPEC
```

3.6 DISJUNCTIVE

Disjunctive questions resemble Verification questions but have multiple question concepts instead of one. Some examples are:

Q1: Was John or Mary here?

```
          (*?*)
   JOHN ⟺ IS LOCVAL (HERE)
          (past)
```

```
          OR
```

```
          (*?*)
   MARY ⟺ IS LOCVAL (HERE)
          (past)
```

Q2: Is John coming or going?

```
                                              ┌──→ UNSPEC₁
          (*?*)
   JOHN ⟺ PTRANS ⟵── JOHN ⟵┤
                                              └─<

          OR

          (*?*)                               ┌──→
   JOHN ⟺ PTRANS ⟵── JOHN ⟵┤
                                              └─< UNSPEC₁
```

Recognizing the Category: All Disjunctive questions are recognized by the following features:

1. There is a top-level OR relation.
2. Concepts under the OR relation have MODE = *?*.

Finding the Question Concept: The question concept of a Disjunctive question is extracted from the parsed question by listing the conceptualizations without their MODE value = *?*. For example:

$$JOHN \overset{(*?*)}{\Longleftrightarrow} PTRANS \longleftarrow JOHN \longleftarrow \begin{cases} \rightarrow UNSPEC_1 \\ \prec \end{cases}$$

OR

$$JOHN \overset{(*?*)}{\Longleftrightarrow} PTRANS \longleftarrow JOHN \longleftarrow \begin{cases} \rightarrow \\ \prec UNSPEC_1 \end{cases}$$

has the multiple question concept:

$$JOHN \Longleftrightarrow PTRANS \longleftarrow JOHN \longleftarrow \begin{cases} \rightarrow UNSPEC_1 \\ \prec \end{cases}$$

$$JOHN \Longleftrightarrow PTRANS \longleftarrow JOHN \longleftarrow \begin{cases} \rightarrow \\ \prec UNSPEC_1 \end{cases}$$

Although Disjunctive questions are much like Verification questions but with multiple question concepts, the processing for these questions is distinct from the processing for Verification questions. A Disjunctive question can rarely be answered appropriately with a yes or no.

3.7   INSTRUMENTAL/PROCEDURAL

Instrumental/Procedural questions are represented by concepts that have a totally or partially unknown instrumentality. Some examples are:

Q1: How did John go to New York?

$$JOHN \underset{(past)}{\Longleftrightarrow} PTRANS \longleftarrow JOHN \longleftarrow \begin{cases} \rightarrow NEW\ YORK \overset{I}{\longleftarrow} *?* \\ \prec \end{cases}$$

Q2: What did John use to eat?

$$\text{JOHN} \Longleftrightarrow \text{INGEST} \xleftarrow{\text{I}}$$
(past)

$$\text{JOHN} \Longleftrightarrow \text{PTRANS} \longleftarrow \text{*?*}$$

→ MOUTH (JOHN)

Sometimes the instrumentality for an act entails a long sequence of acts rather than a single event. In this case, the unknown instrument is more appropriately described as a procedure. Procedural questions are represented in the same way as instrumental ones. The difference lies in what kind of answers are expected: A procedural question is looking for directions; an instrumental question is looking for a short answer. Some examples are:

Q3: How do I get to your house?

→ HOUSE (POSSBY: YOU)

$$\text{ME} \Longleftrightarrow \text{PTRANS} \longleftarrow \text{ME} \xleftarrow{} \qquad \xleftarrow{\text{I}} \text{*?*}$$

Q4: What is a good way to your house?

→ HOUSE (POSSBY: YOU)

$$\text{HUM}_1 \Longleftrightarrow \text{PTRANS} \longleftarrow \text{HUM}_1 \xleftarrow{} \qquad \xleftarrow{\text{I}} \text{*?*}$$

Q5: How will I get word to John?

→ CP (JOHN)

$$\text{ME} \Longleftrightarrow \text{MTRANS} \longleftarrow \text{MOBJECT} \xleftarrow{} \qquad \xleftarrow{\text{I}} \text{*?*}$$
(future)

↳ CP (ME)

Whether a question is looking for an instrumental or a procedural answer is a decision that must be made by interpretive memory processes according to the specific context, the questioner's assumed knowledge state, and other inference processes. The initial parse of a question is not responsible for deciding what kind of answer is most appropriate for a given question. In some contexts, the question "How did John get to your house?" will be best satisfied with an answer like "By car." But in other contexts (e.g., if the obvious route has been altered by several complicated detours), the question asks for a more detailed description. Inferential analysis and content specification are responsible for deciding how much information is being asked for by an Instrumental/Procedural question.

There are many how-questions that appear to be Instrumental/Procedural questions but are not:

Q6: How did you manage to see John?
(Did you make an appointment? Threaten him?)
Q7: How did John find his lost book?
(Did he offer a reward? Look for it himself?)
Q8: How can we eat out tonight?
(Can we cash a check somewhere? Use a credit card?)

Each of *Q6–8* ask about actions or conditions that must precede the act in question. An Instrumental/Procedural question asks about an act that was simultaneous with the main act of the question. If a question asks about an act that precedes the main act of the question, the question is either a Causal Antecedent or an Enablement question.

Q6: How did you manage to see John?

asks what steps had to be taken before you were able to see John. It does not ask for acts that were simultaneous with the act of seeing John (acts such as talking to him or watching him).

Q7: How did John find his lost book?

Finding a lost object is conceptually represented as a change in mental state. Finding a lost book means that the location of the book was for a time unknown (i.e., not accessible to the actor's Conscious Processor), after which the location became known. "How did John find his lost book?" asks for an act that resulted in this change of mental state. John may have found the book by asking Bill whether he knew where it was or by looking through his desk drawers. In any case, the act precedes the state change as a causal antecedent.

Q8: How can we eat out tonight?

If this question were taken as an Instrumental/Procedural question, it could be answered "We'll use forks and knives." The question is much more likely to be asking about the enabling conditions for eating out. Reasonable answers would resemble "We can borrow Bill's car" or "I have an American Express Card." Each of these answers specifies an act or state that will enable the act of eating out.

Knowledge about when questions like *Q6–8* should be understood as Causal Antecedent or Enablement questions instead of as Instrumental/Procedural questions is not something the parser can always be expected to have.

The correct interpretation of questions like these often occurs at a higher level of interpretive analysis. Rules for reinterpreting Instrumental/Procedural questions as Causal Antecedent or Enablement questions are incorporated within the inferential analysis described in Chapter 4.

Recognizing the Category: All Instrumental/Procedural questions are recognized by the following feature:

1. The question involves a conceptualization that has a partially or totally unknown instrument.

Finding the Question Concept: The question concept of an Instrumental/Procedural question is extracted from the parsed question by removing the Instrument slot. For example:

```
                                              ┌→ NEW YORK
    JOHN ⟺ PTRANS ⟵── JOHN ⟵┤                    ⟵─I─ *?*
         (past)                      └<
```

has the question concept:

```
                                              ┌→ NEW YORK
    JOHN ⟺ PTRANS ⟵── JOHN ⟵┤
         (past)                      └<
```

3.8 CONCEPT COMPLETION

Concept-Completion questions include many who-, what-, where-, and when-questions. These questions are very much like fill-in-the-blank questions, insofar as they specify a particular event with one missing component and ask for the completion of that event. Some examples are:

Q1: What did John eat?

```
    JOHN ⟺ INGEST ⟵── *?*
         (past)
```

Q2: Who gave Mary the book?

```
                                  ┌→ MARY
    *?* ⟺ ATRANS ⟵── BOOK ⟵┤
         (past)                └< *?*
```

Q3: When did John leave Paris?

JOHN ⟺ PTRANS ⟵ JOHN ⟵⎰ ⟶
    (past)
      ↑
    TIME: *?*   ⟵ PARIS

Recognizing the Category: All Concept Completion questions are recognized by the following feature[1]:

1. An unknown conceptual component exists somewhere in the question conceptualization.

Finding the Question Concept: The question concept for a Concept-Completion question is identical with the parsed question conceptualization.

3.9 EXPECTATIONAL

Expectational questions ask about the causal antecedent of an act that presumably did not occur. This presupposition is what sets Expectational questions apart from Causal Antecedent questions. Expectational questions are usually phrased as why-not questions. Some examples are:

Q1: Why didn't John go to New York?

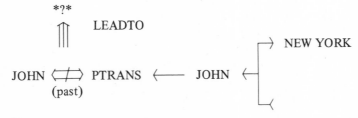

Q2: Why isn't John eating?

     ?
    ⇑ LEADTO
JOHN ⟨╪⟩ INGEST

---

[1]This description holds unless the conceptual question satisfies the specifications of another conceptual category, in which case the other category has precedence over Concept Completion. For example, if the unknown component fills the Instrument slot, the question is Instrumental/Procedural.

Recognizing the Category: All Expectational questions are recognized by the following features:

1. There is a causal chain of two concepts.
2. The first concept is unknown.
3. The causal link is LEADTO.
4. The second concept has a MODE value = *NEG*.

Finding the Question Concept: The question concept of an Expectational question is extracted from the parsed question by taking the second concept from the causal chain and deleting its negative MODE value. For example:

```
 *?*
  ⇑      LEADTO
 |||
                                  ┌──→ NEW YORK
 JOHN ⟨—⟩ PTRANS ⟵——— JOHN ⟨─┤
      (past)                      └──⟨
```

has the question concept:

```
                                  ┌──→ NEW YORK
 JOHN ⟨—⟩ PTRANS ⟵——— JOHN ⟨─┤
      (past)                      └──⟨
```

3.10 JUDGMENTAL

Judgmental questions solicit a judgment on the part of the listener. All Judgmental questions can be appropriately prefaced by "In your opinion. ..." Of course, all questions ask for an opinion of the listener; so such a distinction could be viewed as nothing more than a matter of degree. But without getting into difficult philosophical arguments, Judgmental questions are roughly those that require a projection of events rather than the strict recall of facts. "Where is St. Louis?" does not require a Judgmental answer. This question asks for a specific fact, which a person either knows or does not know. "Where do you think the President will spend Christmas?" is not asking for a hard fact unless the answerer is known to be a close friend of the President.

Judgmental questions are recognized by their explicit reference to the mind of the person being addressed. Some examples are:

Q1: What should John do to keep Mary from leaving?

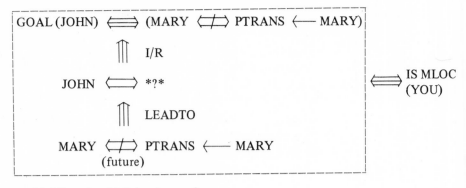

Q2: What should John do now?

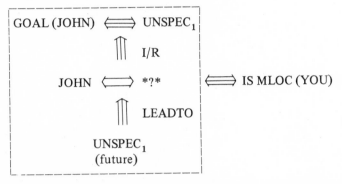

Recognizing the Category: All Judgmental questions are recognized by the following features:

1. There is a top-level MLOC state.
2. The top-level actor is the answerer.
3. The MOBJECT contains a partially unknown conceptualization.

Finding the Question Concept: The question concept for Judgmental questions is extracted from the conceptual question by finding the goal state inside the MOBJECT. If no goal is specified, a default goal must be derived from the context in which the question is asked. For example:

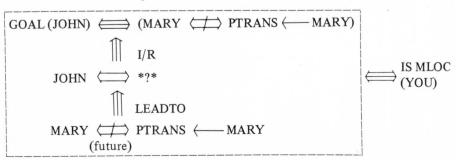

has the question concept:

$$\text{GOAL (JOHN)} \Longleftrightarrow (\text{MARY} \iff \text{PTRANS} \longleftarrow \text{MARY})$$

3.11 QUANTIFICATION

Quantification questions ask for an amount. The amount may be countable, as in how-many questions, or it may be a continuous quantity. All Quantification questions can be phrased as how-questions. Some examples are:

Q1: How many people are here?

$$\text{GROUP} \Longleftrightarrow \text{IS LOC (HERE)}$$
$$\uparrow$$
MEMBERTYP (*HUMAN*)
NUMBER (*?*)

Q2: How many dogs does John have?

$$\text{GROUP} \Longleftrightarrow \text{IS POSSBY (JOHN)}$$
$$\uparrow$$
MEMBERTYP (*DOG*)
NUMBER (*?*)

Some Quantification questions refer to values on physical- or mental-state scales. In this case, the amount in question is a relative value on a finite scale. Some examples are:

Q3: How ill was John?

$$\text{JOHN} \Longleftrightarrow \text{IS PHYSSTATE (*?*)}$$
(past)

Q4: How badly do you want the book?

$$\text{BOOK} \Longleftrightarrow \text{POSSBY (YOU)}$$

$$\Uparrow \quad \text{CANCAUSE}$$

$$\text{YOU} \Longleftrightarrow \text{TOWARD JOY (*?*)}$$

Q5: How does John feel?

$$\text{JOHN} \Longleftrightarrow \text{IS MENTALSTATE (*?*)}$$

Recognizing the Category: All Quantification questions are recognized by the following features:

1. a causal chain or single conceptualization involving a state scale

2. an unknown state-scale value.

Finding the Question Concept: The question concept for a Quantification question is identical with the parsed question conceptualization.

3.12 FEATURE SPECIFICATION

Feature Specification questions ask about some property of a given person or thing. Such questions are similar to Concept Completion questions insofar as they are both fill-in-the-blank questions. The significant difference between the two question types is that Concept-Completion questions ask about missing conceptual components in actions, while Feature Specification questions ask about static properties of objects. Some examples are:

Q1: What color are John's eyes?

$$\text{EYES} \iff \text{IS COLOR (*?*)}$$
$$\uparrow$$
POSSBY (JOHN)

Q2: What breed of dog is Rover?

$$\text{ROVER} \iff \text{IS BREED (*?*)}$$

Feature Specification questions ask about properties that cannot be expressed as a relative value on a scale. For example, colors are conceptualized in terms of names. Although it is possible to represent colors on a wave-length spectrum, people do not naturally think about color in this manner. But it would be misleading to say that Feature Specification questions look for names, while Quantification questions look for relative numerical assignments. Some Feature Specification questions are answered in terms of numerical quantities:

Q3: How much does that rug cost?

$$\text{RUG} \iff \text{IS COST (*?*)}$$

Q4: How old is John?

$$\text{JOHN} \iff \text{IS AGE (*?*)}$$

These questions can be answered in terms of a number, but they are Feature Specification questions because the numerical answer must refer to a specific unit. The unit need not be explicitly stated in the answer, but it is nevertheless there by inference. If John's age is stated as 56, we would infer that he is 56 years old. If the rug is said to cost a hundred, we assume it costs $100. It may cost 100 sheep, but we would infer our own standard monetary unit unless told otherwise.

Feature Specification questions that ask about nonnumeric properties can refer to implicit properties in the same way that the units of numeric properties are often inferred. This happens when questions are phrased "What kind of . . ." or "What sort of . . .":

Q5: What kind of dog is Rover?
Q6: What kind of doctor is John?
Q7: What sort of college is this?
Q8: What sort of bicycle does John have?

By inference, most people would infer that Q5 is asking about the breed of dog and that Q6 is asking for a branch of medical practice. Q7 would normally be understood to be asking about educational orientation, whereas Q8 could be asking about the make or general type. These questions are open to flexible interpretations, which should be sensitive to context. In different contexts, Q5 could be referring to breed (beagle), variety (hound), or lifestyle (housedog). But in any given context, some inference must be made about what property is being sought in order to answer the question.

Recognizing the Category: All Feature Specification questions are recognized by the following feature:

1. There is an unknown property value.

Finding the Question Concept: The question concept for a Feature Specification question is identical with the parsed question conceptualization.

3.13   REQUEST

Requests constitute a special question category distinct from all the other categories presented here. All of the other question categories discussed in this chapter describe inquiry questions. An inquiry is asked by a questioner who is seeking some specific information. All inquiries are appropriately answered by an MTRANS of some sort. But a Request is asked when the questioner wants a specific act to be performed.

Q1: Would you pass the salt?
Q2: Can you get me my coat?
Q3: Will you take out the garbage?

It is not adequate to distinguish Requests from inquiries in terms of whether a verbal response is appropriate in reply. "What time is it?" is an inquiry that can be answered by pointing to a clock on the wall. And many requests are denied verbally:

Would you pass the salt?
No.

Even Requests that are performed are often accompanied by a verbal response:

Would you pass the salt?
Sure, here.

Requests differ from inquiry question types in terms of when they are recognized by the interpreter. Inquiry question types are initially recognized by the question analyzer, whereas Requests are never recognized in this way. All Request questions are assigned some inquiry question type by the question analyzer. It is then up to the inferential analysis to reassign the question category as a Request. This distinction in recognition derives from the fact that all Requests can be literally interpreted as inquiries.

Q1: Would you pass the salt?
Q2: Can you get me my coat?
Q3: Will you take out the garbage?

Each of these questions could be (mis)understood as a Verification question answerable by a yes or no. The question analyzer will always understand a Request literally. Thus, it will recognize *Q1–3* as Verification questions instead of as Requests. The inferential-conversion rules are responsible for finding the less literal interpretations of questions that capture what the questioner "obviously" meant. It is on this higher level of question interpretation that Requests are detected by means of interpretive-inference mechanisms.

3.14   THE QUESTION ANALYZER

The question analyzer is designed to function like a discrimination net that applies various tests to a conceptualized question to determine its conceptual category. The tests within the net are hierarchically organized in order to minimize the test processing. For example, at the head of the net is a test that determines whether a question is represented as a causal-chain structure. If it is, then tests for Causal Antecedent, Goal Orientation, Enablement, Causal Consequent, and Expectational questions are all organized under this one branch of the net.

The most difficult category to recognize are the Concept Completion questions. These questions are characterized by an unknown conceptual component, which may occur anywhere and at any level in the conceptualization. Rather than conduct a search to positively identify such questions, the net is organized so that any question that has passed through a terminal branch without positive identification will be categorized as Conceptual Completion.

Figure 3.1 outlines the organization of the discriminating tests used by the question analyzer.

Is there a causal chain?
no   yes
          └→ Is the first concept an unknown or partially unknown act?
              no   yes
                      └→ Is the causal link LEADTO?
                          no   yes
                                  └→ Does the second concept have a MODE value = NEG?
                                      no   yes
                                            └→ Categorize as EXPECTATIONAL
                                            ──→ Categorize as CAUSAL ANTECEDENT
                      Is the causal link REASON?
                      no   yes
                            └→ Categorize as GOAL ORIENTATION
                      Is the causal link ENABLE?
                      no   yes
                            └→ Categorize as ENABLEMENT
                            ──→ Categorize as CONCEPT COMPLETION
          Is the second concept an unknown act?
 ──←── no   yes
              └→ Categorize as CAUSAL CONSEQUENT

Is the top level concept an OR relation?
no   yes
        └→ Categorize as DISJUNCTIVE

Does the top level concept have an unknown MODE value?
no   yes
        └→ Cateogrize as VERIFICATION

Is the top level concept an MBUILD with actor = YOU?
no   yes
        └→ Categorize as JUDGEMENTAL

Is there an unknown state value?
no   yes
          └→ Is the state a property description?
              no   yes
                    └→ Categorize as FEATURE SPECIFICATION
          Is the state a relative scale description?
 ──←── no   yes
              └→ Categorize as QUANTIFICATION

Is there an unknown INSTRUMENT slot?
no   yes
        └→ Categorize as INSTRUMENTAL/PROCEDURAL
        ──→ Categorize as CONCEPT COMPLETION

FIG. 3.1.   The question analyzer.

4

Recategorizing Questions by Inferential Analysis

This chapter describes inference mechanisms within QUALM that complete the interpretation of a question. When the question analyzer assigns a conceptual category to a question, it does so on the basis of structural features in the Conceptual Dependency representation of that question. Inferential analysis examines the content of a question to see whether this initial categorization of the question is correct.

In the context of talking to a friend on the street, the two questions:

Q1: Do you have a match?
Q2: Do you have a wooden match?

are both recognized by the question analyzer as Verification questions. That is, they are both understood as inquiries deserving yes or no answers. But, whereas *Q2* is best understood as an inquiry, *Q1* should ultimately be understood as a Request for a light. *Q2* should remain an inquiry, because the specification of a wooden match, rather than any other kind of match, suggests that the questioner is interested in something other than merely getting a light. *Q1,* on the other hand, is a standard way of requesting a light.

By the time the inferential analyzer examines *Q1* and *Q2,* both have been tagged as Verification questions by the question analyzer. It is the job of inferential analysis to change the category for *Q1* to a "Request" and to specify that *Q1* is a Request for a light (in the sense of a flame).

4.0 INTRODUCTION

Many questions are not correctly understood if taken literally. Some questions require knowledge of conversational conventions in order to be interpreted correctly, and others can be understood only within their situational context. Many questions can best be answered by taking into consideration what the questioner knows and does not know. All of these factors contribute to the final interpretation of a question. The interpretive analysis of a question must be able to perceive the question within its overall context; interpretive mechanisms must be sensitive to a wide range of information that is "external" to the question. These mechanisms must effectively examine a question, consider contextual factors, appeal to the conventions of dialogue, and conclude that "at this time, in this setting, this question must mean − − −." Such interpretations require understanding by inference.

Inference mechanisms are needed to achieve complete conceptual understanding of a question. When a question is not interpreted correctly on the level of inferential analysis, the answer produced will be inappropriate. Faulty inferential analysis of a question results in an answer that may have been right in another setting, but not in the current one.

There are three inference modules within the interpreter that are designed to recognize what a question is really asking. These three modules contain conversion rules for:

1. Contextual Inference
2. Context-Independent Inference
3. Knowledge-State Assessment.

Each module contains rules of inference that enable the system to alter its understanding of a question. These rules are applied whenever the conceptual category and question concept meet specific criteria. When a conversion rule is applied to a question, it alters the conceptual category assigned to that question and usually alters the question concept as well. Each question is tested by all of the conversion rules, and reinterpretation occurs whenever a rule is applicable. This process of successive reinterpretation continues until all the conversion rules have run their tests. The resulting question concept and conceptual categorization represent the final interpretation of the question.

4.1 CONTEXTUAL INFERENCES

Contextual-inference rules exploit the conversational context in which a question occurs. Conversational context is the situational setting in which a conversation takes place. Three types of inference mechanisms rely on conversational context: conversational scripts, generalized inference mechanisms, and conversational continuity.

Conversational Scripts.   Some conversational settings are very stereotyped, and conversations within these settings can be understood by invoking an appropriate script. An inference rule that is specific to one particular script is a conversational script inference. For example, the conversations that a stockbroker has with his clients all have predictable elements centering around the transactions that a stockbroker can perform. If one is not familiar with the transactions that normally occur in this particular business setting, a dialogue between a stockbroker and his client cannot be fully understood. Conversational scripts are knowledge structures that organize knowledge-based inferences for specific situations in which people interact conversationally.

Generalized Inference Rules. Not all knowledge-based inferences can be organized under specific situational scripts in the way conversational scripts organize inference mechanisms. If John has been helping Mary pack for a trip, and he asks:

Q1: What didn't I pack?
Mary will understand this question to mean:

Q2: What didn't I pack that I should have packed?

There is no conversational script for conversations about packing, because dialogues about packing are not highly stereotyped. But there is a situational script about packing for trips, and this must be used to understand the question. In QUALM, this knowledge is accessed and used by a generalized inference rule. This rule is general in the sense that it would be equally applicable in a context in which John is mailing out Christmas cards and asks Mary:

Q3: Who didn't I send a card to?

Here again, no conversational script goes with sending Christmas cards, but there is a script for sending Chirstmas cards that must be accessed to understand the question. The same general inference rule that operated in the context of packing for a business trip will work in this context. This inference conversion rule will reinterpret *Q3* to mean:

Q4: Who didn't I send a card to who I wanted to send a card to?

Without the inference, the question would admit all sorts of ridiculous answers:

Q3: Who didn't I send a card to?
A3: Abraham Lincoln, Moby Dick, and everyone in Nova Scotia.

The general rule that handles questions like *Q1* and *Q3* is described in subsection 4.1-2. A general rule of this sort, which uses script-related knowledge but which can be applied to a variety of scripts, is called a generalized-inference conversion rule.

Conversational Continuity. A final application of conversational context occurs when a question relies on the continuity of conversation. Many questions do not contain complete conceptualizations, but still make sense because they are understood in terms of previous conversation. Conversational-continuity conversion rules are responsible for understanding in these situations.

> *A:* Did John give the book to Mary?
> *B:* No.
> *A:* Why not?

In this case it is clear that the question "Why not?" is asking "Why didn't John give the book to Mary?"

> *A:* Did John give the book to Mary?
> *B:* I don't know.
> *A:* Why not?

Here "Why not?" means "Why don't you know whether John gave the book to Mary?" General rules of conversational continuity allow us to fill in such missing information.

4.1-1 Conversational Scripts

Many conversations that occur between strangers in the context of an everyday business or service transaction have a highly predictable content. A clerk in a store spends the majority of his time answering such questions as:

> How much is this?
> Do you have this in another color (size, style)?
> Do you expect to get any more in?
> Do you have any . . .?
> Where are the . . .?

Of course a customer can ask a store clerk anything ("Haven't we met before?"), but questions that are appropriate to the role a store clerk assumes are both finite and highly predictable. As for the store clerk, he is expected to do nothing but answer questions and initially offer assistance ("Can I help you?").

The memory processes that predictively anticipate stereotypic exchanges within a common situation are encoded in a conversational script. The term *script,* as it has been presented within the SAM system, has been used primarily to refer to a predictive mechanism that has knowledge of stereotypic sequences of actions. Technically, this type of script is more correctly described as a situational script (Schank & Abelson, 1977), because it describes what events are likely to occur in a given situation. A conversational script is a predictive mechanism that has knowledge of stereotypic conversations.

Many situational scripts have conversational scripts embedded in them. For example, the restaurant script should contain a conversational script for dialogues between the patron and the waiter or waitress. The restaurant script implemented in the SAM system has a minimal version of a complete conversational script.

There is an MTRANS conceptualization in which the patron tells the waiter what he wants, and a branch of events off the main path in which the waiter may MTRANS to the patron that he cannot have what he ordered. This last MTRANS may be followed by an MTRANS from the patron to the waiter specifying another order. This is as much as SAM knows about patron/waiter dialogues in the ordering scene of the restaurant script.

If SAM had a complete conversational restaurant script, it would be able to understand stories in which the patron asks the waiter to describe a specific dish, or to make a recommendation. Social conventions often determine what is and is not included in a conversational script. It is acceptable for a waiter to praise your choice when you place an order ("Oh yes, that's a very good dish"), but it is unlikely that he will tell you when you are making a mistake ("I think that's our worst dish — are you sure you won't reconsider?"). If a waiter tells you that you have made a poor choice, you feel that he is acting outside of his role as a waiter.

Conversational scripts are used in question answering whenever a situation gives rise to stereotyped exchanges. If, after you have consulted a menu in a restaurant, the waiter comes up with pad in hand and says:

Are you ready to order now?
What'll it be?
Are you ready here?
Have you decided yet?
Do you want some more time?
Yes?

all of these questions will be readily understood to be asking for an order. Anyone who has eaten out in a foreign country without any knowledge of the native language will attest to the fact that a waiter who appears with pad in hand at the right point in the script can say just about anything and still get an order. Scriptal situations affect the interpretation of questions just as they affect all script-governed conversation.

In some stereotypic settings, conversational scripts dictate how things are said as well as what things get said. Conversational scripts can affect the stylistic rules of conversation. Style here refers to attitudinal styles, such as formality (business meetings), casualness (parties), or sobriety (funerals). Stylistic features of questions are important because an inappropriate style can constitute a statement in itself. For example, excessively polite inquiries at a party are often used to discourage further conversation.

In addition to stylistic rules, conversational scripts often specify something more on the order of subcultural dialects. A good example of this occurs at auctions, during which the auctioneer uses a highly stylized mode of conversation while interacting with the floor. The rules of conversation in this context extend well beyond verbal conversation into visual signals for bidding; but there are still rules for interpreting verbal questions that must be known in order to understand the interaction. These rules allow us to understand a variety of questions.

> Do I hear $50? → Who will bid $50?
> Who will give me $50? → Who will bid $50?
> Is there $50 out there? → Will anyone bid $50?
> Do we have $50 → Will anyone bid $50?

In this case the auctioneer could say virtually anything that made reference to a number, and the audience would understand it to be a reference either to the bid currently standing or to the bid the auctioneer would like to get:

> I'm at $40, I want $50.
> I've got $40 in the hand, is there $50 in the bush?
> I found $40, I'm looking for $50.

Each of these statements can easily be understood because the conversational script for an auction predicts that an auctioneer will tell the audience two things during bidding: the standing bid and the bid he wants.

Inference mechanisms based on conversational scripts must be script-specific. The interpretive rules for an auctioneer during bidding are very simple:

1. If two numbers are mentioned, the lower one is the standing bid and the higher one is the bid sought.
2. If one number is mentioned, it is the bid sought.

These rules are applied whenever the meaning of a statement does not explicitly refer to the standing bid or the bid sought. These interpretive rules are useless outside of an auction. If John is thinking about buying a $50 chair and asks Mary "Do we have $50?" Mary will not interpret the question to mean "Will you bid $50?" The interpretive mechanisms described in the foregoing should be accessed only when an auctioneer is talking to the audience during bidding.

The notion of conversational scripts and their role in interpretive processing must be included in any question-answering model that claims to be a general model. As far as computer implementation of QUALM is concerned, there is no need to implement conversational scripts in the question interpreter unless we expect the computer to be carrying on conversations in various settings (restaurants, stores, bars, etc.). As long as the computer is confined to the context of answering questions about stories, it has no need to access conversational scripts during question interpretation. In the context of story understanding, conversational scripts are needed during understanding (if a story contains any script-related dialogue) but not during question answering. (John could ask Mary "Your place or mine?" but nobody is likely to put that question to the computer.)

Since SAM and PAM have not dealt with stories containing direct dialogue, no conversational scripts have been implemented in these systems. However, some work has been done that is closely related to the notion of conversational scripts and their application to conversational programs. The application of script-derived predictions has been explored (quite promisingly) in the area of airline reservations with the development of a program called GUS (Bobrow, Kaplan, Kay, Norman, Thompson, & Winograd, 1977). Although this work has been conducted independently and without reference to the general notion of scriptal conversation, GUS clearly relies on script-specific knowledge. GUS assumes the role of an airline-reservations agent in the conversational context of such an agent talking to a client. GUS's script-related predictions guide it through dialogues in which it must determine where the customer wants to go, when, for how long, and so on. We discuss GUS and its relationship to QUALM more fully in Chapter 12.

4.1-2 Generalized Inferences

Many questions require inferencing in order to fill in missing information. These inferences are often made on the basis of scriptal knowledge of the world. When an inference mechanism needs to access knowledge from a script, the mechanism may be designed in one of two basic ways. Some rules that generate inferences by drawing on script-based knowledge can be stated very generally so that one rule will apply over a large set of scripts. Other rules are script specific and can be used only in the context of the one script for which they were designed. This notion of general applicability versus script-specific applicability distinguishes generalized inference mechanisms from conversational-script inference mechanisms. We describe three generalized inference rules here. These rules are very significant because they can be used in a variety of contexts.

Single-Word Questions

In any script containing a host or servant type of role, a question by the person in that role that merely specifies an object or list of objects means "Do you want some (grobs)?" where (grobs) are something normally offered to the consumer in that particular script.

Coffee, tea, or milk? (on an airplane)
Nuts? (from someone fixing you a hot-fudge sundae)

The rule about offering objects that applies to these examples can be stated even more generally:

Rule:
If a role in a script specifies a highly predictable act associated with an object, a question by a person in that role that specifies that object means "Do you want me to (blitch)?", where (blitching) is the act predicted by the script.

Thus, a butler can ask a guest who has just entered the house "Your coat, sir?" and this will be understood to mean "Do you want me to take your coat?" If the guest is about to walk out the door and the butler walks up to him carrying his coat, "Your coat, sir?" means "Don't forget your coat" or "May I help you with (help you put on) your coat?" Similarly, a waitress can approach a man who has just sat down at a table and ask "A menu?" and mean "Do you want a menu?"

But suppose that the man who is sitting at the table says to the waitress "A menu?" Now the question means "Would you bring me a menu?" So if a question in a script situation specifies an object associated with the script, the question should be interpreted as either an inquiry concerning the script act or a request that the script act be performed. Whether the question is an inquiry or a request depends on whether or not the questioner is the script-assigned performer of the act.

So this leads us to the final, most general formulation of the rule:

Rule:
A question that consists of a single noun is either a request or an inquiry about the script-assigned act associated with that object. When the questioner is playing the script role that performs the act in question it is an inquiry about whether or not the act is desired. When the questioner is anyone else it is a request for the act to be performed.

When a script contains multiple events involving an object, each of which is performed by the same actor (as in the case with a butler and a coat), the appropriate act is determined by the current predictions of the script applier (Cullingford, 1976, 1978). If John has just entered a wealthy home, the script applier predicts that the butler may take his coat, but it does not yet predict that the butler will return John's coat to him.

Universal-Set Inference

It does not always make sense to word a Concept Completion question negatively. "Who wasn't elected president in 1969?" is a fairly strange question in any context. But there are reasonable Concept Completion questions that ask about negated concepts. For example, "What didn't I pack?" and "Who haven't I invited?" are Concept Completion questions with negative MODE values, for they ask about things that have not been done. The interpretation of such questions always requires the addition of a constraining feature. Without such a constraint, these questions could be answered:

Q: What haven't I packed? (upon closing the suitcase)
A: This pile of fuzz and the World Trade Center.

Q: Who isn't here? (upon entering a college seminar)
A: Lassie, Kahlil Gibran, and Rosemary Woods.

Q: What haven't I added? (before baking a cake)
A: A pound of dog hair and an oil filter.

It is obvious that all of these questions implicitly place a constraint on potential answers. Although the nonsense answers may be absolutely correct, they are nonsensical because they violate the implicit constraints: "What haven't I packed (that I should have packed)?" "Who isn't here (who should be here)?" "What haven't I added (that belongs in the cake)?" A general rule can be used to specify these constraints on the basis of scriptal knowledge of the world. The rule is invoked whenever we encounter a Concept Completion question with negative MODE value. The appropriate interpretive constraint is derived from the set of potential objects specified by the active script for the act or state in question. This universal set delimits possible answers so that we need to consider only appropriate answers. The script for packing a suitcase specifies that you pack only those objects that you want to have with you for reasons of necessity, convenience, or peace of mind. The script for a college seminar specifies that the professor and registered students attend. The script for baking a cake specifies a set of ingredients.

When a negative Concept Completion question is asked, acceptable answers specify things from the script-defined set of potential considerations. If you do not know the instantiated script-defined limitations, you cannot answer the question. Someone who does not know who belongs in the seminar cannot hope to answer "Who's not here?" In this way scripts delimit the set of acceptable and reasonable answers to negative Concept Completion questions. The more specific a script, the easier it is to find an answer, for the set of appropriate answers will be well defined. "What haven't I packed?" is difficult to answer because it requires knowing what the person packing needs or would like to take with him. A person answering this question needs to know the person who is packing and where he is going in order to come up with good answers. It is much easier to answer "What haven't I added?" in the context of baking a cake, because the ingredients for baking a cake are specified by the script as the ingredients listed in the recipe.

Implicit Requests

Many social interactions are very common and have come to be fairly standardized. Requests that occur within a standard interaction are often phrased in a manner that is not altogether straightforward:

Do you have a match?
Do you know what time it is?
Can you tell me what city this is?

In normal conversation, questions of this sort are never taken literally. That is, no one would ever answer one of these with a simple yes or no unless they were deliberately trying to be difficult. Each of these questions is in fact a request for a specific act or for the communication of information. "Do you have a match?" is a request for a match. "Do you know what time it is?" is an inquiry about the time, and "Can you tell me what city this is?" is an inquiry about the name of a city. The literal interpretation of these questions does not convey their underlying meanings. But how are these underlying meanings recognized? The sentence structure or conceptual syntax of such questions is not sufficient to indicate when the question is an inquiry and when it is a request:

> Do you have a Porsche?
>> (is not asking for the car)
> Can you spell?
>> (is not asking for a demonstration)

We now describe inference conversion rules that transform Verification questions into Requests whenever a Request interpretation is appropriate. Each rule has two parts: criteria and a target interpretation. The criteria describe conditions under which the rule is appropriate. A rule will not be applied if its criteria are not met. If all of the criteria for a rule are satisfied, the question is reinterpreted by replacing the question category and question concept as specified by the target interpretation.

Some of the criteria specifications require facts from general world knowledge concerning the content of the question. Therefore, permanent memory may need to be accessed to verify the criteria. These verification processes may be easily executed or fairly involved. For example, the ATRANS Request Conversion asks whether the object of the conceptualization is of little value. This can easily be confirmed or denied by examining a memory token. But the Performance Request Conversion asks whether it is reasonable to ask that the act described by the question be performed. This is considerably more difficult to establish. The mechanisms that verify these criteria are not described. At this stage it is not clear how the more involved verification processes should be designed. If all of the criteria for a rule apply, the question is reinterpreted according to the instructions under the target interpretation.

Rule 1: ATRANS-Request Conversion

Criteria: 1. Conceptual categorization = Verification.
2. The question concept is of the form:
X $\Longleftrightarrow$ IS POSSBY (*Y*) TIME (*PRESENT*)
where *Y* is the person being addressed.
3. *X* is of little value.

Target Interpretation:
Conceptual categorization ← Request
Question concept ←

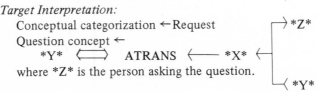

where *Z* is the person asking the question.

Examples:

Rule 1 applies:

Do you have a pencil?   → Would you give me a pencil?

Do you have a quarter?   → Would you give me a quarter?

Do you have a cigarette? → Would you give me a cigarette?

Rule 1 does not apply:

Do you have a coat? (a coat is too valuable to give away)

Did you have a dime? (wrong tense)

Do you have a telephone? (a telephone is too valuable)

Rule 2: MTRANS-Request Conversion

Criteria: 1. Conceptual categorization = Verification.

2. Question concept is of the form:

$$*X* \iff IS\ MLOC\ (*Y*)\ TIME\ (*PRESENT*)$$

where *Y* is the person being addressed and *X* is a conceptualization involving an unknown conceptual component.

3. The unknown component in *X* can be MTRANSed quickly and easily.

Target Interpretation:

Conceptual categorization ← Specification

Question concept ← *X*

Examples:

Rule 2 applies: ·

Do you know what time it is?   → What time is it?

Do you remember Al's address ? → What is Al's address?

Do you recognize this song?   → What song is this?

Rule 2 does not apply:

Do you know John? (this sense of *know* is not represented by an MLOC construction with an unknown MOBJ)

Do you know how to spell? (no unknown component; spell what?)

Does Mary know where John is? (does not address the respondent)

Did you know how to integrate trigonometric functions? (cannot be MTRANSed easily or quickly) (wrong tense)

Rule 3: Performance-Request Conversion

Criteria: 1. Conceptual categorization = Verification.

2. Question concept is of the form:

$$*Y* \iff DO_1\ MODE\ (*CAN*)$$
$$TIME\ (*PRESENT*)$$

where *Y* is the person being addressed and DO_1 is some conceptual action.

3. Performance of the conceptual act DO_1 is a reasonable request.

Target Interpretation:

Conceptual categorization ← Request

Question concept ← *Y* $\Longleftrightarrow$ DO$_1$

Examples:

    Rule 3 applies:

    Can you give me a ride? → Would you give me a ride?

    Could you light the fire? → Would you light the fire?

    Rule 3 does not apply:

    Could you have lit the fire? (wrong tense)

    Are you giving me a book? (MODE value ≠ *CAN*)

    Can John tell Mary? (does not address the respondent)

Criterion 3 is stated vaguely, because the necessary conditions that render a given act "reasonable" are often dependent on the conversational context and the goals of the speaker. For example, in a small hospital where two doctors are conferring over an emergency, the question "Can you perform open-heart surgery?" may very well be a request to perform an operation. But the same question addressed to a doctor at a cocktail party will not be understood as a request.

Rule 4: Permission-Request Conversion

Criteria: 1. Conceptual categorization = Verification.

       2. Question concept is of the form:

          X $\Longleftrightarrow$ DO$_1$ MODE (*CAN*)

                        TIME (*PRESENT* or *FUTURE*)

        where *X* is the person asking the question and DO$_1$ is some conceptual action.

       3. The person addressed has power over *X* with respect to the occurrence of DO$_1$.

Target Interpretation:

    Conceptual categorization ← Verification

    Question concept ← *X* $\Longleftrightarrow$ DO$_1$

    where *Y* is the person being addressed.

Examples:

    Rule 4 applies:

    Can I go to the movies tonight? → Is it all right if I go to the movies tonight?

    Can I take the car today? → Is it all right if I take the car today?

Criterion 3 is stated strongly and should be relaxed to cover social settings or relationships in which the parties are equal. In such a situation it is reasonable to ask for permission in the weak sense of making sure there are no objections. For example, a man could ask his wife "Can I take the car today?" without needing her permission in the sense of her allowing it. He could be asking just to make sure she had not planned to use it herself. This type of request is very different from one made in a relationship of unbalanced power (e.g., a teenager asking a parent for the car).

Rule 5: Function-Request Conversion
Criteria: 1. Conceptual categorization = Verification.
  2. Question concept is of the form:
  $*X* \iff$ POSSBY (*Y*) TIME (*PRESENT*)
  where *Y* is the person being addressed.
  3. The common function associated with *X* can be easily executed.
Target Interpretation:
  Conceptual categorization ← Request
  Question concept ← *Y* $\iff DO_1$
  where DO_1 is the instrumental script commonly associated with *X*.
Examples:
  Rule 5 applies:
  Do you have a light? → Would you offer me a light?
  Rule 5 does not apply:
  Do you have a piano? (playing the piano is not trivial)

A transformation very similar to this but slightly more complex goes into effect when additional information is given about a desired state change. For example:

Do you have air conditioning? It's too hot in here.
should be reinterpreted as
Would you turn on the air conditioning?

Do you have a light? It's dark in here.
should be reinterpreted as
Would you turn on a light?

The application of these conversion rules must be carefully ordered so that some rules will have precedence over others. Consider the request for a cigarette:

Q: Do you have a cigarette?

If the Function Request conversion were applied before the ATRANS Request conversion, this question would be interpreted to ask "Would you smoke a cigarette?" But if the ATRANS Request conversion is applied first, the intended meaning ("Would you give me a cigarette?") is obtained.

The inference mechanisms described in this section are context dependent in the sense that contextual information may suppress them. For example, suppose that John has been out drinking and phones Mary around 3 A.M. to tell her he will be home late. If, in this context, Mary asks John "Do you know what time it is?" she is probably not really asking for the time. The preceding rules will work most of the time, but not always. Higher-level predictive processes can interfere with and suppress them.

Implicit Causality

How-questions are subject to wide variations in conceptual representation. At the beginning of Chapter 3 we saw eight distinct conceptual senses for questions beginning with *how*. Many of these senses are recognized by the parser, but others are left for higher memory processes to discern. In Chapter 1 (sub-sections 1.1-3 and 1.1-4), we saw that in some contexts the question "How will we eat tonight?" should be understood as an Enablement question, whereas in other contexts it is asking about instrumentality. The parser does not attempt to determine which causality is more appropriate for such a question. The parser always represents "How will we eat tonight?" as an Instrumental/Procedural question.

Two inference mechanisms within inferential analysis determine when an Instrumental/Procedural question should be reinterpreted as a Causal Antecedent or Enablement question: namely the Causal-Antecedent Conversion and the Enablement conversion. The Causal-Antecedent conversion operates independently of the context in which a question is asked, and thus is not presented until Section 4.2. But the Enablement conversion is sensitive to context and so is presented now.

Rule 6: Enablement Conversion
Criteria: 1. Conceptual categorization = Instrumental/Procedural.
   2. Question concept is of the form:
      $*X* \Longleftrightarrow DO_1$
      where DO_1 describes a script instantiation.
   3. One or more of the enabling conditions for DO_1 are not satisfied.
Target Interpretation:
   Conceptual category ← Enablement
   Question concept ← $*X* \Longleftrightarrow DO_1$
Examples:
   Rule 6 applies:
   How did you write this book? (you can't write) →
                        How were you able to write this book?

How will we eat out tonight? (without any money) →
                                How will we be able to eat out tonight?
How did John eat at Leone's? (because John was barefoot) →
                                How was John able to eat at Leone's?
Rule 6 does not apply:
How did John go to New York? (no violated enablements)
How are you contacting John? ("contacting" does not describe a script)

4.1-3 Conversational Continuity

Questions that occur in dialogue are often incomplete, yet people rarely have difficulty understanding the intended question in these cases. There are rules of conversational continuity that enable people to conceptually complete a partial question. When information is left out in dialogue, conversational continuity is usually maintained by filling in information from the last conceptualization communicated. In this section we present a basic rule for question interpretation that relies on conversational continuity. Two additional rules are given as variations on the basic rule; these deal with pronominalization and incomplete questions.

The Basic Rule

Jane: Did John go to class yesterday?
Bill: No.
Jane: Why not?

Jane: Did John go to class yesterday?
Bill: I don't know.
Jane: Why not?

In the first dialogue, "Why not?" refers to the fact that John did not go to class yesterday. In the second, it refers to the fact that Bill did not know whether John went to class yesterday. A simple rule explains how to complete an incomplete question concept that has been asked within dialogue.

Continuity-Completion Rule: Complete a partial question in terms of the last concept communicated to the questioner.

In the first dialogue, the last thing the questioner heard before asking "Why not?" was "No." Since this was an answer in response to a question, it communicated some conceptual information to the questioner. In this case, it conveyed the information that John did not go to class yesterday. Given the incomplete question "Why not?" the rule tells us to combine "Why not?" with the concept of John's not going to class yesterday to get the complete question "Why didn't John go to class yesterday?" In the second dialogue, the last thing the questioner heard was "I don't know." This was also a response to an earlier question, conveying "I don't know if John went to class yesterday." So by using the rule, we combine "Why not?" with "I don't know if John went to class yesterday," to get "Why don't you know if John went to class yesterday?"

In addition to Causal-Antecedent and Expectational questions, this rule also works for many other incomplete questions:

A: Does it rain in Portland?
B: Yes. (It rains in Portland)
A: How much? (How much does it rain in Portland?)

A: Are you leaving for New York?
B: Yes. (I am leaving for New York)
A: Today? (Are you leaving for New York today?)

A: Is John still in charge?
B: No (John is not still in charge)
A: Says who? (Who says John is not still in charge?)

The Last MLOC Update

The Last MLOC Update (LMU) is a temporary storage buffer that enables a question answerer to remember the last concept he communicated to the questioner. Each time a new exchange occurs in dialogue, the LMU is updated with the last concept communicated, and the previous contents of the LMU are lost. This simple device is sufficient for all of our conversational-continuity inference rules. Some examples are:

Q: Does it rain in Portland?
A: Yes. (LMU = It rains in Portland)
Q: How much?

Q: Did Mary get the book from Susan?
A: No. (LMU = Mary did not get the book from Susan)
Q: Who did?

Q: Did John leave for New York?
A: Yes. (LMU = John left for New York)
Q: When?

The contents of the LMU must be a complete conceptualization, even if the answer from which it is derived is incomplete. This is not a problem, because the memory retrieval unit of QUALM always produces a complete conceptualization, even if the answer generated is a short one (see Chapter 6). Entering a new concept into the LMU is the last process performed by the memory search unit before the conceptual answer is passed to the generator.

If the next question received by the interpreter is conceptually incomplete, conversational-continuity rules are responsible for combining the current question with the LMU concept to form a complete conceptual question. For example, the question "When?" can be combined in a straightforward manner with the LMU concept of John's having left for New York to form a complete conceptual question: "When did John leave for New York?"

Pronominal Reference

A slight variation on the basic continuity-completion rule is needed when pronominal reference must be resolved in a question. Whenever a pronoun appears in a question, the last concept communicated to the questioner (the LMU) will contain the pronominal referent.

A: Is John still in charge?
B: No, Bill is. (Bill is in charge)
A: Who's he? (Who's Bill?)

In this case the pronominal referent for "he" is easy to find. The last concept communicated (Bill is in charge) contains only one male human in its conceptualization, Bill. So "he" must refer to Bill.

If there is more than one candidate for pronominal reference among those memory tokens appearing in the last concept, then a pattern match between the question concept and the last concept determines the correct referent.

A: Did Mary get the book from Susan?
B: No. (Mary did not get the book from Susan)
A: Who gave it to her? (Who gave the book to Mary?)

In this example the pronominal reference is a little harder to find. The last concept communicated (Mary did not get the book from Susan) has only one inanimate object, the book. So the referent for "it" is resolved to be the book. But there are two possible candidates for "her." Both Susan and Mary are female humans in the LMU. The correct referent must be found by matching the question concept against the LMU to find which component of the last concept communicated corresponds to the pronoun in question. The conceptual representation for "Mary did not get the book from Susan" is:

$$
\text{MARY} \Longleftrightarrow\!\!\!\!\!/\!\!\!\Longrightarrow \text{ATRANS} \longleftarrow \text{BOOK} \longleftarrow
\begin{cases}
\rightarrow \text{MARY} \\
\text{—} \langle \text{SUSAN}
\end{cases}
$$
$$\text{(past)}$$

ACTOR = MARY
OBJECT = BOOK
RECIPIENT = MARY

The conceptual representation for "Who gave it to her?" is:

$$
? \quad \overset{\Longrightarrow}{\text{(past)}} \quad \text{ATRANS} \longleftarrow \text{PHYSOBJ} \overset{\displaystyle \overset{\longrightarrow}{} \text{HUM}_1}{\underset{\displaystyle \overset{\longleftarrow}{} *?*}{\Big|}}
$$

$$
\begin{aligned}
\text{ACTOR} &= *?* \\
\text{OBJECT} &= \text{PHYSOBJ} \\
\text{RECIPIENT} &= \text{HUM}_1
\end{aligned}
$$

where HUM^1 has the properties of being human and female. A simple pattern match that recognizes corresponding slots in two conceptualizations and checks property list values can determine that "her" (the recipient) corresponds to the filler of the recipient slot of the LMU: Mary. Therefore the question is interpreted to mean "Who gave the book to Mary?"

A: Did Susan give the book to Mary?
B: No. (Susan did not give the book to Mary)
A: Was it given to her by Ann? (Was the book given to Mary by Ann?)

This example is identical with the last one in processing complexity. In Conceptual Dependency, the representation for this dialogue is identical[1] with the previous dialogue:

A: Did Mary get the book from Susan?
B: No. (Mary did not get the book from Susan)
A: Did Ann give it to her? (Did Ann give the book to Mary?)

Both LMUs — "Did Susan give the book to Mary?" and "Did Mary get the book from Susan?" — are represented in part by:

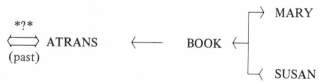

Both "Was it given to her by Ann?" and "Did Ann give it to her?" are represented conceptually by:

---

[1]This is not exactly true, but it is close enough for the point at hand. In the next subsection we see how Conceptual Dependency distinguishes between active and passive constructions as well as between "Susan gave the book to Mary" and "Mary got the book from Susan."

$$
\text{ANN} \overset{\underset{*?*}{}}{\underset{(\text{past})}{\Longleftrightarrow}} \text{ATRANS} \longleftarrow \text{PHYSOBJ} \left\{ \begin{array}{l} \longrightarrow \text{HUM}_1 \\ \\ \longleftarrow \text{ANN} \end{array} \right.
$$

The referent for "it" can only be the book, and a pattern match against the LMU determines that "her" (HUM_1) must correspond to Mary.

Pronominalization is actually a problem for internalization. Use of the LMU in pronominal reference illustrates how techniques developed for QUALM can spill over into other processing domains.

Focus-Based Continuity

In the last section, we said that the questions "Did Ann give it to her?" and "Was it given to her by Ann?" were represented by the same conceptualization. This was an oversimplification of the representations, but for the purposes of the pronominalization rule described in subsection 4.1-3, it was an adequate statement. There are, however, situations in which it is necessary for the conceptual representation to distinguish between active and passive constructions. This distinction is accomplished by placing a focus flag on the component of the conceptualization that was emphasized by the sentence structure (Goldman, 1974). Using focus flags, we represent "Ann gave the book to Mary" by:

$$
\underset{\substack{\uparrow \\ | \\ \text{focus}}}{\text{ANN}} \overset{}{\underset{(\text{past})}{\Longleftrightarrow}} \text{ATRANS} \longleftarrow \text{BOOK} \left\{ \begin{array}{l} \longrightarrow \text{MARY} \\ \\ \longleftarrow \text{ANN} \end{array} \right.
$$

and we represent "The book was given to Mary by Ann" by:

$$
\text{ANN} \overset{}{\underset{(\text{past})}{\Longleftrightarrow}} \text{ATRANS} \longleftarrow \underset{\substack{\uparrow \\ | \\ \text{focus}}}{\text{BOOK}} \left\{ \begin{array}{l} \longrightarrow \text{MARY} \\ \\ \longleftarrow \text{ANN} \end{array} \right.
$$

This representation of focus is used when Concept Completion questions must be interpreted in terms of previous dialogue.

DIALOGUE 1

A: Did Susan give the book to Mary?

B: No (Susan didn't give the book to Mary)

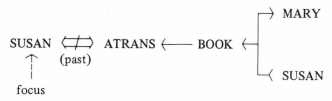

focus

A: Who did? (Who gave the book to Mary?)

```
                                                    ┌─→ MARY
   *?*     ⟺     ATRANS  ←── BOOK  ←─┤
          (past)                                    └─⟨ *?*
```

DIALOGUE 2

A: Was Mary given the book by Susan?

B: No (Mary wasn't given the book by Susan)

```
                                                    ┌─→ MARY
                                                       ↑
                                                       │
   SUSAN  ⟺̸     ATRANS  ←── BOOK  ←─┤   focus
          (past)
                                                    └─⟨ SUSAN
```

A: Who was? (Who was given the book by Susan?)

```
                                                    ┌─→ *?*
   SUSAN  ⟺     ATRANS ←── BOOK  ←─┤
          (past)
                                                    └─⟨ SUSAN
```

DIALOGUE 3

A: Was the book given to Mary by Ann?

B: No. (The book wasn't given to Mary by Ann)

$$\text{ANN} \langle\!\!\overset{\underline{\quad}}{=}\!\!\rangle \text{ ATRANS } \longleftarrow \text{ BOOK} \longleftarrow \begin{cases} \longrightarrow \text{MARY} \\ \\ \longrightarrow \text{ANN} \end{cases}$$

(past)   ↑
                 ¦
                focus

A: What was (What was given to Mary by Ann?)

$$\text{ANN} \langle\!\!\overset{\underline{\quad}}{=}\!\!\rangle \text{ ATRANS } \longleftarrow \text{ *?* } \longleftarrow \begin{cases} \longrightarrow \text{MARY} \\ \\ \longrightarrow \text{ANN} \end{cases}$$

(past)

In these dialogues the question concept must be inferred on the basis of the LMU. The interrogative pronouns (who, what) must be assigned to a role slot in a complete conceptualization. This conceptualization must be derived from the conversation.

The rule that infers the complete conceptual question uses only the LMU. When the unknown component of an incomplete question does not have an obvious role filler on the basis of a pattern match, then we assign the unknown component to the role that received the focus flag and complete the concept without further alterations. In DIALOGUE 1, focus fell on the ACTOR slot; so "who" is assigned to the ACTOR slot. In DIALOGUE 2, focus fell on the TO slot; so "who" is assigned to the TO slot. In DIALOGUE 3, focus was assigned to the OBJECT slot; so "what" assumes the OBJECT slot.

Knowledge-Based Continuity

More complicated questions that can be interpreted in terms of the basic rule for conversational continuity require that general world knowledge be combined with the LMU to the questioner in order to conceptually complete a question.

A: I want to make a withdrawal.
B: Checking or savings?
(Do you want to withdraw from a checking account or a savings account?)

To understand this question, we must know that "checking" and savings" refer to types of bank accounts. It is also necessary to know that a withdrawal has to do with a bank account; that is, a withdrawal is a transaction in which money is taken from a bank account. Once these connections are made, the question can be fully interpreted in terms of the LMU.

This kind of knowledge would be found in the conversational script (subsection 4.1-1) for bank transactions. So conversational scripts must be accessed along with the LMU in order to complete a particular class of partial questions.

4.2 CONTEXT-INDEPENDENT INFERENCES

Context-independent conversion rules may be used by the interpreter in any context. These general rules are structured in the same way as contextual inference rules; each one has a set of criteria and a target interpretation. A rule is activated only when its criteria are satisfied. If all the criteria are satisfied, the rule changes the question's conceptual categorization and question concept according to directions specified under the target interpretation. These transformations are designed to produce a target interpretation that captures an intended question, as opposed to a precisely literal question.

Q: Do you do your homework?
A: Almost never.

This question is technically a verification type that could be answered by a simple yes or no. But the answer given specifies the frequency of the act in question. To produce this answer, we had to apply to the question a general interpretive rule that reconceptualizes the question to mean "How often do you do your homework?"

Rule 7: Simple-Request Conversion
Criteria: 1. Conceptual Categorization = Expectational.
   2. Question concept is of the form:
    $*Y* \Longleftrightarrow DO_1 \text{ TIME (*PRESENT*)}$
   where *Y* is the person being addressed.
Target Interpretation:
 Conceptual category ← Request
 Question concept ← $*Y* \Longleftrightarrow DO_1$
Examples:
 Rule 7 applies:
 Why don't you listen? → Would you listen?
 Why don't you come here? → Would you come here?
 Why don't you pay me now? → Would you pay me now?
 Rule 7 does not apply:
 Why are you paying me now? (wrong conceptual category)
 Why didn't you pay me then? (wrong tense)
 Why didn't John eat a hamburger? (wrong tense)

Rule 8: Frequency-Specification Conversion
Criteria: 1. Conceptual categorization = Verification.

2. Question concept is of the form:
  X MANNER (*REPEATEDLY*)
  where *X* is a conceptual event.
Target Interpretation:
  Conceptual category ← Specification
  Question concept ← *X* FREQUENCY (*?*)

Examples:
  Rule 8 applies:
  Does it snow in Portland?   →   How often does it snow in Portland?
  Do you eat at Clark's?   →   How often do you eat at Clark's?
  Do you do your homework? →   How often do you do your homework?
  Rule 8 does not apply:
  Did the train arrive this morning? (MANNER ≠ *REPEATEDLY*)
  Is John going to New York? (MANNER ≠ *REPEATEDLY*)

The parser is capable of recognizing when an action should have MANNER = REPEATEDLY by accessing scripts in memory. When an action is typically something that occurs again and again, it describes a situational script. Any such situational script has a descriptive tag that says this script is normally recurrent.

Rule 9: Duration-Specification Conversion
Criteria: 1. Conceptual categorization = Verification.
     2. Question concept is of the form:
        X TIME (*W*)
        where *X* is a concept event and *W* specifies an interval of time.
Target Interpretation:
  Conceptual category ← Specification
  Question concept ← *X* TIMEDURATION (*?*)

Examples:
  Rule 9 applies:
  Have you lived in Italy long? → How long have you lived in Italy?
  Did it rain this morning?   → How long did it rain this morning?
  Did it hurt for a while?   → How long did it hurt?
  Rule 9 does not apply:
  Do you watch football? (would be transformed first by the frequency-specification conversion)
  Did John go to New York? (does not describe an event over an interval of time)

The last two conversion rules (8 and 9) are optional conversions in that they do not precisely stay with the immediate meaning of the question. "Do you beat your wife?" does not have to be understood to mean "How often do you beat your wife?" These conversions should be sensitive to how talkative the system is: They should be used only if the system wants to be talkative and to prolong conversation. If the system is more businesslike and less conversational, these conversions should be ignored. Softer conversion rules of this sort are closer to transitional rules of conversation than to strict interpretive processing.

Rule 10: Agent-Request Conversion

Criteria: 1. Conceptual categorization = Verification.

2. Question concept is of the form:

$$*X* \Longleftrightarrow POSSBY\ (*Z*)\ MODE\ (*CAN*)$$

or

$$*Z* \Longleftrightarrow ATRANS \longleftarrow *X*\ MODE\ (*CAN*)$$

Target Interpretation:

Conceptual category ← Request

Question concept ←

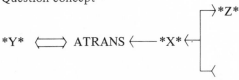

where *Y* is the person being addressed.

Examples:

Rule 10 applies:

Can I have a cookie?	→ Would you give me a cookie?
Could we get a collie?	→ Would you get us a collie?
Can Rover have your leftover bone?	→ Would you give Rover your leftover bone?

Rule 10 does not apply:

Can I have swine flu? (is not represented by a POSSBY state; this is a physical-state description)

Does John have a car? (MODE value ≠ *CAN*)

Can John see Mary now? (is not a POSSBY or ATRANS)

4.3 KNOWLEDGE-STATE-ASSESSMENT INFERENCES

The correct interpretation of a question may rely on knowing something about the questioner's knowledge state and goal states. If a mathematician is at a party for university faculty, and someone he has just met asks him:

Q1: What field are you in?

he should interpret *Q1* to mean:

Q2: What academic field are you in?

Using this interpretation, he can respond on an appropriate level of description: "I'm in mathematics." But if he is at a professional mathematics conference, *Q1* should be understood to be asking:

Q3: What specialty field are you in?

Q3 should be answered with a more exact description: "I'm in algebraic topology." These interpretations are based on assumptions about what the questioner knows and does not know.

Knowledge-state-assessment rules are sensitive to beliefs about the questioner's knowledge state. Each rule has criteria that specifies a conceptual categorization and a condition concerning the questioner. If all the criteria are satisfied, the rule is applied by changing the conceptual categorization and question concept according to the directions under the target interpretation. The implementation of these rules is dependent on some sort of memory model of the questioner. How this modeling of the questioner is to be carried out is still an open problem. A complete model of question answering processes must at some point take into account what the questioner knows and does not know, what he wants, and why he asks the questions he does. This problem is discussed from the viewpoint of memory retrieval in Chapter 9.

Rule 11: Goal-Orientation Conversion
Criteria: 1. Conceptual categorization = Concept completion.
          2. The qustioner knows the answer
Target Interpretation:
    Conceptual category ←Goal orientation
    Question concept ← the conceptual answer to the concept-completion question.
Examples:
    Rule 11 applies:
    What are you doing? (to wife packing suitcase)   → Why are you packing a suitcase?
    What have you done? (to a child holding a torn picture in hand) →
                              Why did you tear up the picture?
    What are you doing? (to a friend throwing the I-Ching) — may or may not be transformed, depending on whether the person asking knows what the I-Ching is.

Rule 12: Specification-Constraint Conversion
Criteria: 1 Conceptual categorization = Specification.
          2. The questioner knows certain specifiers.
Target Interpretation:
    Conceptual category ←Specification

Question concept ← same as before but with added constraints on known specifiers.

Examples:

Who is John Dean? (Don't give his name or sex.)
Who is the Secretary of Defense? (Don't give his title or information that can be inferred from the title — such as being a presidential appointee.)

A Specification question asks for a feature description of something. For example, "Who is President?" is a Specification question that is best answered by specifying the name of the President. But other feature descriptions could be used, some of which would convey different overtones. If "Who was the President in 1976?" were answered "Betty Ford's husband," the answer suggests that you might recognize her name more readily than his. The way in which people answer Specification questions is strongly determined by what they think the questioner knows and does not know.

Rule 13: Obvious-Request Conversion

Criteria: 1. Conceptual categorization = Verification.

2. Question concept is of the form:

$$*Y* \Longleftrightarrow DO_1 \ TIME \ (*PRESENT*)$$

or

$$*Y* \Longleftrightarrow DO_1 \ TIME \ (*FUTURE*)$$

where $*Y*$ is the person being addressed, and the questioner is assumed to desire the performance of DO_1.

Target Interpretation:

Conceptual category ← Request
Question concept ← $*Y* \Longleftrightarrow DO_1$

Examples:

Are you going to walk the dog? (probably a request)
Are you taking out the garbage? (almost certainly a request)
Would you let your son marry one? (not a request)

When a question has passed through inferential analysis, it has completed the interpretive phase of its processing. Inferences about the intended meaning of the question have been made, and the conceptual categorization is final. Processes can now be executed that extract an answer from memory.

For some questions, the memory search will indicate that the conceptual focus of a question must be established before an answer can be formed. In this case, further interpretive processes are invoked after the memory search is initiated. The heuristics involved in focus establishment will be described in Chapter 7. But for other questions, interpretive processes are completed before the memory search is conducted.

Inferential analysis is based on a theory of human inference processes. Each conversion rule described here represents a cognitive process that people use when they understand questions. These mechanisms are used without conscious awareness, both during understanding and generation. Only when someone purposely violates one of these inferences and takes a question "literally" are we forced to acknowledge that a question was intended to mean something other than what it said explicitly. The processes of inference can be formalized as manipulations of conceptual information within inferential analysis.

Part II

MEMORY SEARCHES: FINDING AN ANSWER

INTRODUCTION

Once a question has been sufficiently understood by inferential analysis, the memory search can begin to look for an answer. Chapters 5, 6, and 7 describe those processes in QUALM involved in finding a conceptual answer that can be passed to the generator. The generator translates conceptual representations into natural language. Generation,[1] like parsing, is not part of the Q/A model. The generator that interfaces with QUALM inputs a conceptual answer and translates it into English. In the same way that QUALM can interchange parsers, a generator for any language can be attached to QUALM to produce answers in that language.

The processes of finding and formulating an answer are split up into roughly two basic processes: content specification and memory search. Content specification determines what kind of answer should be produced and how to look for it, while the memory search does the work of actually finding information. Content specification provides direction for the memory search. Occasionally the memory search finds something that indicates that the question must be analyzed further before the memory search can continue. This is the case when the focus of a question must be established. Although focus establishment is more properly an aspect of question interpretation, knowledge-based focus heuristics are de-

---

[1]Although the term "generation" may sound suggestive of the entire process that finds an answer and produces a natural-language response, it is used here in a more restrictive sense. In this volume, generation is a technical term referring to the process that receives a complete conceptual representation and produces a natural language translation of that conceptual information.

scribed here because they are invoked only when the content specification predicts a possible need for them and the memory search confirms that they are in fact needed. The intuitive division between understanding questions and finding answers becomes difficult to maintain when the memory search invokes heuristics that are essentially interpretive.

DECIDING HOW TO ANSWER A QUESTION

Once a question has been understood by decomposition into a conceptual category and a question concept, it is time to decide how we wish to answer it. Should the answer be honest? Should it be misleading? Should it be detailed? Or should it provide as brief a response as possible and still be correct? To a large extent, these issues can be addressed only in terms of a theory of conversation that accounts for why people say the things they do. Although we do not attempt here to solve problems in conversation, it is appropriate to design mechanisms in QUALM that integrate instructions derived from conversational goals into the Q/A processes.

The factors that determine what people say and how they say it are motivational factors concerned with the context and purpose of conversation. If a model of Q/A does not acknowledge the role that these factors must play in the question-answering process, it cannot be viewed as a comprehensive model of human question answering. Although factors of social interaction are not yet very well understood, we can still specify how such factors affect and control question answering. That is, QUALM does not know why it says what it does, but it is ready to answer questions talkatively or minimally if a higher motivating process should appear that can tell it what stance to assume. Until a controlling process appears to interface with QUALM, we can arbitrarily set variables within QUALM that result in different answers to the same questions.

In the context of the following story, QUALM can supply the following answers during a question-answering session with SAM:

John went to New York by bus. Then he went to Leone's. The hostess gave John a menu and he ordered lasagna. John ate and asked for a check. When the check came, he discovered that he didn't have any money, so he had to wash dishes.

Q1:   Where did John go?
A1a: New York.
A1b: John took a bus to New York.

Q2:   Did John eat?
A2a: Yes.
A2b: Yes, John ate some lasagna.

Q3:   Did the waitress give John a menu?
A3a: No.
A4b: No, the hostess gave John a menu.

Q4:   Did John pay the check?
A4a: No.
A4b: No, John discovered that he had no money, so he had to wash dishes.

Q5:   Who gave John a menu?
A5a: The hostess.
A5b: The hostess gave John a menu.

Content specification can be thought of as an interface device that takes information about the general attitude or mood of the system (from any processes outside of QUALM that can specify such things) and integrates this information into the retrieval instructions, which produce an appropriate answer. One kind of instruction it gives to the memory search incorporates attidudinal variables, that is called an elaboration option. Another kind of instruction that content specification may pass to the memory search is a category-trace instruction. These instructions take into account what kinds of processes were activated during inferential analysis in order to understand a question. That is, some answers reflect the interpretive processing which was used to understand them. In Chapter 5 the content-specification unit is explained and specific elaboration options and category-trace instructions are described. These specific rules are not intended to be a complete set of all the elaboration options and category-trace instructions that a general question answerer must have. They are purely representative and are intended to illustrate the general idea of content specification.

CARRYING OUT ORDERS

Once we know how to search memory for an answer, somebody has to do the actual digging. This is the job of the memory search. The memory search is defined by a set of default-retrieval heuristics. These default heuristics are generally augmented by specific instructions from content specification. But if no special guidance is provided by content specification, the memory search will resort to its standard default processes to produce an answer.

Memory searches are organized according to three levels of description within a story representation: script structures, planning structures, and causal-chain representations. When a question asks about static properties or features of things, the memory search resorts to checking information stored in memory tokens. The heuristics are designed to take as much advantage as possible of a story representation. As such they are intimately connected to the specific features and properties of script- and plan-generated memory representations.

In fact, the design of these story representations has been altered and extended to accommodate retrieval heuristics at the same time that the retrieval heuristics have been designed to fit the story representations.

For the most part, the information needed to produce answers to questions about stories exists within the story representation that was generated at the time of understanding. But there are questions that can be answered only by activating predictive memory processes in conjunction with the story representation. For example, suppose that we ask, "Why didn't John order a hamburger?" in the context of a story in which he orders a hot dog. To answer this question, we must activate processes that can provide information about why John did what he did instead of something else. This information cannot be found in the story representation alone. Special processes that are activated during the memory search when the story representation is not enough are described in detail in Chapter 8. These situations should be considered exceptions to the rule: Most questions about a story can be answered on the basis of inferences that were made at the time of understanding and stored in the story representation.

In Chapter 6, the default retrieval heuristics of QUALM are described, along with brief descriptions of story representations generated by SAM and PAM.

ANSWERING BETTER BY UNDERSTANDING MORE

At times, the processes of question interpretation and memory retrieval are not as neatly divided as first one, then the other. In Chapter 7, we describe question-answering processes in which the initial interpretation of a question is followed by a memory search; this leads to a need for further analysis of the question, which in turn requires conducting a memory search, after which a final memory search for the answer is completed. The processing flow of control for these questions is outlined in Fig. II.1. The focus of a question directs attention to a specific conceptual component of the question. Focus can be very important in determining what a question is asking. For example,

Q4: Was it the waitress who gave John a menu?

is a question that directs attention to the waitress. A conceptually equivalent question that does not carry such a strong focus is:

Q5: Did the waitress give John a menu?

To see that focus affects the answers that a question will take, we need only point out that *Q5* can be answered:

Q5: Did the waitress give John a menu?
A5: No, the waitress gave Mary a menu.

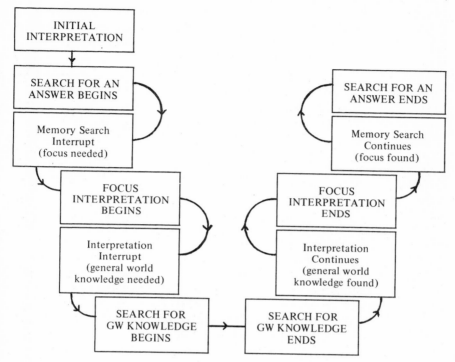

FIG. II.1. Answering better by understanding more: knowledge-based focus establishment.

But the same answer cannot be smoothly offered in response to *Q4:*

Q4: Was it the waitress who gave John a menu?
A5: No, the waitress gave Mary a menu.

Q4 demands an answer such as:

Yes, the waitress gave John a menu, or
No, somebody else gave John a menu.

Q4 carries a very strong presupposition that John was given a menu by someone; the question is, Who? *A5* carries no such presupposition.

Focus in a question can be established many ways and at different points in the process model. One heuristic for focus establishement in QUALM has been implemented for the SAM system and is described in Chapter 7. This is a knowledge-based heuristic. That is, for the identification of focus, it relies on general world knowledge rather than on syntactic constructions (as in *Q4*) or on intonational devices (which might be used in spoken dialogue).

GENERATION INTO ENGLISH

Once a final conceptual answer has been produced by the memory search, all that remains to be done is generation into English (or whatever language is desired). The program that generates from Conceptual Dependency into English is not part of QUALM; it is an independent system that merely interfaces with QUALM. The generator is based on an original program by Neil Goldman (1975), which has since been expanded in terms of its vocabulary and finesse. In the course of setting up an interface between QUALM and the generator, a few minor additions were made to the generator. The most important of these from a theoretical viewpoint is the use of mixed concepts.

QUALM's understanding of an answer can often be most effectively communicated to the generator in a mixed format of some connectives and some Conceptual Dependency. For example, in answering a why-question, a specific retrieval heuristic is designed to produce an answer consisting of two causally linked concepts. In all cases, the causality between these two concepts is so specific that they can always be joined together by the connective "and so." For example, "John discovered that he had no money, and so he had to wash dishes," or "The waitress told John that they didn't have any hot dogs, and so John ordered a hamburger." Because the retrieval heuristic can reliably predict that any answer obtained via that heuristic can be expressed by using those connectives, the generator should not have to search for an appropriate connective.

Here mixed concepts come to the rescue. The generator has been extended to accept information structures from QUALM that are part English and part Conceptual Dependency. Mixed formatting is used whenever a retrieval heuristic can predict the connective relationships between concepts. When SAM answers "John was angry because the hamburger was burnt, and so he left," this answer originally entered the generator as a mixed concept of three conceptualizations and two English connectives of the form "*X* because *Y* and so *Z*."

This is the only aspect of QUALM that could conceivably be described as language dependent. If a generator for another language were attached to QUALM, the connectives that QUALM inserts in its mixed concepts would have to be altered for the new language. In its current implementations, QUALM uses only the connectives:

1. because
2. and
3. so
4. and so
5. and then.

The formatting for mixed concepts in specific retrieval heuristics is described as needed in Chapter 6.

In Fig. II.2, the processes of the memory search are outlined. The question "Did the waitress give John a menu?" enters the content-specification unit as a

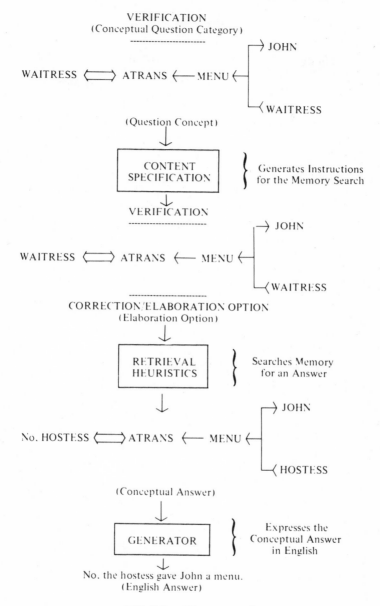

FIG. II.2.   Memory search.

question concept and a conceptual question category. Content specification consults the system's intentionality and specifies an elaboration option to guide the retrieval heuristics. A conceptual answer (representing "No, the hostess gave John a menu") is found by the retrieval heuristics and passed to the generator for translation into English.

5 Content Specification

Somewhere within the question-answering model must be a process that controls the amount of information that goes into an answer:

Q: Did John apply to Yale?
Aa: No.
Ab: No, his advisors told him he didn't have a chance.
Ac: No, his advisors told him he didn't have a chance, and so he applied to Harvard instead.

One of the ways that correct answers to a question may vary is in the amount of information communicated. A question-answering system must be capable of adjusting responses to yield varying amounts of information.

5.0 INTRODUCTION

If a *Q/A* model always answers the same questions in exactly the same way, it has clearly failed to simulate the way people answer questions. There are two ways in which people vary their answers to questions. On a low level, generational mechanisms can produce answers that are conceptually equivalent, but that are worded differently:

Q1: Why did John order a hamburger?
A1a: The waitress told him they didn't have hot dogs.
A1b: Because he was told by the waitress that they didn't have hot dogs.
A1c: Because the waitress informed him that there were no hot dogs.

On a higher level, answers to questions vary in their conceptual content:

Q2:   Did John eat a hot dog?
A2a: No.
A2b: No, the waitress told John they didn't have any hot dogs.
A2c: No, the waitress told John they didn't have any hot dogs, and so John ordered a hamburger.

Each of these answers constitutes a reasonable response to Q2; yet they differ in the amount of information they convey. In fact, answers can vary not only in terms of their relative content, but also in terms of the kind of content they communicate. For example, if Q2 had been answered "Yes" in the context of a story in which John did not eat a hot dog, then the content of this answer would have to be described as dishonest (if we thought the answerer knew better) and wrong (if we thought we knew better).

In this chapter we look at a mechanism within the memory-retrieval part of QUALM that is responsible for determining how much and what kind of information goes into an answer. This part of QUALM is called the content-specification unit. To determine how a question should be answered, content specification takes into account the conceptual category of each question and the factors that describe the "attitudinal" mode of the entire system. The content-specification unit produces a system of descriptive instructions to instruct and guide the memory-retrieval processes as they look for an answer.

The primary challenge of content specification is precisely how these instructions to memory retrieval are formalized. It is not enough to say "give a minimally correct answer," or "bring in everything you can find that's relevant." The instructions generated by content specification must tell the retrieval heuristics exactly how to produce a minimally correct answer and exactly what must be done to come up with everything relevant.

One of the interesting aspects to this problem is that initial results from the retrieval processes can affect how the rest of the search should be conducted. That is, the content-specification unit cannot give the retrieval heuristics a set of instructions that will work in all cases regardless of what the memory search finds. Content-specification instructions must anticipate in a very general way what kinds of things the retrieval heuristics can produce, and formulate instructions that are sensitive to different retrieval results. For example, a Verification question will require different instructions depending upon whether the initial search finds the question concept in memory. An affirmative answer is elaborated differently from a negative answer.

The general system of instructions generated by the content-specification unit are described in terms of two basic mechanisms: elaboration options and category-trace instructions. As soon as a question has been fully interpreted, its conceptual categorization and question concept are passed to the content-specification unit. Here the question may be tagged with an elaboration option or a category-trace instruction, which will be consulted when retrieval heuristics are executed. If no such special instructions are attached to the question, standard retrieval heuristics (described in Chapter 6) are executed.

But before we can proceed with a description of elaboration options and category-trace instructions, we must first identify those factors that are ultimately responsible for conceptually different answers. In QUALM, the variables that affect the content of an answer are described as intentionality factors.

5.1 INTENTIONALITY

The factors that affect human question answering are not easy to pin down. Questions are answered differently, depending on the context, relationship with the questioner, type of conversational dialogue, purpose of the dialogue, and everybody's mood. Answers to simple questions are affected by such things as:

1. You know the questioner and despise him.
2. You want the questioner to think well of you.
3. You are taking an oral exam for a Ph.D.
4. You are preoccupied with other things.
5. You want to mislead the questioner.
6. You find the topic of discussion:

   a. emotionally painful
   b. in poor taste
   c. intellectually stimulating
   d. sexually stimulating
   e. boring
   f. absurd

The list could go on forever. If we seriously tried to bring all possible variables into our Q/A model, we would quickly find ourselves immersed in some rather deep waters of social psychology. A theory of human conversation (of which Q/A is a part) must eventually touch upon theories of social interaction. But not yet. At this stage it is appropriate to make a few simplistic assumptions.

As far as QUALM is concerned, the attitudinal orientation of a question answerer can be described by a two-dimensional decomposition into (1) mood, and (2) reliability. This descriptive decomposition falls far short of specifying a complete attitudinal orientation. The attitudinal factors that it does endeavor to specify are perhaps better described as factors of intentionality. We view intentionality as the subset of attitudinal factors that are strongly goal oriented. To be dishonest or extremely informative are attitudinal stances that relate to some ultimate purpose; hence they are intentional. Because we are concerned with designing a mechanism that controls the sort of answers QUALM produces, strongly intentional orientations are reasonable factors to be explored. If it is not already obvious, it should be understood that our notion of intentionality is a very loose part of QUALM, and absolutely no claims for psychological validity are being made.

5.1-1   Mood

The first dimension of intentionality we will call mood. Variables of mood can be viewed on a continuum. This continuum is split up into six segments, and the names assigned to each segment are meant to be purely suggestive:

1. talkative
2. cooperative
3. minimally responsive
4. uncooperative
5. rude
6. condescending/sarcastic.

These attitudinal stances are partially ordered in terms of which moods imply which other moods. To be talkative implies cooperativeness, and being condescending, sarcastic, or rude implies being uncooperative. But not all mood relationships are so clear. In some contexts, minimal responsiveness can be construed as rudeness (e.g., at a casual party), whereas sarcasm tends to be rude only when the content of a sarcastic remark is insulting.

5.1-2   Reliability

The second dimension of intentionality is reliability. The reliability factor can assume only two orientations:

1. honest
2. deceptive.

If the system is operating with honest reliability, its answers to questions will be correct to the best of its knowledge. If the system does not know the answer to a question, it will say so. When the system is operating with deceptive reliability, answers to questions may be either correct or incorrect. The system may give an answer that it knows to be incorrect; it could say it does not know the answer although it does; it could guess at answers; or it could give the right answer. Any of the six moods can assume either an honest or deceptive reliability.

5.1-3   Intentionality and Answers

Roughly speaking, the mood of the system controls the form of the answer, while the reliability of the system controls the content of the answer. As soon as a question has been assigned a final interpretation, each elaboration option and category-trace instruction checks the mood and reliability factors of the system to see whether special retrieval and answer-formation instructions should be attached to that question before retrieval heuristics are executed. Each set of instructions is constrained by specific moods and reliabilities that determine whether those instructions should be executed.

It is much more difficult to implement deceptive reliability than honest reliability, because deception in conversation is motivated by various conversational goals; people have reasons for speaking deceptively, and there are more ways for an answer to be wrong than right. The actual implementation of QUALM has therefore been limited to a system operating with honest reliability. Until we have a theory of conversation, we cannot hope to model deceptive answers in any theoretically sound way.

The system of intentionality proposed here is adequate for a Q/A model. It would not be adequate in a general model of interactive dialogue. Question answering by itself is largely passive; everthing is done in response to the questioner. But fully interactive dialogues that maintain mixed initiatives require active goal orientations.

A theory of mixed-initiative dialogue must (1) identify what kinds of goals people have in conversation, and (2) describe the mechanisms that manifest these goals. No one in the field of AI has proposed a system of general conversational goals. But many people have worked on specific mechanisms that assume one particular goal and converse accordingly (Bobrow et al., 1977; Collins, 1976; Shortliffe, 1974). Of these efforts, the most interesting one from the view point of conversational theory is the work by Collins on Socratic dialogues. Collins analyzed transcripts of Socratic dialogues in an effort to extract general principles that could be incorporated in a teaching program. His analysis produced 23 goal-oriented strategies that are used according to a hierarchy of goals and subgoals. These strategies motivate the teacher in a Socratic conversation.

To a large extent, a Q/A model can be devised without reference to theories of conversation. In Chapter 11, we discuss more carefully how Q/A becomes unavoidably tangled up with rules of conversation.

5.2 ELABORATION OPTIONS

Elaboration options provide the system with an ability to elaborate its responses to questions. Elaboration options are summoned for a question only if the intentionality of the system indicates that an elaboration is appropriate. If the intentionality "wills" an elaboration, an appropriate elaboration option is given to the question immediately after interpretation. This option is then activated during memory retrieval only if an initial memory search produces information that meets a set of criteria specified by the option. An elaboration option consists of four parts:

1. intentionality threshold (IT)

2. question criterion (QC)
3. initial-answer criterion (AC)
4. elaboration instructions (EI).

The intentionality threshold specifies what sort of intentionality the system must be running under in order for the elaboration option to be assigned to the question. The question criterion describes what conceptual category the question must have in order for it to receive the Elaboration Option.[1] If either the intentionality of the system or the conceptual category of the question fails to meet the specifications of the intentionality threshold and the question criterion, then the elaboration option is not tagged to the question. The initial-answer criterion specifies the type of conceptual answer that the memory search must initially return in order for the Elaboration Option to be executed. And the elaboration instructions specify exactly how an elaboration is extracted from memory and integrated into the conceptual answer.

In the following elaboration options, the answer criterion and elaboration instructions will be described nontechnically. In an actual implementation of these options, the answer criterion would specify a test to be applied to the initial answer, and the elaboration instructions would specify a function designed to retrieve information from memory and integrate it with the initial answer for a final conceptual answer. Of the options described here, only the first four — the Verification, Short-Answer, Single-Word, and Correction/Explanation Options — have actually been implemented to run in SAM and PAM. The processes that carry out the elaboration instructions for the Correction/Explanation option are described in Chapter 7.

Rule 1: Verification Option
IT: Talkative
QC: Verification
AC: Initial answer is yes.
EI: Final conceptual answer is "Yes, *X*" where *X* is the conceptualization found in the story representation that matches the question concept.

Examples:
Did John go to New York?
Yes, John went to New York by bus.

Did John eat?
Yes, John ate lasagna.

Did someone pick John's pocket?
Yes, a thief picked John's pocket.

---

[1]In one case (the inquiry-explanation option) a MODE specification is needed in addition to the conceptual category.

Did John pay the check?
Yes, John paid the bill.

Answers produced using this option often appear to be volunteering more information than the question specifically asks for. When the question "Did John eat?" is answered "John ate lasagna," we are told not only that John ate but also what he ate. This happens whenever the question concept matches a concept in the story that encodes more information than the question concept contained. The matching heuristic does not require an exact match between the question concept and a conceptualization in the story representation. In order for a match to occur, a conceptualization must have everything in the question concept, but it can also include more than is in the question concept.

Rule 2: Short-Answer Option
IT: Minimally responsive, uncooperative, or rude
QC: Verification
AC: Initial answer is yes (or no).
EI: Final conceptual answer is yes (or no).
Examples:
Did John eat lasagna?
No.

Did the waitress bring John a menu?
No.

Did the hostess bring John a menu?
Yes.

Did John go to New York?
Yes.

The initial-answer criteria for this option is superfluous, for it does not weed out any questions. This option and the next are perhaps better described as anti-elaboration options because the answers they produce are minimal. The technical realization of elaboration options is a control structure for retrieval heuristics. This control can result in a nonelaboration as well as an elaboration.

Rule 3: Single-Word Option
IT: Minimally responsive, uncooperative, or rude
QC: Concept completion
AC: Initial answer is found.
EI: Final conceptual answer is the conceptual component that matched the unknown component of the question concept.
Examples:
Who gave John a menu?
The hostess.

What did John eat?
Lasagna.

Where did John go?
New York.

Who went to Leone's?
John.

The other way that a concept-completion question can be answered is by generating back the entire conceptualization (Where did John go? — John went to New York). In the implementation of QUALM used for SAM and PAM, the default—retrieval heuristics for concept-completion questions produce a long answer, and the single-word option must be activated to produce a short one. It could as easily have been the other way around. The single-word option is actually more of a suppression option than an elaboration option in the sense of extending an answer.

Rule 4: Correction/Explanation Option
IT: Cooperative or talkative
QC: Verification
AC: Initial answer is no.
EI: 1. Use the focus heuristic[2] to make a Concept Completion question.
  2. Answer the Concept Completion question.
  3. If an answer is found, append this conceptual answer to the answer no.
  4. If no answer is found for the Concept Completion question, make an Expectational question,[3] answer it, and append the conceptual answer to the answer no.

Examples:
Did the waitress give John a menu?
No, the hostess gave John a menu.
(answers the Concept Completion question: Who gave John a menu?)

Could John pay the check?
No, John had no money.
(answers the Expectational question: Why couldn't John pay the check?)

Did the waitress serve John a hot dog?
No, the waitress gave John a hamburger.
(answers the Concept Completion question: What did the waitress give John?)

---

[2] The focus heuristic is described in Section 7.3.

[3] This means to enter memory retrieval with the question category = Expectational instead of Verification. The question concept does not need to be changed.

Did John eat the hamburger?

No, John was angry because the hamburger was burnt, and so he left.

(answers the Expectational question: Why didn't John eat the hamburger?)

The first part of the Correction/Explanation instruction attempts to correct the question concept. If the question concept to be verified is almost right except for one conceptual component (e.g., the actor or the tense), an appropriate elaboration makes the necessary correction. The second part of the Correction/Explanation instruction is used when no correction is possible. In this case the concept in question could have happened but did not. The Correction/Explanation option then endeavors to explain what interfered or what was responsible for a different turn of events.

Rule 5: Inquiry/Explanation Option

IT: Talkative or cooperative

QC: Verification with mode (*NEG*)

AC: Initial answer is yes.

EI: Find and explain apparent inconsistency.

Examples:

Weren't you going to California this week?

Yes, but my husband got sick, and so I postponed it.

Aren't you a member here?

Yes, but I don't have my card with me.

Can't you drive to work?

Yes, but I'd rather not unless I have to.

The questioner thinks that the nonnegated concept in question is true (you *were* going to California, you *are* a member, you *can* drive to work), but he finds it surprising or inconsistent with other information. He is looking for some explanation that will allow him to integrate the question concept more satisfactorily. It is up to the person being addressed to supply the necessary explanatory information. There are some general rules for finding such explanations.

If the question concept describes an act, the explanation can be found by answering an Expectational question.

Aren't you going to New York? → Why aren't you going to New York?
(I couldn't get my car started.)

Isn't he taking the job? → Why isn't he taking the job?
(He decided to hunt around some more.)

If the question concept describes a state, the explanation is harder to find. If the question asks about an enablement condition, it can be answered by answering an Enablement question. But finding which Enablement question should be generated is more than a trivial manipulation of the question concept.

> Aren't you a member here?   →   Can you get in here?
> (I don't have my card with me.)

> Aren't Porsches terribly expensive?   →   How can you afford a Porsche?
> (My parents gave it to me.)

The correct interpretation of questions like these require additional inferences about the questioner's knowledge state, beliefs, and expectations. Still other states lend themselves to elaboration strategies that are much more conversational:

> Isn't British Columbia beautiful?
> (Yes, and it's a great place to catch salmon.)

Rule 6: Request-Explanation Option
IT: Talkative, cooperative, or minimally responsive
QC: Request
AC: Initial answer is no.
EI: Make an Expectational question and append the answer no.
Examples:
Would you pass the salt?
No, I can't reach it.

Can we balance the checkbook now?
No, I have a headache.

Are you going to walk the dog now?
No, I have to make a phone call first.

When a request is denied, it is a standard civility to offer an explanation for the denial.

Rule 7: Delay-Specification Option
IT: Talkative, cooperative, or minimally responsive
QC: Request
AC: Answer is yes, but with expected delay.
EI: Specify the expected time lapse and append this to yes.
Examples:
Would you pass the salt?
Yes, as soon as I put this down.

Will you take me to a ball game?
Yes, maybe next week.

Are you going to take out the garbage?
Yes, in a minute.

When someone is willing to fulfill a request but cannot do so immediately, the person making the request must understand that it will be taken care of eventually.

Rule 8: Condition-Specification Option
IT: Talkative, cooperative, or minimally responsive
QC: Request
AC: The answer is yes if certain conditionals are met.
EI: Specify the condition and append to yes.

Will you go to the store?
Yes, if I can get the car started.

Can we get a new car?
Yes, as soon as I get a raise.

Will you give me the furniture, the house, and the car?
Yes, if you'll leave me alone.

When someone agrees to a request, he is involving himself in a social interaction that may have many consequences beyond the simple performance of the act. If John asks Mary to do his laundry for him all the time and Mary agrees, her agreement indicates a great deal about their relationship. Conditionals are often used on these higher levels of social interaction to clarify relationships and goals. If Mary agrees to do his laundry only if he marries her, she has used the request as a vehicle for higher levels of communication.

Rule 9: Inference-Anticipation Option
IT: Talkative
QC: Verification
AC: Answer is yes, but with misleading inferences.[4]
EI: Correct the misleading inference after yes.
Examples:
Do you have a bicycle?
Yes, but I never ride it.

Aren't those terribly expensive?
Yes, but this one was given to me.

Is your brother applying for a scholarship?
Yes, but he doesn't have a chance.

This is a way to prolong or contribute to conversation. When an elaboration describes something running counter to normal expectations, the elaboration is

---

[4]Before we can formalize a notion of "misleading inferences," we must first be able to model the inferences that someone is likely to make when he hears an answer to a question. This problem is discussed further in subsection 5.2-1.

pointing out something that is at least minimally interesting and that may be pursued for further explication.

The elaboration options described thus far have all used very simple tests for their initial-answer criteria. These tests were all independent of the specific retrieval heuristics that found the initial answer. Another type of elaboration option can be designed to rely on the specific retrieval heuristics that are successful in finding an answer. It is difficult to give examples of these now, before retrieval heuristics have been discussed. But the next elaboration option is an example of a retrieval-oriented mechanism for content specification.

The basic idea involves replacing the initial-answer criteria with retrieval criteria (RC) specifying a particular retrieval heuristic. If this heuristic succeeds in finding an answer, the option is executed. The following rule is an example of an elaboration option with retrieval criteria. The retrieval mechanism specified is described in subsection 6.4-2.

Rule 10: Mental-State-Description Option
IT: Talkative
QC: Causal Consequent
RC: Interference/Resolution search
EI: If the actor of the resolution concept undergoes a mental-state change at some point between the interference and the resolution concept, return a mixed-format answer of the form:

> "[M] because [I] and so [R]"

where

[M]   is the mental-state change
[I]   is the interference concept
[R]   is the resolution concept.

This elaboration option is responsible for an answer like:

Q: What happened when the waiter served the hamburger?
A: John became angry because the hamburger was burnt, and so he left.

On the other hand, the default-retrieval heuristics for an Interference/Resolution search would have produced the answer:

A: The hamburger was burnt, and so John left.

5.2-1 Preventative-Inference Simulation

Often the answer criterion of an elaboration option can be satisfied by a simple examination of the initial answer. It may be enough simply to see whether the initial response is yes or no. But some answer criteria require additional memory processing. For example, the answer criteria for the Inference-Anticipation option requires some very involved memory processes. The Inference-Anticipation option is responsible for elaborations like:

Q1: Do you like Indian food?
A1: Yes, but New Haven has no good Indian restaurants.

This elaboration is generated by a mechanism that checks the LMU[5] after the initial response "Yes" is given. The LMU resulting from the answer "Yes" in this case contains the conceptualization for "I enjoy eating Indian food." The elaboration option triggered in this situation must look something like:

> IF (1) the LMU describes an act with
> MANNER value = HABITUAL, and
> (2) an enabling condition for that act is not satisfied,
> THEN augment the initial response with a description of the missing enablement.

This mechanism is responsible for exchanges like:

Q2: Does John shop at Bloomingdale's?
A2: Yes, but he can't afford it.

Q3: Do you usually drive to work?
A3: Yes, but right now my car isn't running.

To simulate the inference processes used by speakers in dialogue, we find the conversational context critical in guiding the flow of inference. Actual dialogue is often instrumental to the achievement of common or individual goals:

Q4: Do you want to play tennis?
A4: Sure.

Q5: Do you have a racket?
A5: No, but I can borrow one.

In this conversation, the two participants share a common goal: They want to play tennis. Given this goal orientation, there is an obvious purpose behind *Q5*. The person asking *Q5* wants to know the status of the enabling condition of having a racket. When the purpose of *Q5* is understood in this way, it is easy to see how a simple "No" answer would result in a misleading inference. The elaboration in *A5* addresses itself to the goal implicit in the last question. In this way a misleading inference (that they cannot play because they need a racket) is prevented by the elaboration. Without knowledge of the conversational context

---

[5]The LMU was introduced in subsection 4.1-3.

and instrumentality, an elaboration might be constructed that prevents a totally irrelevant inference:

Q6: Do you want to play tennis?
A6: Sure.
Q7: Do you have a racket?
A7: No, but I used to have one.

This elaboration prevents us from inferring that the respondent never had a racket. This assurance seems out of place because we cannot relate it to the purpose of the dialogue. Appropriate elaborations that prevent undesirable inferences are motivated by conversational goals. Inference simulation must be directed by underlying conversation, so it tends to be a problem closer to conversation theory than to question answering per se.

5.3 CATEGORY-TRACE INSTRUCTIONS

Category-trace instructions are responsible for producing answers that reflect the interpretive processing a question undergoes. In many situations, appropriate answers to questions actually indicate that the question underwent successive interpretations. For example, in Chapter 4 we described a Frequency-Specification conversion within context-independent inferential analysis. This transformation was responsible for recognizing when Verification questions should be understood to be asking how often an event takes place:

Q1: Do you eat out very often?
A1a: About twice a week.

Q2: Do you see each other?
A2a: Only during holidays.

Q3: Is there much rain?
A3a: Only in December.

Once these questions have ultimately been interpreted as Specification questions, the memory search can recognize them only as such and answer them by specifying a frequency. Answers to Verification questions that have been reinterpreted as Specification questions are different from answers to those that were initially interpreted as Specification questions. Each of *Q1–3* can be answered with an initial response of yes or no:

Q1: Do you eat out very often?
A1b: Yes, about twice a week.

Q2: Do you see each other?
A2b: Yes, but only during holidays.

Q3: Is there much rain?
A3b: No, only in December.

But if *Q1–3* were rephrased as questions that would be initially interpreted as Specification questions, these prefaces of yes and no would be out of place:

Q4: How often do you eat out?
A1b: Yes, about twice a week.

Q5: How often do you see each other?
A2b: Yes, but only during holidays.

Q6: How often does it rain?
A3b: No, only in December.

Q4–6 are conceptually equivalent to *Q1–3*, but they cannot be answered in the same ways. *Q4–6* can be answered with *A1a–3a,* but not with *A1b–3b*. The answers *A1b–3b* are appropriate for *Q1–Q3* because they reflect the interpretive processing that *Q1–3* undergo. Because *Q4–6* do not require the same reinterpretation as *Q1–3*, answers that reflect reinterpretive processing are inappropriate for these questions.

Category-trace instructions are designed to construct answers that reflect the interpretive processing of a question. The only information that must be recorded about a question's interpretive processing is a history of its conceptual categorizations as it passes through inferential analysis. A trace of interpretive categorizations is easy to maintain in a simple list. We call this list the category trace. Each of the questions *Q1–3* have a category trace = (Verification, Specification/[Frequency]). Questions *Q4–6* have a simple category trace = (Specification/[Frequency]).

Category-trace instructions are dependent on two factors: the intentionality of the system and the category trace of the question. Each category-trace instruction has three parts:

1. intentionality threshold (IT)
2. trace criterion (TC)
3. instruction execution (IE).

The intentionality threshold specifies under what intentionality factors the trace instructions are appropriate. The trace criterion specifies what kind of category trace a question must have in order to qualify for the trace instructions. If either the intentionality-threshold or the trace-criterion specifications is not met, the trace instructions are not applied to the question. The instruction execution describes the processes that derive a final conceptual answer in the event that the trace instructions are executed.

Rule 11: Verifying-Frequency Instructions
IT: Talkative, cooperative, minimally responsive

TC: Verification/Specification (frequency)
IE: The answer is yes or no, followed by frequency specification.
Examples:
Do you eat out much?
No, very rarely.

Did John study in college?
Yes, night and day.

Does it snow in Portland?
Yes, about once every year or two.

Does the computer ever crash?
No, never.

Rule 12: Verifying-Duration Instructions
IT: Talkative, cooperative, minimally responsive
TC: Verification/Specification (duration)
IE: The answer is yes or no, followed by duration specification.
Examples:
Was Nixon in office long?
Yes, about 6 years.

Did John stand there for more than an hour?
No, he was there about 40 minutes.

Have you lived in Italy long?
No, only a month.

Are you leaving soon?
Yes, as soon as I get my papers.

5.3-1 Category-Trace Instructions vs. Elaboration Options

There is a very fundamental difference between answers that result from category-trace instructions and those derived from elaboration options. By looking at the answers alone, the distinction is not apparent. Both of the answers

No, the hostess gave John a menu.
Yes, about once every year or two.

appear to have the same form. They are both yes or no answers followed by an elaboration of some sort. The difference between a compound answer derived from a category-trace instruction and one derived from an elaboration option is the order in which conceptual components of the answer are found during the memory search. When a question goes into the memory search with an elaboration option, the initial answer can be handed to the generator before the elaboration is found. In fact, elaboration options are designed so that the initial answer is a prerequisite condition for the application of an elaboration option. If asked,

Q7: Did McGovern win in 1972?

it is possible to generate the response "No" as soon as the question concept is found to be false. An elaboration (Nixon won in 1972) can then be found and generated after the initial response "No."

With questions that are answered by a category-trace instruction, the initial answer (yes or no) depends on the elaboration. The last part of the answer must be found before the first part can be generated. To answer "No" in response to "Does John go to the opera?" we must know how often John goes to the opera. To answer "Yes" to "Has John been to Europe very often?" we must know how often John has been to Europe. But to answer "No" to "Did McGovern win in 1972?" we do not have to know that Nixon won in 1972.

Category-trace instructions also differ from elaboration options in terms of the system intentionality required to activate them. Category-trace constructions are almost mandatory: The system must be operating in an uncooperative or rude intentionality in order for a category-trace construction to be suppressed. The intentionality threshold for many elaboration options is much higher. Some are triggered only if the system is talkative.

5.3-2 Hardly Ever Is Never Very Often

Some subtle difficulties are involved in the formation of compound category-trace answers. The problems arise in finding the appropriate initial response. Consider how many ways you could answer:

Q8: Do you go to New York very often?

A8a: No, only on Sundays.
(Once a week is not very often.)
A8b: Yes, every Sunday.
(Once a week is very often.)
A8c: No, hardly ever.
(Hardly ever can never be very often — if it could, we could say "Yes, hardly ever.")
A8d: No, never.
(Never is not very often — if it were we could say "Yes, never.")
A8e: Yes, whenever I can.
("Whenever I can" must be very often.)
A8f: No, only when I have to.
("Only when I have to" cannot be very often.)
A8g: Yes, whenever I have to.
("Whenever I have to" must be very often.)

A8h: No, but whenever I can.
("Whenever I can" must not be very often.)
A8i: Yes, but only when I have to.
("Only when I have to" must be very often.)
A8j: No, but whenever I have to.
("Whenever I have to" is not very often.)

The choice of an initial answer here is dependent on whatever cut off point is selected for "very often." *A8e* and *A8h* show how "whenever I can" can take either initial response, but there is something about this type of answer that makes it more consistent with a yes than a no. Thus, *A8h* must be constructed with the connective "but" to signal a violation of expectations.

Do you go to New York very often?
No, whenever I can.

sounds very strange, while

Do you go to New York very often?
No, but whenever I can.

seems perfectly fine. The same thing happens with *A8f, A8i, A8g,* and *A8j.* "Only when" answers are consistent with "No" (*A8f*), and "whenever" answers are consistent with "Yes" (*A8g*). If "only when" answers are combined with "yes," or if "whenever" answers are combined with "No," a but-construction is needed to counter the violated expectation.

5.4 ELABORATING UPON ELABORATION OPTIONS

It may appear odd that this chapter on content specification seems to ignore totally the problem of knowledge-state assessment; that is, the content of an answer should address gaps in the questioner's knowledge state. If the mechanisms that control memory retrieval are not motivated by a model of what the questioner does and does not know, then where will knowledge-state assessment fit in?

If we had a theory of knowledge-state assessment, it would interface with QUALM during content specification. Each elaboration option and category-trace instruction would specify knowledge-state-assessment criteria (KSAC), which would apply tests at the time of memory retrieval to make sure the elaboration is not telling the questioner something he already knows.

Knowledge-state assessment is discussed in Chapters 9 and 11. This is an area that needs attention. A theory of knowledge-state assessment would be a significant contribution to theories of question answering and conversation. When such a theory is sufficiently developed, QUALM will be ready to interface with knowledge-state models during inferential analysis and content specification by refining the conversion rules and elaboration options proposed here. In the same way that content-specification mechanisms are sensitive to intentionality factors without knowing what a theory of intentionality should look like, the interpretive mechanisms and memory retrieval controls proposed for QUALM have been designed to accommodate input from a knowledge-state model, even if we do not know exactly what that model will look like.

6 Searching Memory

Before information can be extracted from the memory, it must be found. If memory organization and retrieval heuristics are designed with care, searching processes should be able to zero in on the desired information without having to sift through everything in memory. If a system is trying to answer the question:

Q: Is New Haven in Connecticut?

It should not begin by looking at:

Lassie is a collie.
I burnt an English muffin this morning.
Elvis Presley is dead.
The integers under addition form an abelian group.

The time required for a search that examines irrelevant information without any sense of direction grows linearly with the amount of information in memory. That is, the more you know, the longer it will take to remember something. This does not sound like a very promising theory of memory. The processes that search memory must know where they are going before they begin; it is not sufficient to flit around like a blind bat.

6.0   INTRODUCTION

The memory search heuristics invoked for a question are determined by its conceptual question category. There are three levels of story representation in which answers to questions may be found:

1. the causal chain representation
2. script structures
3. planning structures.

Each of these represents a different level of understanding and detail. Not all stories have representations on each level. SAM generates story representations that have a causal chain and script structure, while PAM generates story representations made up of a causal chain and plan-based structures. But in a system that accesses both scripts and plans during its understanding, story representations will use all three descriptive levels. The retrieval heuristics described here were designed with such a system in mind.

Once the inferential analysis has settled on a conceptual question category, and content specification has determined a search strategy, the memory search can begin to look for an answer. Because each question category requires different processing by the memory search, the description of retrieval heuristics is organized according to conceptual question categories. But before we describe techniques specific to each conceptual question category, we must first mention a fundamental process used for most of the categories: the matching search.

Very often the first order of business when searching any level of story representation is to find a conceptualization that matches the question concept. This process is called the matching search. Roughly speaking, the matching search looks for a conceptualization having everything that the question concept has, and perhaps having additional things not found in the question concept. So if the question concept represents "John took a bus" (as would be the case for the question "Why did John take a bus?"), and the script summary for the bus trip represents "John went to New York by bus," the matching search will accept this script summary as a match. The Conceptual-Dependency representations for these two concepts differ only in that "John went to New York by bus" specifies a destination for the PTRANS, while "John took a bus" contains no destination. The term *answer key* is used to refer to that conceptualization from the story representation which matches the question concept when the matching search is successful.

The heuristics described here do not represent a complete or definitive set of search strategies. This is more of a beginning, representing those heuristics that have been implemented in a computer program and that appear adequate for large classes of questions in the context of story understanding. Unless there is an indication to the contrary, all retrieval heuristics described in this chapter have been implemented in the versions of QUALM used by SAM and PAM.

6.1   CAUSAL ANTECEDENT

A Causal Antecedent question may find its answer in either the causal chain representation, script structures, or planning structures. In each case, the first step is to find an answer key.

6.1-1   Script-Structure Retrieval Heuristics

The matching search for Causal Antecedent questions begins with a search of script structures. Each script instantiation that is referenced by the script-structure representation has a pointer to a single conceptualization called the script summary. For example, in the Leone's story, the script instantiation of the bus ride to New York has a script summary that represents John's having gone to New York by bus. The script instantiation of his restaurant episode has a script summary representing John's having eaten lasagna at Leone's. For a more detailed discussion of script summaries, what they are, and how they are created for a story representation, see Cullingford (1976, 1978). Searches of the script structure for Causal Antecedent questions access only these script summaries when looking for an answer key.

If the matching search succeeds at the script-structure level, the question is answered according to script-specific retrieval heuristics. That is, each script specifies a set of retrieval heuristics, which are organized according to conceptual-question categories. These heuristics apply only to questions that locate an answer key in the script structure search. It is probably more illuminating to discuss how a few specific questions are handled by script-specific heuristics, than to describe all the heuristics of all currently implemented scripts.

Suppose that we asked "Why did John go to New York?" in the context of the Leone's story. This is a Causal Antecedent question with a question concept representing "John went to New York." The matching search accesses the script structure of the story representation and determines that the top-level script under which the entire story is embedded is the trip script. It then examines the script summaries from the trip-script instantiation and all script instantiations embedded within the trip script. When it checks the script summary for the bus-script instantiation (John went to New York by bus), it finds the answer key.

Because the matching search succeeded while examining a trip-script instantiation, a special heuristic specific to that script is now invoked. The heuristic first determines whether the answer key was a summary of a script instantiation that was a part of (1) the going, (2) the destination, or (3) the returning leg of the trip script. An answer is then produced that is dependent upon in which leg of the trip script the matched script summary was found.

If the answer key was found in the "going" leg of the script, as was the case when we asked "Why did John go to New York?" then the answer is produced by concatenating the script summaries of all scripts instantiated in the destination leg of the trip. In the Leone's story there is only one script instantiated in the destination leg of the trip script: the restaurant script. So the conceptual answer to "Why did John go to Leone's?" involves the script summary of the restaurant-script instantiation: "John went to New York." But before the final conceptual answer can be sent to the generator, a small manipulation must be performed on the script summary so that its statement relates back to the question. In this case some indication of an enabling relationship is appropriate. This can be achieved by generating a sentence of the form: "Because X wanted to Y," where X is the actor of the answer key and Y is the conceptual action of the script summary (or summaries) in the destination leg of the trip script. To achieve this, we give the generator a mixed conceptual structure of the form:

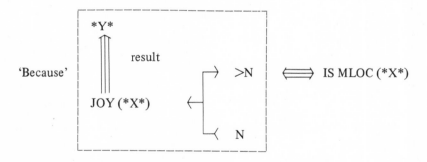

where *X* is the actor of the answer key and *Y* is the script summary (or summaries) from the destination leg of the trip script. This general answer format is applied to the script instantiations in the destination leg of the script to produce a conceptual answer for the generator. Thus the answer "Because John wanted to go to Leone's" is produced in response to "Why did John go to New York?"

If the question concept is matched in the destination leg of the script, the answer is produced by finding the maincon of the script instantiation whose summary matched the question concept. The maincon of a script instantiation is the conceptualization corresponding to the main act of that script. See Cullingford (1976, 1977) for a description of maincons in scripts. When the maincon is found, the conceptual answer is produced by generating:

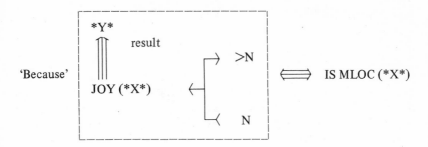

where *Y* is the maincon and *X* is the actor of the maincon. In the case of the restaurant script, the maincon is the patron eating his meal. So if we were to ask "Why did John go to Leone's?" the question concept (John went to Leone's) would match the script summary for the instantiation of the restaurant script (John went to Leone's). Because this match is made in the destination leg of the trip script, the question is answered by manipulating the maincon of the restaurant script to get "Because John wanted to eat some lasagna."

If the matching search succeeds in the returning leg of the trip script, a canned answer is returned by generating a conceptualization that is translated: "Because ACTOR(SS) wanted to go home," where ACTOR(SS) is the actor from the matched script summary. So if the Leone's story described John's leaving Leone's to take a subway and then a bus from New York, the questions "Why did John leave Leone's?" and "Why did John leave New York?" would both be answered "Because John wanted to go home."

6.1-2 Planning-Structure Retrieval Heuristics

If no match is found for the question concept on the level of script structures, planning structures are tried next. The matching search examines the causal-chain representation and plan-related inferences (if there are any), looking for an answer key. If the question concept is matched, plan-based retrieval heuristics are invoked in an effort to produce an answer. These heuristics are designed to produce a goal-oriented answer whenever possible (see Section 3.2).

Once the answer key is found in the story representation, its immediate causal antecedents are extracted from the causal chain of events. If there are no immediate causal antecedents, then the memory search on the level of planning structures has failed. Otherwise each of these antecedents is checked to see whether it is tagged as an act that instantiates some plan. Any act that is tagged as being part of a plan instantiation will have a pointer to the immediate goal motivating that plan. If a plan instantiation is found, its immediate goal forms the basis of the conceptual answer. In the dragon story, in which John rescues Mary from a dragon, the Causal-Antecedent questions — "Why did John kill the dragon?" and "Why did John get on his horse?" — are both answered in terms of plan-instantiated goals:

Q: Why did John kill the dragon?
A: Because he wanted Mary to not die.

Q: Why did John get on his horse?
A: Because he wanted to be near Mary.

If none of the direct antecedents yields a goal via plan instantiation, then no goal-oriented answer can be found. In this case, the same list of antecedents is searched for a concept that was motivated by a state. When one is found, its causal motivation is used to form the conceptual answer. This is how the question about Mary's marrying John (in the dragon story) is answered:

Q: Why did Mary agree to marry John?
A: Because she was indebted to him.

The manipulation of conceptualizations to form a final conceptual answer is similar to manipulations described previously for script-structure retrieval heuristics. These plan-based retrieval heuristics are described further in the discussion of retrieval heuristics in PAM (subsection 9.3-2).

6.1-3   Causal Chain Retrieval Heuristics

These heuristics are employed if the question concept has been found in the causal chain representation but no answer could be found using plan-based retrieval heuristics. In this case we expect an answer to be found on the basis of (1) inferences made by the script applier at the time of understanding, or (2) scriptal world knowledge.

Nonstandard Inference Search

When the script applier generates a causal-chain representation, it tags some conceptualizations as being inferences. This tag is used to indicate a lesser degree of certainty about these conceptualizations. There is another tag for conceptualizations that were found in the main path of a script. For example, looking at a menu is in the main path of the restaurant script, but leaving because you have to wait for a table is not. For a description of different inference paths in scripts, see Cullingford (1978). If the answer key has a causal antecedent that is tagged as an inference but not as a main-path conceptualization, then this nonstandard inference is used to generate a conceptual answer. For example, in the Leone's story, if we ask "Why couldn't John pay the check?" the question concept (John couldn't pay the check) is matched against the conceptualization in the causal chain representing "John discovered he couldn't pay the check." This answer key has as a causal antecedent the inference "John had no money," which is used to form a conceptual answer. The final answer is "Because John had no money." A mixed concept of the form "Because CA" (where CA is the selected causal antecedent) is used to construct the final conceptual answer.

Interference Search

If no inference-tagged causal antecedent is found, we then check to see whether the answer key itself is tagged as a script resolution (Lehnert, 1977; Cullingford, 1978). If so, its corresponding interference concept is picked up to form an answer. "Why did John have to wash dishes at Leone's?" is a question answered in this manner. John's washing dishes is a script resolution for the interference of not being able to pay the check. So the question is answered "Because John discovered he couldn't pay the check."

Script-Internal Goal Structures

If all these other heuristics fail, we then resort to answering the question on the basis of scriptal world knowledge alone. This is done by analyzing the answer key in terms of its place within a specific script. All scripts contain a goal/subgoal structure that is strongly correlated with hierarchies of scenes within a script and subscript maincons of each scene (see Fig. 6.1). For example, "Why did John order lasagna?" asks about the maincon of the ordering scene in the restaurant script. The script-based answer "Because he wanted to eat lasagna" references the maincon of the eating scene. Of course, a script-based answer of this sort is acceptable only when no other information exists. Had the story mentioned that John always ate lasagna at Italian restaurants, this information would provide a better answer than the obvious connection of wanting to eat what you order.

Although some retrieval heuristics on the level of script structures are very script specific, the heuristics that look for goals are generalizable across scripts. Although each script has a different goal structure, some structural features, like scenes and maincons, are universal to all scripts. The rules that manipulate these structural features are very general. For example, if scene N does not come after the main act of the script, then the goal behind the maincon of scene N is the maincon of scene $N + 1$. For example, the goal behind ordering is eating.

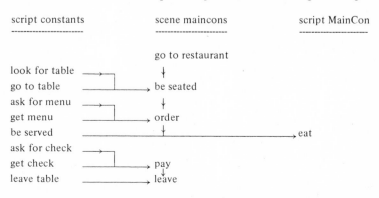

script constants	scene maincons	script MainCon

```
                          go to restaurant
look for table  ──────┐         ↓
go to table     ──────┴──────→ be seated
ask for menu    ──────┐         ↓
get menu        ──────┴──────→ order
be served       ──────────────→ ↓ ──────────────────────→ eat
ask for check   ──────┐
get check       ──────┴──────→ pay
leave table     ──────────────→ leave
                                  ↓
```

FIG. 6.1.   Restaurant-script goal hierarchy.

If the question concept cannot be matched against any of the conceptualizations in the script structures, plan-related inferences, or causal chain, then no conceptual answer can be produced and the memory search returns a conceptualization to the generator that translates into "I don't know." The same answer is returned if the question concept is matched but all of the above heuristics fail to produce an answer.

6.2 GOAL ORIENTATION

The set of retrieval heuristics for Goal Orientation questions largely overlaps with heuristics for Causal Antecedent questions. This is quite reasonable because a Goal Orientation question is a particular type of Causal Antecedent question. This being the case, it is easiest to describe retrieval for Goal Orientation questions in terms of how it differs from Causal Antecedent retrieval.

Like Causal Antecedent questions, Goal Orientation questions can find answers in either the causal-chain representation, planning structures, or script structures. As before, the first step is to match the question concept against a conceptualization in the story representation.

6.2-1 Script-Structure Retrieval Heuristics

The matching search begins with script structures and uses the same script-specific heuristics that Causal Antecedent questions used for script structures. Thus far, all of the script-specific heuristics developed for Causal Antecedent questions return answers that identify a goal orientation. As long as this continues to be the case, retrieval for Causal Antecedent and Goal Orientation questions will be identical on the level of script structures.

6.2-2 Planning-Structure Retrieval Heuristics

If the matching search fails at the script-structure level, heuristics applicable to planning structures are invoked. Here there is a slight departure from the plan-related retrieval processes used for Causal Antecedent questions. Once an answer key is found in the story representation, its immediate causal antecedents are extracted from the causal chain of events. If there are no immediate causal antecedents, then the memory search on the level of planning structures has failed. Otherwise each of these antecedents is checked to see whether it is tagged as an act that instantiates some plan. Any act tagged as being part of a plan instantiation will have a pointer to the immediate goal motivating that plan. If a plan instantiation is found, its immediate goal forms the basis of the conceptual answer. A manipulation of the immediate goal, identical with those manipulations used in Causal Antecedent questions, becomes the final conceptual answer, which is passed to the generator. In this way we can answer:

Q: For what purpose did John kill the dragon?
A: So Mary would not die.

Q: For what purpose did John get on his horse?
A: So he could be near Mary.

in the context of the dragon story:

> John loved Mary but she didn't want to marry him. One day, a dragon stole Mary from the castle. John got on top of his horse and killed the dragon. Mary agreed to marry him. They lived happily ever after.

If no plan instantiation is found for a Causal Antecedent question, a search looks for a motivating state. In Goal Orientation questions this search is not conducted. Because Goal Orientation questions ask about the goal or ultimate intentionality behind an action, they cannot be answered in terms of motivating states. It is reasonable to answer:

Q: Why did Mary agree to marry John?
A: Because she was indebted to him.

But it is not appropriate to answer:

Q: For what purpose did Mary agree to marry John?
A: Because she was indebted to him.

So if no plan instantiation is found, no further heuristics are invoked, and the matching search for a Goal Orientation answer has failed on the planning-structure level.

6.2-3 Causal Chain Retrieval Heuristics

Again we have a slight departure from the causal-chain retrieval heuristics used for Causal Antecedent questions. Neither the nonstandard inference search nor the interference search produces a goal-oriented answer; so neither of these searches is executed for Goal Orientation questions. It would not be appropriate to answer:

Q: For what purpose did John order a hamburger?
A: Because the waitress said they had no hot dogs.

But the script-internal goal structures do provide goal-oriented answers. So the goal structure of a script is used to answer Goal Orientation questions:

Q: For what purpose did John order a hamburger?
A: So he could eat a hamburger.

If either no answer key is found, or all of the above heuristics fail to find an answer, a conceptualization is given to the generator representing "I don't know."

6.3 ENABLEMENT

Enablement questions are a special case of Causal Antecedent questions. As such, their processing is similar. Answers to Enablement questions may be found in either the script structures, planning structures, or on the causal-chain level. The matching search examines the entire story representation at each level to find an answer key.

6.3-1 Script Structure Retrieval Heuristics

Each script has specific entry conditions to be satisfied before a default-path script execution can be achieved. For example, the entry conditions for the restaurant script are that the patron be hungry and that he have some money. It is possible to execute the script without these states being satisfied, but if a script is entered with an entry-condition violation, the script applier anticipates specific difficulties within the script that are not part of the default-path script instantiation. For example, in the Leone's story, John goes into Leone's without any money. The inference about John's not having money has been generated before he enters Leone's. So when the script applier hears that John cannot pay the check, it has anticipated this particular inference and is ready to link this anomalous turn of events with the entry-condition violation. For a more complete description of this process, see Cullingford (1978).

If the story had made no mention of any difficulty with the check, the script applier would have had to make an inference about an alternative entry condition to account for John's being able to pay the check. In this case, it would check the credibility assigned to the inference that John has no money, determine that there is some uncertainty about it, and conclude that John must have had some money with him after all. The inference that John had no money would then be eliminated from the story representation.

In one version of the Leone's story, we are told that John took a bus back to New Haven after washing dishes at Leone's. In this case the inference about John's not having any money has been substantiated by the fact that John could not pay the check at Leone's. But the default entry condition for the bus script is having some money. So when the bus script is activated, the script applier anticipates some difficulty because the script's entry condition is not satisfied. Yet "John took a bus to New Haven," without further mention of the bus trip, creates a default-path instantiation of the bus script. The script applier must somehow reconcile this with the fact that the entry condition for that script was violated. It first checks the credibility assigned to the conceptualization representing John's having no money. But this concept is now tagged with a credibility value of absolute certainty. So it cannot delete this concept from the story representation. It then looks to see whether there are any alternative entry conditions that can replace the condition of having money. When it looks for an alternative entry condition, it finds a resolution for the apparent inconsistency: To execute a default path through the bus script, one could have a bus ticket instead of money. The script applier then concludes that this alternative entry condition must have been satisfied and incorporates this inference into the story representation, though with less than absolute certainty.

When the matching search is conducted for an Enablement question on the level of script structures, the question concept is checked against script summaries of all instantiated scripts in the story representation. If an answer key is found in one of the script summaries, the entry conditions for the script are examined. If an alternative entry condition is found, and the credibility value assigned to it is less than absolute certainty, the final conceptual answer is produced by generating "Probably EC," where EC is the entry-condition conceptualization. This is how the question about the return bus ride is answered in the Leone's story:

Q: How was John able to take the bus to New Haven?
A: Probably John had a ticket.

6.3-2 Planning-Structure Retrieval Heuristics

The plan applier decomposes goal-oriented behavior into plan instantiations for goals and subgoals. This organization allows us to determine when an action has been carried out in order to further a specific plan. If the matching search can locate the answer key in the story representation, it checks to see whether the conceptualization matched has a SUBGOAL link pointing to a subordinate goal whose achievement contributes to or furthers the satisfaction of the answer-key goal. If such a pointer exists, an answer is generated by concatenating the subgoal conceptualizations. If only one subgoal exists, the answer refers to the single subgoal. This heuristic would be used to answer:

Q: How was John able to prevent Mary from dying?
A: John killed the dragon.

6.3-3 Causal Chain Retrieval Heuristics

If the previous heuristics fail to produce an answer, the answer key is located in the causal chain representation, and its direct causal antecedents are examined. If one of the causal antecedents is connected to the matched conceptualization by an ENABLES link, that antecedent is taken to be the conceptual answer.

Enablement links are generated by the script and plan appliers either when (1) the chronology of the causal chain calls for an enabling relationship, or (2) a necessary enabling condition is recognized for a specific act. This heuristic would be used to answer a question like:

Q: How was John able to leave a tip?
A: John had some money.

If no conceptualization in the story representation is found to match the question concept, or if none of the heuristics described produces an answer, the generator is given a conceptualization corresponding to "I don't know."

6.4   CAUSAL CONSEQUENT

Answers to Causal Consequent questions are found on the level of either script structures or causal-chain representation. When a Causal Consequent question is answered on the script-structure level, the answer is described in terms of a broad overview of the story. When it is answered on the causal-chain level, a much finer degree of detail is described. Whenever a question can be answered on varying levels of detail, it is appropriate to answer on the same level on which the question was asked.

A script-structure answer is sought first, for a question that can be answered on that level references an entire script instantiation and is therefore asking about an overview of something. If a question concept cannot be found on the script-structure level, it is asking about something within a particular script and therefore deserves to be answered in terms of acts within the script instantiation — acts that are on the same finer level of detail as the question itself.

An important feature of Causal Consequent questions is their ambiguity in terms of chronological ordering. In the context of the Leone's story,

Q: What happened when John got off the bus?

could reasonably be answered with either:

A: He thanked the driver, or
A: He went to the subway.

The first answer describes an event that happened before John actually got off the bus, while the second describes an event that took place after John got off. In addition to answers that strictly precede or follow the question concept, an answer to a Causal Consequent question can occur at the same time as the act in question:

Q: What happened when John took the subway?
A: A thief picked John's pocket.

Causal Consequent questions actually say, "Tell me about something that happened at about the same time as (blitch) took place." Of course, the best answers describe the most interesting thing possible, and the retrieval heuristics must incorporate some notion of relative interest values when searching for an answer.

6.4-1 Script-Structure Retrieval Heuristics

The matching search begins with script structures, trying to find the answer key in the summaries of those scripts that were instantiated for the story representation. If the question concept matches one of these script summaries, the question is asking about a relatively rough time reference: Acceptable answers can describe events that took place anywhere within the course of the referenced script instantiation. "What happened when John took the subway?" is one such question. The question concept (John took the subway) matches the script summary for the subway trip (John went to New York by subway) and is therefore asking for events that occurred anytime during the subway trip.

Weird-Event Search

When the answer key is a script summary, the memory search first looks to see whether the corresponding script instantiation contained any events that were recognized as weird by the script applier. A weird event is a conceptualization that script applier cannot find in any of its currently active scripts, and that itself triggers a script that is unusual or inappropriate in the context of currently active scripts. See Cullingford (1978) for a description of weird events within the context of a script. In the Leone's story, John's being pickpocketed is recognized as a weird event and is tagged as such in the subway-script instantiation. If a weird event is found, it is picked up as the conceptual answer to the question. This is how the Causal Consequent question about the subway trip is answered:

Q: What happened when John took the subway?
A: A thief picked John's pocket.

Interference/Resolution Search

If no weird event is found within the script in question, the memory search looks to see whether anything mildly interesting occurred during that script. It does this by checking for interference/resolution pairs. If there were one or more such pairs, a conceptual answer is formed by concatenating them in the form 'I1 and so R1, and then, I2 and so R2, and then . . ." where In and Rn are the nth interference and resolution in that script. This is how we answer:

Q: What happened when John went to Leone's?
A: John discovered that he couldn't pay the check, and so he had to wash dishes.

Main-Act Search

If the script has no weird events or inference/resolution pairs, then a test is executed to see whether the script summary matches the main act of the script. In some scripts the main act and the script summary convey the same information (e.g., the pickpocket script), while in others they are different. If it turns out that the main act is different from the script summary, then the main act of the script is returned as the conceptual answer.

> John went to Leone's. He ordered lasagna. When he left he gave the waitress a large tip.

Q: What happened when John went to Leone's?
A: John ate lasagna.

6.4-2 Causal-Chain Retrieval Heuristics

If the script-structure memory search fails to produce an answer key, then a matching search begins on the causal-chain representation. If the question concept cannot be found in the causal chain, the generator is given a conceptualization representing "I don't remember anything."

Default-Path Departures

If a match is made, the memory search checks to see whether the answer key is an instantiation of a maincon in a script scene. Most scripts are partitioned into scenes, each of which has one main act of primary importance. For example, the restaurant script has scenes for entering, seating, ordering, eating, paying, and leaving. See Cullingford (1978) for a detailed description of script scenes. If the answer key describes the main act of a scene, the memory search examines each act of the script instantiation that forms a part of that scene, looking for a conceptualization that is not tagged as an act on the default path of the script. If it finds such an act, it returns that conceptualization as the conceptual answer.

For example, the main acts of the bus-script scenes are getting on, sitting down, and getting off. So if we ask "What happened when John got off the bus?" in the context of the Leone's story, the underlying question concept (John got off the bus) matches a concept in the causal chain that is tagged as the main act of the getting-off scene. Other conceptualizations from the getting-off scene are then checked to see whether there was one that did not come from the default path of the bus script. One such conceptualization is found, and it becomes the answer:

Q: What happened when John got off the bus?
A: John thanked the driver.

The same processing of default-path departure answers the question:

Q: What happened when John sat down on the bus?
A: John talked to an old lady.

Resolution Search

The memory search next checks to see whether the answer key was tagged by the script applier as a script interference. If so, its corresponding resolution is returned as the conceptual answer:

Q: What happened when John couldn't pay the check?
A: The management told John he would have to wash dishes.

Chronological-Consequent Search

If no answer is produced by the other heuristics, but an answer key was found in the causal chain, then the next act in the causal chain is taken as the conceptual answer:

Q: What happened when John ordered lasagna?
A: The waitress took the order to the chef.

Q: What happened when John told the waiter he couldn't pay the check?
A: The management told John he would have to wash dishes.

In an early version of SAM, Causal Consequent questions were answered by picking up all the conceptualizations following the question concept in the causal chain up to the next one explicitly stated in the story:

Q: What happened when the hostess gave John a menu?
A: John read the menu, the waiter saw that John was at the table, the waiter went to the table.

Q: What happened when John ordered the hamburger?
A: The waitress gave the order to the cook, the cook prepared the hamburger, the cook gave the hamburger to the waitress, the waitress served John the hamburger.

This heuristic was designed primarily as a way of displaying all of the inferences SAM makes. It was never intended to be taken as a serious model of what people do or as a heuristic for providing natural answers. One of its immediate faults lies within its reliance on knowing whether or not a conceptualization in the story representation was explicitly mentioned in the text of the story. A number of psychology experiments (Bower, 1976; Bransford & Franks, 1971) have shown that people cannot differentiate what they are explicitly told from what they infer. Furthermore, the type of information that gets confused appears to be exactly the mundane scriptal information with which we are working. Because our question-answering model is attempting to model human cognitive processes, we do not want to develop memory mechanisms that rely on capabilities people do not have. Consequently, this early heuristic has been replaced by the chronological-consequent search, which returns the single concept immediately following the answer key in the causal chain.

6.5   VERIFICATION

The initial memory search for a Verification question is quite straightforward. A matching search is executed to examine all conceptualizations in the script structures, planning structures, and causal-chain representation. If a match is made, the credibility value of the matched conceptualization is checked. If it has absolute certainty, the answer "Yes" is passed to the generator. If it has a credibility that is less than absolutely certain, the answer "Probably" is returned. If no answer key if found, the initial answer is "No."

Verification questions often carry elaboration options from content specification (see Chapter 5). After an initial answer of yes, no, or probably is produced, the memory search checks to see whether the question is carrying an elaboration option or category-trace instruction. If it carries neither, the initial answer is the final conceptual answer. Otherwise an elaboration must be produced according to the instructions in the elaboration option or category-trace instruction.

If a Verification question is carrying an elaboration option, it will specify two things for the memory search: the answer criteria (AC) and the elaboration instructions (EI). The initial response is compared with the answer criteria. If the answer-criteria test is passed, the elaboration instructions are executed. If the answer-criteria test fails, the initial answer becomes the final conceptual answer, which is passed to the generator. At present, three elaboration options applying to Verification questions have been implemented: the Verification option, the Short-Answer option, and the Correct/Explanation option (see Section 5.2). These options are responsible for answers like:

Q: Did the waitress give John a menu?
A: No, the hostess gave John a menu.
   (Correction/Explanation option)

Q: Did John pay the check?

A: No, John was angry because the hamburger was burnt, and so he left.
(Correction/Explanation option)

Q: Did John order lasagna?
A: Yes, John ordered lasagna.
(Verification option)

Q: Did John go to New York?
A: Yes, John went to New York by bus.
(Verification option)

Q: Did John go the the Friar's Club?
A: No.
(Short-Answer option)

6.6   DISJUNCTIVE

Disjunctive questions are similar to Verification questions in terms of the retrieval heuristics used to answer them. It is useful to think of Disjunctive questions as Verification questions having multiple question concepts instead of one.

Initially, a matching search of the entire story representation (script structures, planning structures, and causal chain representation) is conducted for each of the question concepts until one of them is matched. As soon as a match is made, the matched concept is passed to the generator as the final conceptual answer. If no match is made, the initial answer is "Neither." Once an initial answer is produced, the question is checked to see whether there is an attending category-trace instruction or elaboration option.

There is a focus problem with Disjunctive questions. Occcasionally, a Disjunctive question can be answered simply yes or no, depending on whether any of the conceptualizations in the question concept can be verified.

Q: Did John or Mary go shopping?

may be asking:

Q: Who went shopping – John or Mary?

or it might be asking:

Q: Did anyone go shopping?

in a context in which John and Mary are the only obvious candidates and the questioner is more interested in the act of shopping than in the actor. Knowing which way a Disjunctive question should be answered depends on contextual factors and inferences about what the questioner is really interested in.

However, an answer that is derived by passing the answer key to the generator is always adequate — at its worst, it supplies more information than the questioner was looking for. Saying that Mary went shopping will satisfy the questioner regardless of whether he was interested in who went or just that someone went. The focus issue for Disjunctive questions is therefore less crucial than it is in other conceptual question categories. (These problems will be pursued in Chapter 7).

6.7 INSTRUMENTAL/PROCEDURAL

Answers to Instrumental/Procedural (I/P) questions may be found in either the script structures, planning structures, or on the causal chain level. The matching search begins with script structures. Not all scripts have script-specific retrieval heuristics for I/P questions. The only script implemented thus far that has special heuristics for I/P questions is the trip script.

6.7-1 Script-Structure Retrieval Heuristics

The matching search among script structures examines summaries for each script that appears as a top-level instantiation in the "going" or "returning" legs of the trip script. If the question concept matches one of these summaries, an answer is produced by combining other script summaries from the trip-script structure. If the answer key is found in the going leg of the trip, the answer is formed by concatenating all of the summaries for each script in the going leg of the trip up to and including the matched summary:

Q: How did John get to New York?
A: John went to New York by bus.

Q: How did John get to Leone's?
A: John went to New York by bus, and then he went to Leone's by subway.

If the question concept matches a script summary from the returning leg of the trip, the same heuristic is used, but with the script summaries in the returning leg of the trip:

Q: How did John leave Leone's?
A: John went from Leone's by subway.

Q: How did John get to New Haven?
A: John went from Leone's by subway, and then John went from New York to New Haven by bus.

6.7-2 Planning-Structure Retrieval Heuristics

If no answer is found in the script structures, inferences from planning structures are invoked. On this level, retrieval for I/P questions is identical with retrieval for Enablement questions. If the matching search can locate the answer key in the story representation, it checks to see whether the answer key has a PLANACT link pointing to a subordinate goal. If such a pointer is found, an answer is produced by concatenating the PLANACT conceptualizations:

Q: How did John prevent Mary from getting hurt?
A: John killed the dragon.

Retrieval from planning structures for Enablement and I/P questions is identical because there does not seem to be a conceptual distinction between the plans that are enablements to a parent goal and those that are instrumental to a parent goal. At present, there is only one relationship between a goal and its plans: A plan contributes to the achievement of its parent goal. In the questions and stories considered, Enablement and I/P questions appear to be conceptually equivalent when the answers are derived from goal/plan relationships. The questions:

Q: How was John able to prevent Mary from getting hurt?
Q: How did John prevent Mary from getting hurt?

can both be answered:

A: He killed the dragon.

If at some point we encounter a question that demands a distinction between instrumental and enabling plans, the representation will be forced to reflect this difference, and the retrieval heuristics will be altered accordingly.

6.7-3 Causal Chain Retrieval Heuristics

On the causal chain level, the matching search runs through the causal chain looking for an answer key. If one is found, the answer key is checked to see whether it has an instrument slot. If so, that conceptualization is returned as the final conceptual answer:

Q: How did John get to the table?
A: John walked to the table.

If no instrument slot is found in the matched conceptualization, or if no conceptualization in the causal chain is matched, a conceptualization is passed to the generator representing "I don't know."

6.8 CONCEPT COMPLETION

To answer Concept Completion questions requires little more than a matching search. The question concept for a Concept Completion question has an unknown conceptual component. In the memory search, this unknown component is treated as a wild card; it will match anything. The matching search examines all levels of the story representation. Script structures, planning structures, and the causal-chain representation are all searched for an answer key.

When a match is made, short answers are produced if the Single-Word option is in effect (see Section 5.2).

Q: Who gave John a menu?
A: The hostess.

Otherwise, the entire answer key is generated to produce a long answer:

Q: Who gave John a menu?
A: The hostess gave John a menu.

6.9 EXPECTATIONAL

In terms of the initial memory-search processing that must take place, Expectational questions are unlike all of the conceptual-question categories discussed so far. For all of the other question categories, a matching search was initially executed to locate the question concept in the story representation. But an Expectational question asks about something that did not happen, whereas a conceptual story representation contains only those things that took place. So an answer key for an Expectational question cannot be found in the story representation. Therefore Expectational questions do not conduct the kind of matching search for the question concept, that is undertaken for other question categories. A matching search is conducted, but it operates on a data structure that is created at the time of the memory search to augment the story representation. A detailed account of Expectational questions and of the memory search processes that answer them is given in Chapter 8.

6.10 JUDGMENTAL

Judgmental questions are similar to Expectational questions insofar as they must access information outside of the story representation in order to produce an answer. Questions like "What should John do now?" require the answerer to project himself into John's place (i.e., into the situational context of the story) and make a projection concerning John's behavior on the basis of whatever scripts and plans the answerer has at his disposal.

These questions have been implemented by Jaime Carbonell (1977) in his script-based version of the Goldwater machine. The POLITICS program currently processes Conceptual Dependency input and produces Conceptual Dependency answers. Given an input statement and some questions, POLITICS can respond with answers reflecting a conservative political ideology:

INPUT: Russia massed troops on the Czech border.

Q: What will Russia do next?
A: RUSSIA MAY ORDER ITS TROOPS INTO CZECHOSLOVAKIA.

Q: What can the United States do?
A: THE UNITED STATES CAN DO NOTHING; IT CAN INTERVENE MILI-
TARILY IN CZECHOSLOVAKIA BY SENDING TROOPS; OR IT CAN
INTERVENE DIPLOMATICALLY BY TALKING TO RUSSIA ABOUT
CZECHOSLOVAKIA.

Q: What should the United states do?
A: THE UNITED STATES SHOULD INTERVENE MILITARILY.

To implement Judgmental questions for SAM and PAM, we would have to set up
an interactive communication between the question answerer and the script or
plan applier (much like the interaction implemented for Expectational questions that we describe in Chapter 8). In this interaction the script or plan applier
would be given a processing state encountered at some point during understanding, along with possible goals specified in the question and a request to project
the predicted behavior of whatever character was in question. For example,
suppose that we read the following story:

John went into a restaurant. The waitress gave him a menu, and he decided
he wanted a hamburger.

Now suppose we are asked:

Q: What should John do now?

To answer this question, we would ask the script applier for the next conceptualization involving John:

A: John should order a hamburger.

Suppose we had read:

John loved Mary but she didn't want to marry him. One day a dragon stole
Mary from the castle. She was never seen again.

and were asked:

Q: What should John have done to save Mary?

To answer this question, the plan applier would have to be given: (1) the story
representation as it stood before the statement that Mary was never seen again,
and (2) John's goal of saving Mary. It could then predict a plan that John could
invoke for attaining his goal. This plan would be used to produce an answer:

A: John should have killed the dragon.

No difficulties are anticipated in implementing these questions. Many of the necessary mechanisms already exist for the Expectational questions. These questions have not been implemented for SAM and PAM, largely because they have been implemented in the POLITICS system.

6.11   QUANTIFICATION

Quantification questions are very much like Concept-Completion questions, but their answers are found in memory tokens rather than in the chronological story representation. A fact such as how many people were in Leone's would be stored under the memory token for Leone's patrons. It would not be placed in the script structures, planning structures, or causal chain conceptualizations.

The internalization processing that follows the initial parse should be able to identify which memory token is being referenced; so the only work remaining for the retrieval heuristics is to look up the appropriate property under that memory token. For example, if the story had mentioned that there were 20 people on the bus going to New York, a memory token for that group of people would be created at the time of understanding. Say that the memory token was given the pointer GN005. Under that memory token would be the property NUMBER, and the value assigned to the property NUMBER would be 20. Now if we parse a question that asks "How many people were on the bus going downtown?" the internalization program would be responsible for recognizing that this question references GN005. The internalized conceptualization representing the question would therefore be:

$$\text{GN005} \Longleftrightarrow \text{IS NUMBER VAL (*?*)}$$

The question concept consists of two parts, the referent and the unknown property:

(REF GN005 PROP NUMBER)

The retrieval heuristic is then very simple. The conceptual answer is produced by performing a GET (the function that accesses property list values) on the name GN005 and on the property NUMBER.

6.12   FEATURE SPECIFICATION

Feature Specification questions are answered the same way as Quantification questions. The question concept consists of a tokenized referent and an unknown property value. A simple retrieval on the property list of the specified memory token produces the answer. For example,

Q: How old was John?

is parsed and internalized as:

GN001 $\Longleftrightarrow$ IS AGE VAL (*?*)

The interpreted question concept is (REF GN001 PROP AGE), and the answer is produced by getting the value of the property AGE under the name GN001. In the event that a fuzzy property reference is given in the question (What kind of dog is Rover?), the retrieval looks for any descriptive property that is not in a list of standard descriptors to avoid (SEX, AGE, COLOR, WEIGHT, NATION-ALITY, etc.). The first property it finds that is not on this list is returned as the conceptual answer. This heuristic should be replaced by a type-specific default heuristic. For example, a memory token of type DOG should default to BREED when a general descriptor is needed. But such a type-specific search would require a taxonomy of memory token types. Although such a taxonomy must eventually be proposed, it is too early to develop anything other than an ad hoc system of memory token hierarchies. The primitive heuristic described above will stand until a memory token taxonomy can be proposed.

6.13 CONCLUDING REMARKS ON RETRIEVAL HEURISTICS

The one conceptual question category that does not dictate retrieval heuristics is Requests. In a complete model of question answering, a large portion of the memory search should be devoted to the processing required to execute a Request. This aspect of the theory would naturally be limited to whatever simulated world in which the computer can function. For example, Winograd's (1972) SHRDLU explores the Request aspect of memory searches in its manipulation of a blocks world.

Because the programs implemented in conjunction with QUALM function to demonstrate story understanding, there has been no natural opportunity for exploring Requests in terms of memory searches. The questions that people can ask about stories are called inquiries. These have formed the basis for the research presented here. In the context of story understanding, we need not concern ourselves with whether the computer is willing to light our cigarettes.

7

Focus Establishment

The focus of a question is that conceptual component of the question to which attention is directed. When focus is misplaced, answers to questions appear to miss the point:

Q1: Why does Carter carry his own luggage?
A1: He wants us to know he's one of the people.
A2: It would be silly for him to carry Billy's things around.

A1 answers a question that focused on the fact that the President is violating a social convention of his office: The President does not carry his own luggage. The focus falls on Carter:

Q2: Why does Carter (of all people) carry his own luggage?

A2 answers the same question but with focus on the fact that people normally carry their own luggage instead of other people's. The focus here falls on whose luggage Carter carries:

Q3: Why does Carter carry his own luggage (instead of someone else's)?

7.0 INTRODUCTION

If *A1* seems to be a more natural answer to *Q1* than *A2*, it is only because we know that Carter is President, and that presidents are not subject to the same social conventions as the rest of us. It would not make much sense to answer:

Q4: Why does John Doe carry his own luggage?
A4: He wants us to think he's one of the people.

Unless there is something special about John Doe that suggests he is not one of the people. This particular example of focus establishment is based on general knowledge about the world and is discussed in subsection 7.1-4. But first we describe other ways in which focus manifests itself.

7.1 DIFFERENT KINDS OF FOCUS

Attention can be directed to a particular component of a question by many different means. Four general strategies used by speakers for focus placement are:

1. stress-intonation patterns
2. syntactic construction
3. contextual determinants
4. knowledge-based determinants.

The first strategy, stress intonation, is a function of acoustic processing and cannot be detected in written language without the use of italics, underscoring, or some other visual device designed to mimick spoken stress. The second strategy, syntactic construction, is a grammatical device. The last two strategies, contextual focus and knowledge-based focus, are functions of conceptual processing that cannot be discussed without reference to memory processes and information in memory.

7.1-1 Stress-Intonation Patterns

One way that a question can be constructed with a clear focal assignment is by using various intonation patterns. Of course this does not occur in written language, but it is used all the time in spoken language.

Q5: Did the *WAITRESS* bring John a menu?

A stress pattern for *Q5* that emphasizes the word *waitress* by a rise in tonal frequency and perhaps volume serves to place the focus of the question on the waitress. With the proper intonation, *Q5* is functionally equivalent to asking:

Q6: Was it the waitress who brought John a menu?

in terms of where the attention is focused and what kinds of answers are appropriate.

In actual speech, intonation can be combined with syntactic construction to express attitudes of irony, disbelief, or sarcasm. A classic story illustrating the way intonation can turn around the meaning of entire sentences involves two readings of a fictitious telegram:

Joseph Stalin
Kremlin
Moscow

You were right and I was wrong. You are the true heir of Lenin. I should apologize.

Trotsky

The same telegram read with feeling becomes an entirely different message:

Joseph Stalin
Kremlin
Moscow

YOU were right and I was WRONG? YOU are the true heir of Lenin? I should *apologize??!!*

Trotsky!!!!!!

7.1-2 Syntactic Constructions

Certain syntactic constructions function as focus operators:

Q6: Was it the waitress who brought John a menu?

This question is constructed to place emphasis on the conceptual component of the waitress. Any appropriate answer to *Q6* will address this aspect of the question concept. *Q6* can be answered naturally with:

A6a: No, the hostess brought John a menu.

but it would be odd to answer *Q6* with:

A6b: No, the waitress brought John a hamburger.

Q6 effectively asks "Did the waitress bring John a menu? If not, who brought John a menu?" The question tends to convey a presupposition that somebody brought John a menu; the question is, Who? So the focus for *Q6* falls on the actor who brought John a menu.

7.1-3 Context and Focus

Syntactic constructions and stress-intonation patterns are aspects of a question that the parser must recognize. Although syntactic construction and stress-intonation patterns can be used to establish the focus of a question, there are also times when the focus does not rely on anything that the parser can be expected to handle. Often, the context of a question is essential in establishing its focus. To see how context can affect focus, we consider a question asked in the contexts of two different stories:

Context 1

John had just bought a new car. He was so happy with it that he drove it at every possible opportunity. So last night when he decided to go out for dinner, he drove over to Leone's. When he got there he had to wait for a table. . . .

Q7: Why did John drive to Leone's?

Appropriate answers to this question are "Because he just got a new car and he liked to drive it whenever he could," or "Because he was very happy with his new car," or "Because he enjoyed driving," and so on. The point is that the question here is interpreted to be asking about driving. The focus of the question is on the transportational instrument used when John went to Leone's. Now consider another story:

Context 2

John had a crush on Mary. But he was so shy that he was happy to just be in her proximity. So he was in the habit of following her around a lot. He knew that she ate at Leone's very often. So last night when he decided to go out for dinner, he drove over to Leone's. When he got there he had to wait for a table. . . .

Q8: Why did John drive to Leone's?

The question now has a different meaning. Appropriate answers are "Because he knew that Mary ate there," or "Because he hoped to run into Mary there," or "Because he wanted to see Mary," and so on. Here the question has been interpreted to be asking about Leone's. The focus of the question is on John's destination.

Because *Q7* and *Q8* elicit different answers, they cannot be conceptually equivalent. Yet lexically, *Q7* and *Q8* are identical questions, they differ only in terms of interpretive focus. This assignment of focus must be a function of the context in which the question occurs. The conceptual representation of a question is not complete if it does not include focus specification whenever appropriate. It follows that the conceptual representation of some questions must therefore depend on the context in which the question occurs.

When the focus of a question is sensitive to context, it tends to be interpreted in terms of what information is present in memory. In the first context we do not know why John chose to go to Leone's in particular, but we do know why he drove. In the second context we have no information about John's choice of transportation, but we do not know why he elected to go to Leone's. People do not consider an alternative interpretation of a question that they cannot answer when there is a natural interpretation that can be answered. This suggests that there are questions for which memory must be accessed before a full interpretation is achieved. A discussion of this problem and some proposed solutions is presented in Chapter 9.

7.1-4 World Knowledge and Focus

In some cases the focus of a question can be established only by accessing world knowledge in memory and applying various inference processes in order to see where the question was likely to be focused. In these cases the establishment of focus occurs in the interpreter or the memory search.

For example, suppose I tell you that our friend John roller-skated to McDonald's last night. You may very well ask:

Q9: Why did he roller-skate to McDonald's?

and I could answer back:

A9a: Because he was hungry.
A9b: Because his bicycle was broken.

A9a addresses the question as an inquiry about John's destination. *A9b* answers the question in terms of John's mode of transportation. If *A9a* seems an odd answer, it is because it addresses an unnatural focus assignment. *Q9* is more naturally interpreted as asking about John's roller-skating than about his destination. This focus preference is a function of evaluating what is most interesting about the question. John's going to McDonald's is far more commonplace than his roller-skating (assuming that John is an adult). This interest evaluation must be made in terms of world knowledge and by knowing what things are relatively common or unusual.

Of course if the reader knows that John is an eccentric who roller-skates everywhere and never goes to McDonald's because he abhors fast food, then this knowledge will be used to understand that John's going to McDonald's is more interesting than roller-skating.

Focus Rule #1
Specific Knowledge has Priority
Over General Knowledge During
Focus Establishment

But in the absence of specific knowledge, there is a default hierarchy of world knowledge in terms of relative interest values. No matter where the interest evaluations come from, the same interpretive rule always holds: When different components of a question are competing for the focus, it is natural to emphasize the most unusual aspect of the conceptual question.

Another knowledge-based focus assignment is concerned with placing focus on the most variable aspect of a question:

Q10: Did the waitress bring John a menu?

Suppose that the answer to this question is no and that we want to elaborate the negative response.

A10a: No, the waitress brought John a hamburger.
A10b: No, the hostess brought John a menu.

A10a results when the focus of *Q10* is placed on the menu. The elaboration is predicated on the belief that what is important about this question is what the waitress brought John. *A10b* results when the focus is placed on the actor, the waitress. Here the elaboration is produced by understanding *Q10* to be concerned with who brought John the menu. When focus is assigned to the menu, *Q10* carries a weak presupposition that the waitress brought John something. When focus is assigned to the waitress, the presupposition is that somebody brought John a menu. Focus is being placed on that component of the question concept that is most open to correction or variation.

Focus Rule #2
Focus Favors Variation
Over Expectation

It may well be that both *A10a* and *A10b* are perfectly correct answers. But one of them is likely to be more appropriate. Finding a focus that will result in the most appropriate answer requires knowledge of the world, of stereotypic occurrences, and of points of variation within a stereotypic situation. We return to this particular type of focus problem and propose a script-based processing solution for it in Section 7.3

7.2 WHEN FOCUS IS ESTABLISHED

Syntactic constructions and intonational patterns allow us to identify the focus of a question without any inferencing or higher-memory processing. In either case, the parser can recognize the focus of the question and mark the component receiving emphasis in its resulting conceptual representation. In our computer models, intonational patterns are not considered because we are processing written rather than spoken input. But syntactic constructions should be recognized by the parser when they function in terms of focus establishment. The parser should be able to input

Q1: Was it the waitress who brought John a menu?

and output a concepualization that marks the focus of the question:

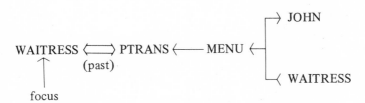

The current parser used in SAM and PAM recognizes and assigns focus in some cases. The parser design has not incorporated comprehensive focus recognition, largely because of design priorities. For example, the recognition of various cleft-sentence constructions is both a straightforward and a relatively peripheral problem that is not expected to pose any interesting theoretical questions.

One of the basic processing principles that applies to the problem of focus establishment is the desirability of not doing something you do not have to do. Some questions can be answered without ever considering the focus of the question. If the answer to

Q2: Did the waitress bring John a menu?

is yes, then it is not necessary to know the focus of the question. We can conduct a memory search that finds a concept corresponding to the waitress bringing John a menu the answer "Yes" is returned; and no more processing is required. Focus is needed to answer *Q2* only if the initial answer is "No" and if elaboration is desired. It is therefore appropriate to relegate focus establishment to the answer elaborator in cases like *Q2,* where focus is not needed unless an elaboration option is being exercised.

7.3   A SCRIPT-BASED FOCUS HEURISTIC

The focus heuristic about to be described is executed when the Correction/Explanation option is exercised to augment a negative response to a Verification question. In this case, the focus of the question must be identified to correct the question concept. Before launching into a description of the actual heuristic, we discuss various Correction/Explanation elaborations to see what is involved in producing these answers.

Suppose that we are asking questions in the context of the following story:

John went to a restaurant and the hostess gave him a menu. When he ordered a hot dog the waitress said they didn't have any. So John ordered a hamburger instead. But when the hamburger came, it was so burnt that John left.

Q1: Did the waitress give John a menu?
A1: No, the hostess gave John a menu.

Q2: Did the waitress serve John a hot dog?
A2: No, the waitress served John a hamburger.

Q3: Did John eat the hamburger?
A3: No, the hamburger was burnt.

Each of these Verification questions has been answered with an appropriate elaboration. The problem we are concerned with is where these elaborations come from. If we consider *Q1, Q2,* and *Q3,* it becomes clear that each of the elaborations offered here is itself the answer to a question:

Did the waitress give John a menu?
Yes   No
Who gave John a menu?
The hostess gave John a menu.

Did the waitress serve John a hot dog?
Yes.   No.
What did the waitress serve John?
The waitress served John a hamburger.

Did John eat the hamburger?
Yes.   No.
Why didn't John eat the hamburger?
The hamburger was burnt.

It appears that these elaborations are obtained by asking and answering some new question. So the problem of finding an elaboration becomes one of finding a question to ask (and answer). Once we have asked the right question, finding an answer is not hard: The secondary question can simply be fed back into

QUALM to be processed as if it were just another top-level question. The difficulty is in asking the right secondary question. How do we know which question will lead to a good elaboration?

It should be clear that many secondary questions could be generated. In fact, many secondary questions would lead to correct elaborations.

Q4: Did the waitress give John a menu?
A4: No, the waitress gave John a hamburger.

A4 comes from answering the secondary question "What did the waitress give John?" It is important to realize that there is nothing incorrect about *A4* as a response to *Q4*. It is absolutely true that the waitress gave John a hamburger. Yet somehow this answer seems less natural or less appropriate than "No, the hostess gave John a menu." In generating a secondary question, we must be concerned with finding the one that leads to the most natural response.

All secondary questions that lead to reasonable elaborations can be derived from the original question concept in some manner. *A1* and *A2* are the result of Concept Completion questions created from the original question concept. "Who gave John a menu?" comes from replacing the waitress with an unknown actor in the question concept underlying "Did the waitress give John a menu?" "What did the waitress serve John?" is the result of an unknown object in place of the hamburger in the concept underlying "Did the waitress serve John a hot dog?" *A3* is a response to an Expectational question: "Did John eat the hamburger? — No. — (Why not?) — The hamburger was burnt." How do we know when to generate a Concept Completion question and when to generate an Expectational question? And if a Concept Completion question is to be used, which one?

For the moment, let us just worry about finding the right Concept Completion question. Each possible Concept Completion question is derived by replacing a conceptual component in the original question concept with an unknown. The problem we face is one of knowing which conceptual component should be replaced. Consider all the possible Concept Completion questions that could have been generated from Q1:

Did the waitress give John a menu?
(question concept)

Who gave John a menu?
(Replace actor slot.)

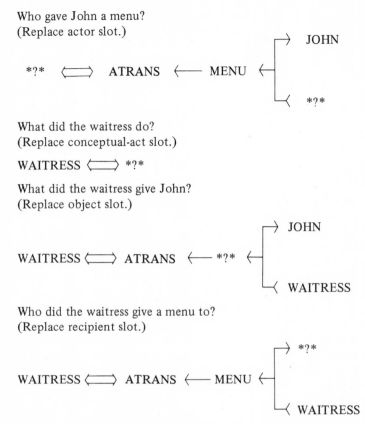

What did the waitress do?
(Replace conceptual-act slot.)

WAITRESS ⟨⟹ *?*

What did the waitress give John?
(Replace object slot.)

Who did the waitress give a menu to?
(Replace recipient slot.)

By focusing on different conceptual components in the question, we can generate different secondary questions for elaborations. Some of these secondary questions lead to an elaboration and some do not. For example, in the context of our original story "What did the waitress give John?" can be answered and will therefore provide an elaboration. But "Who did the waitress give a menu to?" cannot be answered (unless the answer is no one) and therefore does not lead to a good elaboration.

Although many secondary questions can be generated, more than one of which may lead to a correct elaboration, one question generally leads to the most natural elaboration. Knowing which question will give the best elaboration is equivalent to knowing which conceptual component of the question should receive attention. There is an implicit focus in these questions that singles out the proper conceptual component. In Q1 the focus is on the waitress. In Q2 focus falls on the hot dog. The problem is how to identify the implicit focus in these questions.

A basic principle in question answering can be used to guide all problems in focus establishment.

Focus Rule #3
Focus Should Always Fall
On That Conceptual Component
That Is Most Interesting

The only problem is to determine which component in a conceptual question is relatively interesting. To find out what expectations the person asking the question has, we must use knowledge about the world.

Once we have answered the question "Did the waitress give John a menu?" with "No," we have contradicted an implicit expectation on the part of the questioner. There was some expectation that the waitress might have or should have given John a menu. In elaborating our answer, we wish to address this expectation and explain why it was violated. If we consider the source of this expectation, we can determine different degrees of certainty in the conceptual components of the expectation. These variations in certainty derive from the notion of script constants and script variables.

Every script contains a set of very strong expectations. When we hear that John went to a restaurant, we expect certain activities to have taken place. For example, we expect that John sat down, he got a menu, he ordered, he ate, and he must have paid the check. These acts are called script constants. If our expectations of a script constant are violated, we want to be able to account for the contradiction. So if we hear that John went to a restaurant but did not pay the check, we want to know why not. Some explanation is expected and will be sought.

Within each of the expected script constants, there is often room for a certain amount of variation (see Table 7.1). We know that John must have gotten

TABLE 7.1

Script Constants
Patron goes to restaurant
Patron sits down
Patron receives menu
Patron orders
Cook prepares meal
Meal is served
Patron eats
Patron receives check
Patron pays check
Patron leaves restaurant

Script Variables
How patron gets to restaurant
Who gives patron menu
What patron eats
Who serves the meal
Who brings the check

---

a menu, but it is not clear where the menu comes from. He might get it from the waitress, or from the hostess, or it may be sitting on the table and he picks it up himself. The source of the menu is a script variable. Naturally what John orders is a script variable, as well as who brings him the check (it could be the waiter/waitress, or the host/hostess). Some script variables take default assignments in the absence of explicit information. For example, I would assume that the waiter/waitress brings the check unless I am told otherwise. But I would make no assumptions about what is eaten in the absence of any explicit information.

When a script-based expectation has been violated, we can examine it in terms of script constants and script variables to see what aspects of the conceptualization are most interesting. Assuming that variations are more interesting than expectations, we can assign focus on the basis of script variables.

Given the question concept underlying *Q1* (Did the waitress bring John a menu?), we examine this concept for script constants and variables. By accessing the restaurant script, we can determine that there is a script constant that corresponds to John's getting a menu. Furthermore, there is a variable component within that constant act: the actor. So focus is assigned to the actor slot, and a Concept Completion question is generated by leaving the actor slot unknown.

The same technique can be applied to *Q2* (Did the waitress serve John a hot dog?). By examining the restaurant script, we see that John's being served is a script constant. What John is served and who serves him are script variables. So a Concept Completion question is generated by replacing the actor and object of the PTRANS with unknowns.

Q3 (Did John eat the hamburger) requires some additional processing. In this case the focus heuristic sends us looking for the answer to "What did John eat?" But when we search the causal chain for a concept corresponding to John's eating something, we cannot find anything. Now a very strong expectation has been violated. John's eating is a script constant. If nothing in the story representation corresponds to this script constant, we must account for this unexpected omission. We must find out why John did not eat anything. So to finally elaborate the answer to *Q3,* we must answer the question "Why didn't John eat a hamburger?" Whenever a script constant is violated, we account for it by generating an Expectational question.

So we can now determine when a correction/explanation elaboration requires a Concept Completion or an Expectational question. And in the case of a Concept Completion, we can determine which conceptual component should receive the focus and thereby determine which of all the possible questions will result in the most natural elaboration. In effect, we can find which secondary question will yield the most appropriate elaboration when the initial response to a Verification question is no. The establishment of focus in the original question was part of

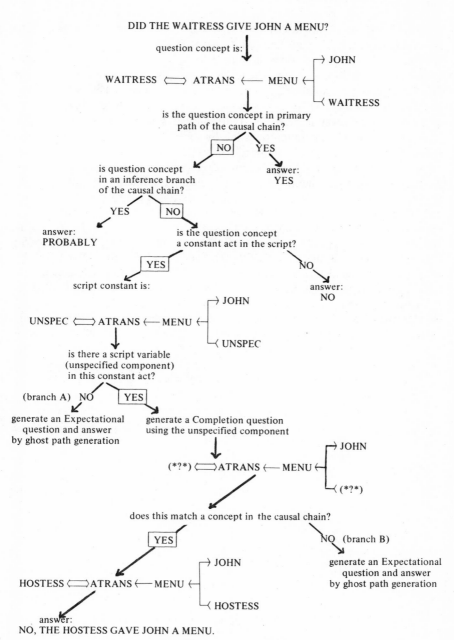

DID THE WAITRESS GIVE JOHN A MENU?

question concept is:

WAITRESS $\Longleftrightarrow$ ATRANS $\longleftarrow$ MENU $\longleftarrow$ → JOHN
                                                                    ⟨ WAITRESS

is the question concept in primary
path of the causal chain?

NO   YES

is question concept   answer:
in an inference branch   YES
of the causal chain?

YES   NO

answer: is the question concept
PROBABLY   a constant act in the script?

YES   NO

script constant is: answer:
                                                     NO

UNSPEC $\Longleftrightarrow$ ATRANS $\longleftarrow$ MENU $\longleftarrow$ → JOHN
                                                                        ⟨ UNSPEC

is there a script variable
(unspecified component)
in this constant act?

(branch A) NO   YES

generate an Expectational   generate a Completion question
question and answer   using the unspecified component
by ghost path generation

(*?*) $\Longleftrightarrow$ ATRANS $\longleftarrow$ MENU $\longleftarrow$ → JOHN
                                                                      ⟨ (*?*)

does this match a concept in the causal chain?

YES   NO (branch B)

                        → JOHN   generate an Expectational
                                        question and answer
                                        by ghost path generation

HOSTESS $\Longleftrightarrow$ ATRANS $\longleftarrow$ MENU $\longleftarrow$
                                                                  ⟨ HOSTESS

answer:
NO, THE HOSTESS GAVE JOHN A MENU.

FIG. 7.1.   Flow of control for verification questions.

171

this task, and a script-based technique for focus establishment was invoked using the notion of script constants and script variables.

Figure 7.1 outlines the flow of control for a Verification question with the Correction/Explanation option. The initial memory search tries to find the question concept in the causal-chain representation. If an answer key is found with absolute credibility, the answer is yes. If it is found with less than absolute credibility, the answer is probably. If no answer key can be found, we try to generate a Concept-Completion question by looking for a script constant with a script variable in the question concept. If we can identify a variable component within a constant act, a Concept Completion question is generated according to the script-based focus heuristic. If this Concept Completion question can be answered, we have our elaboration. (Did the waitress give John a menu? — NO. — Who gave John a menu? — THE HOSTESS GAVE JOHN A MENU.) If the question concept has a constant act but no variable component, an Expectational question is generated and answered. (Did John pay the check? — NO. — Why didn't John pay the check? — JOHN DISCOVERED HE HAD NO MONEY.) If a variable is found but the resulting Concept Completion question cannot be answered, we generate an Expectational question for the final elaboration. (Did John eat a hamburger? — NO. — Why didn't John eat a hamburger? — THE HAMBURGER WAS BURNT.) The retrieval processing for these Expectational questions is described in Chapter 8.

8
Understanding
What Did Not Happen

Expectational (why-not) questions can be characterized by the fact that they ask about things that did not happen. This poses a special processing problem in terms of memory retrieval. A story representation that contains information about events that occurred does not readily lend itself to questions about things that did not occur. Also, some Expectational questions make more sense than others.

Q1: Why didn't Ford beat Carter?

is a perfectly reasonable question. But

Q2: Why hasn't Canada declared war against Mexico?

seems to be a silly question. It is as if some things that do not happen make more sense than other things that do not happen. How do we distinguish reasonable Expectational questions from unreasonable ones?

8.0 INTRODUCTION

In this chapter we dicusss Expectational questions and the processing required to answer them. Degrees of reasonableness in Expectational questions are discussed and explained in terms of predictive-knowledge structures. Finally, the retrieval heuristic used by SAM to answer Expectational questions is described.

8.1 AROUSED EXPECTATIONS

When people read stories, their understanding process involves a predictive element that makes use of certain expectations. Skillful writers are aware of the expectations they set up, and they exploit these to catch the reader off guard or to dramatize important points. If you read that John just robbed a bank and that the police are pursuing him in a car chase, you expect to hear some resolution. John will either be captured, or be killed, or outwit the police and escape. You expect to hear about some such outcome. You do not expect to hear about the results of John's last medical exam or about whether he supports the Equal Rights Amendment. Although this is an example in which the reader may be conscious of being in suspence and wanting to find out what happens next, most of the predictions that occur during understanding occur on a much lower level and do not receive conscious attention.

Suppose you read that John wants to buy a sweater and that he goes into a department store. In this case you have some expectations about what John is going to do next and what you might hear about next: He might look at a store directory, ask for information at a counter or information booth, he might go directly to the sweater department, or these things may be skipped over, and you might hear about John's looking at sweaters or buying one. These are relatively low-level expectations that come from a department-store script. They are not likely to create a sensation of suspense or strong interest. If a story goes on long enough merely setting up and confirming low-level expectations, we are likely to feel bored by it.

All predictions made during the understanding process are made on the basis of knowledge about the world. A tremendous amount of knowledge is used in story understanding, including knowledge about stereotypic situations, activities, human relationships, and motivations. People have a sense of what is normal and routine in the world, and this prototypical knowledge is responsible for expectations aroused during understanding. Scripts and plans are knowledge structures that act as predictive mechanisms to generate expectations at the time of understanding.

8.2   VIOLATED EXPECTATIONS

When an expectation is not explicitly substantiated by the text but is weakly confirmed by subsequent text, it can be incorporated into the memory representation as an inference. Inferences derived from expectations in this way are made at the time of understanding are are incorporated in the memory representation as explicit concepts in memory. But what comes of an expectation that was violated by subsequent text? There are only two possibilities: (1) the story representation could maintain a record of failed expectations in some manner; or (2) missed predictions could be ignored in the construction of the story representation and therefore be effectively forgotten.

There are certainly some violated expectations that must be incorporated into the story representation. If you read a murder mystery with a good twist, you might remember that you had thought the butler guilty until the last chapter. In fact the twist may be a predominant feature in your story representation. Long after you have forgotten the characters and the plot, you might remember that the book led you down a clever garden path and surprised you at the end.

Thus, some expectations aroused at the time of understanding should be incorporated in the story representation. But should all expectations be recorded? The number of low-level expectations that are violated in a short story can easily run into the hundreds. It is hard to believe that there is any good reason for preserving all such violated expectations in memory. Some criteria must be invoked in an effort to determine which are worthy of inclusion to memory.

This problem about expectations in the memory representation is just one aspect of a much larger issue. A theory of text comprehension must inevitably make some claims about what does and does not belong in the memory representation for a story. Clearly there are times when a story representation should include some information about the understanding process that occurred at the time the story was read. Sometimes an expectation is aroused at the time of understanding that is later violated, and we remember how we had made wrong assumptions. Is this a critical aspect of text comprehension? Would you say that someone did not comprehend a detective novel if he failed to recall how he had been misled by it? The question-answering task is a good place to look for criteria whenever a problem arises over what does and does not belong in a story representation.

8.3 ANSWERING QUESTIONS ABOUT EXPECTATIONS

John went to a restaurant and ordered a hot dog. But the waitress told him they didn't have any, so he ordered a hamburger instead. When the hamburger came it was so burnt that John left.

Q1: Why didn't John eat a hot dog?
A1: Because the waitress told him they didn't have any.

Q2: Why didn't John pay the check?
A2: Because the hamburger was burnt.

Both questions ask about things that did not happen in the story. John did not eat a hot dog and he did not pay the check. The questions seem to be asking for the causality behind nonevents. In only one situation does it make sense to talk about the causality behind something that did not happen: There must have been a time during understanding when there was an expectation that the act in question was going to occur. The question is then asking for the event or circumstance that interfered with such an expectation. The stronger the expectation, the more sense the question makes.

If we are asked "Why didn't John swim across the lake?" after reading the burnt hamburger story, the question makes no sense. We cannot begin to answer it, for we never had any expectations about John's getting across a lake or going swimming. If we are asked "Why didn't John order a salami sandwich?" the question makes more sense, because there was an expectation that John would order something. Because there was no expectation that he should order a salami sandwich in particular, the question strikes us as being a little odd (why a *salami sandwich?*). But if we are asked "Why didn't John eat a hot dog?" the question seems completely reasonable, for we at one time expected John to eat a hamburger. As soon as we read the first sentence we knew that John ws a patron in a restaurant, that he had decided he wanted a hot dog, and that he ordered a hot dog. Given this much information, we have several low-level expectations from the restaurant script about what will happen next. Knowing what normally happens in restaurants, we expect that the order will be communicated to a cook, who will prepare the hot dog; then it will be served to John, who will eat it; and he will be given a check, which he will then pay before he leaves the restaurant.

These expectations make it possible to skip a lot of intermediary information. "John went to a restaurant and ordered a hot dog. John ate the hot dog quickly and left." The second sentence follows the first smoothly only because the first set up expectations about what would happen next — and these expectations included John's eating a hot dog. In the burnt hamburger story, the use of the conjunction "but" at the beginning of the second sentence is a warning device. It effectively tells us to watch out for something unexpected. But something can be unexpected only if we had expectations to the contrary. Because John's eating a hot dog was an expectation aroused when he entered the restaurant and ordered, the question "Why didn't John eat a hot dog?" is reasonable.

8.4   ANSWERING QUESTIONS ABOUT POSSIBILITIES

John's investigative report on the city court system was turning up some volatile political information. He had received threats in the mail but he didn't ease up on his story. One night a sniper fired at his bedroom window.

The processing for Expectational questions has not yet been implemented for plan-based stories. But when it is, we would like to produce answers such as:

Q3: Why didn't John quit his story?
A3: He must have felt very committed to his work.

Q4: Why didn't John ask for police protection?
A4: I don't know. Maybe he didn't think it would help.

In this story we have some slightly less stereotypic expectations about the behavior of investigative reporters and of politicians with shady dealings. When we hear that John has been threatened because of his work, we recognize that John is in a state of danger. Although we do not know exactly what might happen, we do expect him either to comply with the threatening agent (to remove the threat) or to protect himself in some way. And so the questions about John's quitting his story and asking for police protection are not unreasonable. It would make much less sense to ask "Why didn't John buy municipal bonds?" At the time of understanding, we have an expectation about John's getting hurt, and this initiates some general expectations about his behavior.

In the reporter story, there were general expectations about what was likely to happen. We expected something might happen to John, but we did not know whether he would get shot, be blown up, or experience harm to his home or family. We expected John to do something about it, but we did not know whether he would quit, seek more publicity, ask for police protection, or dig harder. Our expectations were expressed as general intentionalities and motivations rather than specific acts. Suppose we had asked:

Q5: Why didn't they threaten John over the phone?
Q6: Why didn't they shoot at his livingroom window?

Q5 and *Q6* ask about specific actions that may have been feasible in the story but that did not take place. These questions are fundamentally different from *Q3* and *Q4* in terms of specificity. They relate to general predictions made at the time of understanding, but they go into a deeper level of detail concerning specific actions that are consistent with these general expectations. It is harder to answer these questions, for we had no expectations which related specifically to these acts. One is tempted to answer "Because the story just didn't go that way." But if you feel compelled to give a more cooperative answer, you try to discover why the story took the turn it did instead of the one suggested by the question. So *Q6* might be answered "Maybe the light was on in the bedroom," even though there is nothing explicit in the story supporting the choice of a target room.

A question that asks about an event that could feasibly have happened but that was not predicted at the time of understanding is asking about a possibility. The processing required to answer questions about possibilities is very different from that required when a question asks about a specific expectation aroused at the time of understanding. Questions about possibilities require inferences that were not made at the time of understanding. To answer why they did not snipe at the livingroom window, we must first understand that this was an option they could have exercised in place of sniping at the bedroom window. Because no predictions were made at the time of understanding outlining all the possible ways they could have sniped at John, recognizing that this was an option requires an inference that was not made at any time before the question was asked. Once this recognition is made, we know the question makes a certain amount of sense. Had we asked "Why didn't they offer John a season pass to the opera?" the question would fail to make sense because this is not recognizable as a reasonable plan of action for people who are trying to scare John off.

8.5 CLASSIFICATION OF EXPECTATIONAL QUESTIONS

The last few sections have discussed very generally the ways an Expectational question can relate to story representations. We classify Expectational questions into two general classes: (1) those that ask about specific expectations aroused at the time of understanding; and (2) those that ask about possibilities within a general expectation. If an Expectational question does not make sense, it either fails to reference a specific expectation aroused at the time of understanding, or fails to specify a plausible option within a general expectation. Expectational questions asked about specific expectations are differentiated from those asking about possibilities by the processes required to answer them. The remainder of this chapter describes the processing of Expectational questions that ask about specific expectations aroused at the time of understanding.

8.6 SCRIPT-BASED EXPECTATIONS

When scripts are used in understanding stories, they are applied to the understanding process in a strongly predictive manner (Cullingford, 1975, 1976, 1978). As soon as a script situation has been recognized, inferences are made concerning what has taken place and predictions are made about what is likely to happen next. Hearing that John went to a restaurant triggers the restaurant script, which then makes predictions about John's looking for a table, sitting down, getting a menu, deciding what to have, ordering, being served, eating, paying, and leaving the restaurant. If the next piece of text says that John ordered lobster, the previous predictions up to the ordering prediction become incorporated in the story representation as inferences about what must have happened between John's going to the restaurant and his ordering. Inferences are made about John's looking for a table, finding one, sitting down, getting a menu, and deciding what to eat.[1]

Whenever a script is triggered in the understanding process, specific predictions are made on the basis of the stereotypic knowledge specific to the given script. Scripts by definition are knowledge structures of highly specific expectations. So a script-based prediction made at the time of text understanding will be a very specific conceptualization (e.g., the gas-station attendant takes the cap off the gas tank, the clerk in the grocery store puts the items purchased in a bag, the waitress brings a check to the table). It may happen that a story will deviate from the most routine path through a script.

Deviation from the default path of a script can occur when a script interference is encountered. In this event, earlier predictions made by the script applier be-

---

[1] In actuality the predictions and inferences that would be made here are much more numerous. A few of the major ones are delineated here only to illustrate the inference processing.

come obsolete and must be updated by a new set of predictions. For example, "John ordered a hamburger" results in a path of predicted concepts taking John through the remainder of the restaurant script. Included in this path of predictions are conceptualizations for the cook's preparing a hamburger, John's being served the hamburger, and John's eating the hamburger. But suppose that the next input sentence is "The waiter told John they didn't have hamburgers." Now all the previous predictions about a hamburger are rendered obsolete. Having been told that the restaurant has no hamburgers, we no longer expect John to get one. The old predictions are therefore discarded, and new ones are loaded according to the expectations of the script. In this case, two paths of script instantiation are anticipated: John may reorder and carry on from there; alternatively, he may decide to leave the restaurant.

Consider the story:

John went to a restaurant and ordered a hamburger. But the waiter told him they didn't have any, and so John left.

The final story representation for this would be a causal chain containing conceptualizations for John's entering a restaurant, sitting down, ordering a hamburger, being told there were none, and leaving. The story representation would have no record of the expectations that were present in the system just before the processing of the second sentence. These expectations were effectively "forgotten" when the system revised its scriptal predictions in the course of understanding the second sentence. "Forgotten" here means that no record of these predictions was entered into the story representation.

Now suppose that we wanted to answer the question "Why didn't John eat a hamburger?" This question makes sense only if we recognize that the concept of John's eating a hamburger was an expected act at some point during understanding. But how can we recognize that the question makes sense if the story representation has no record of the failed expectations? This question cannot be answered unless the question concept can be related to the story representation as an act that would have taken place if only (something) had not happened. The question requires that we identify the one event in the story that wiped out our expectation that John would eat a hamburger. If we can identify the concept responsible for this revision in expectations, then we have an answer:

Why didn't John eat a hamburger?
Because the waiter said they didn't have any.

8.7   HOW TO REMEMBER THINGS YOU FORGOT

Although it is useful to know that answerable Expectational questions ask about failed expectations or possibilities that were alive at the time of understanding, we still have the problem of answering these questions on the basis of a story representation that has no history of failed expectations or alternative outcomes. We have described two classes of why-not questions: those asking about script-based expectations and those asking about plan-related possibilities. In this section we describe a retrieval mechanism for answering why-not questions about script-based expectations. Realizing that a story representation does not contain all failed low-level expectations, we require a process that can reconstruct the failed expectations that were alive at some point during the understanding process.

8.7-1 Ghost-Path Generation

If something is lost, it is reasonable to start looking for it at the place it was last seen. The same idea holds when trying to recover a lost expectation. We must first go back to whenever we last had the expectation. Although we can't turn back time, we can pretend to go back in time by reconstructing processing states that occurred during understanding. The past processing states we are interested in are those which involve changes in the predictions current at the time.

When an expectation has been violated, it was last seen alive just before it was replaced by some other expectation. So if we are looking for lost expectations, it makes sense to look for them at those points in the story where there were shifts in the current predictions, where one set of predictions was replaced by another. We must be able to examine the story representation and find points in the story where predictions were revised.

When the knowledge structure responsible for comprehension is a script, there are some general script structures that reflect predictive shifts very simply. For example, script-interference points are always places where script predictions are revised. A script interference is an event that is not normally expected in a smooth execution of the script, but that is encountered frequently enough to have stereotypic resolutions within that script. If John goes to a restaurant and is told he must wait 15 minutes for a table, he has encountered a script interference. Fifteen-minute waits are not always assumed when one goes to a restaurant, but they occur often enough so that there are standard courses of action from which to choose when such an interference is encountered. John can go to another restaurant, can stand and wait, go for a walk, have a drink at the bar, or slip the maitre-d' a tip. These are all stereotypic resolutions when one cannot immediately be seated at a restaurant.

Not all unexpected events are script interferences, even if they interfere with script execution. Suppose that John goes to a restaurant, and when he orders the waitress ignores him, opens a Bible, and proceeds to read from the Book of Revelations. This is an unexpected occurrence from the point of view of the restaurant script, and it interferes with the script. But because this occurrence is so completely removed from the restaurant script, the script cannot suggest what should be done in response. John will have to resort to plans in order to figure out how to handle the strange behavior of the waitress. If John encounters this situation very often, he will incorporate it in his script as an interference point along with whatever resolutions he has learned to respond with. But most of us do not have this interference in our restaurant script.

Script-interference points are important because they are places where script-generated predictions are revised. If John goes to a restaurant and orders a hamburger, the restaurant script predicts that his waiter/waitress will relay his order to the cook, the cook will prepare a hamburger, John will be served the hamburger, he will eat it, be billed for it, he will pay, and leave. But suppose that John goes to a restaurant, orders a hamburger, and is informed that they do not serve hamburgers. Now we no longer expect his waiter/waitress to relay the hamburger order; we do not expect the cook to prepare a hamburger; and John is not expected to get a hamburger, eat one, be billed for one, or pay for one. Being told that you cannot have what you ordered is a point of interference in the restaurant script. Its standard resolutions are to order something else or leave. As soon as this script interference is encountered, expectations about what is going to happen change.

When the script applier is processing a story, it recognizes any interference points that are encountered. Interference points in a script are labeled as interferences. Their corresponding resolutions are also tagged accordingly. So when a script interference is encountered, the script applier can easily tag it as such in the story representation. For example, suppose that SAM reads the following story:

John went to a restaurant and the hostess gave him a menu. When he ordered a hot dog the waitress said that they didn't have any. So John ordered a hamburger instead. But when the hamburger came, it was so burnt that John left.

The causal-chain representation looks something like this (in reality there are many more states and acts):

John enters restaurant
John is seated
John gets a menu from the hostess
John orders a hot dog
(I1)   The waitress tells him they don't have any
(R1)   John orders a hamburger
Waitress serves John the hamburger
(I2)   The hamburger is burnt ⟶
John gets angry
(R2)   John leaves the restaurant ⟵

In this story there are two inference/resolution pairs: The waitress telling John there are no hot dogs is resolved by his ordering a hamburger, and the hamburger

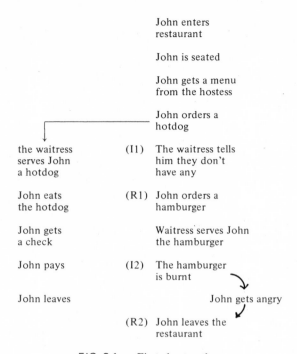

FIG. 8.1.   First ghost path.

being poorly prepared is resolved by his leaving. These interferences and corresponding resolutions are tagged as such in the story representation.

When a why-not question is subsequently asked, we can easily identify those points in the story representation where expectations changed during understanding. We need only look for conceptualizations in the causal chain which are tagged as interferences. At each point of interference, we know that a new set of expectations was generated by the script applier. The next problem is to reconstruct the expectations that were alive just before each point of interference. To reconstruct these expectations, we must simulate to some extent the state of the script applier just before each interference was encountered.

To simulate states of the script applier, we ask it to process another story. We want to know what the prediction queue of the script applier is when it understands the original story up to a point of interference but no further. To see this we will effectively ask the script applier to process the story over again, but this time we will only give it a truncated version of the story, which cuts off just before an interference point.

To see what script predictions were alive just before the waitress told John there were no hot dogs, we will feed back to the script applier the causal chain from the story representation up to but not including the waitress's telling him there are no hot dogs. The script applier is asked to understand this sequence of conceptualizations as a story. When it is done processing, it has a prediction queue and is ready to check the next input conceptualization against this queue. We have recaptured the state of the prediction queue as it was at the time of understanding just before the sentence describing the waitress's response to John's order was encountered.

Part of the prediction queue consists of a default path through the remainder of the script, instantiated according to what has been seen thus far. That is, the script applier has predicted what is likely to happen if the execution of the restaurant script runs smoothly from now on without any more surprises. Given that John ordered a hot dog, the script applier predicts that the waitress will give that order to the cook, the cook will prepare the hot dog, the waitress will serve it to John, John will eat it, receive a check for it, pay, and leave. The script applier can generate this causal chain, completing a default path through the script on the basis of predictions in its prediction queue. This script completion chain is called a ghost path (see Fig. 8.1). Each ghost path generated by the script applier is a causal chain, along with a pointer to the place in the original story representation where the ghost path starts its branch from the actual story.

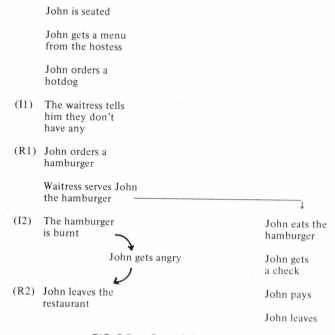

FIG. 8.2.   Second ghost path.

If we want to see the predictions that were alive just before the hamburger came back burnt, we go through the same procedure. The casual chain up to that point is handed to the script applier to be understood. When processing is finished, a ghost path that completes script instantiation is generated. This ghost path effectively recaptures expectations that were aroused at the time of story understanding but subsequently revised (see Fig. 8.2).

8.7-2 Using Ghost Paths

Once ghost paths have been generated, the processing needed to answer expectational why-not questions is fairly straightforward. Given a ghost path, we examine it for the question concept (nonnegated). When the question concept is located, we follow the ghost path up to its origin, to the point at which it branches off the original story representation. Each branch occurs immediately before a script interference. The answer to our Expectational question is that interference conceptualization. In this way we can answer:

Q1: Why didn't John eat a hot dog?
A1: Because the waitress told John they didn't have any hot dogs.

Q2: Why didn't John eat the hamburger?
A2: Because the hamburger was burnt.

In the event that a match can be made in more than one of the ghost paths, we trace the most recent path (the path whose branch from the story representation occurs closest to the end of the chain) back to the branching point and subsequent interference. So the question:

Q3: Why didn't John pay the check?

would be answered:

A3: Because the hamburger was burnt.

When SAM answers *Q3,* a slightly more involved answer can be produced:

A4: John was angry because the hamburger was burnt, and so he left.

This is due to the fact that paying the check is a pure script constant, while eating a hamburger and eating a hot dog are acts that include script variables (see Section 7.3 for a description of script constants and script variables). When a pure script constant has been violated, more explanation is needed than when acts with script variables are violated. If John did not eat a hamburger, it is possible that he ate something else; the violation of the concept may be restricted to the instantiation of the variable component. But when John does not pay the check, there is no shift in a role instantiation that could explain why not. So when a constant act is encountered as the concept underlying an answer, the retrieval heuristic is instructed to piece together in a causal template an answer including not only the interference (the hamburger was burnt), but also its corresponding resolution (John left) and any intermediate mental-state changes (John was angry). This retrieval heuristic is controlled by the Mental-State-Description option of content specification (see Section 5.2).

9 Finding the Best Answer

Some questions can be answered with many different answers, each of which is right and makes sense. When a memory representation contains information for many potential answers, retrieval is more complicated. The situation of multiple answers arises very easily. Even in stories that SAM can understand completely on the basis of scripts, we see how one event could be explained by several causal antecedents:

Q: Why did John wash dishes at Leone's?
A1: Because he couldn't pay the check.
A2: Because he had no money.
A3: Because he was pickpocketed on the subway.

How does the memory search decide which answer should be returned? Should retrieval heuristics be aware of all the possible choices for an answer? Or should the memory search somehow "know" where to look for the best answer and be oblivious to other possibilities? If a heuristic is aware of many answers, it must be able to make a choice. What rules can be formalized for finding the best answer? If a heuristic is blind to all but one answer, how can we be certain it will see the best one? In this chapter we explore strategies for finding a best answer and discuss issues of memory representation that are related to this problem.

9.0 INTRODUCTION

Why-questions are difficult to answer because they often have many answers that are plausible, acceptable, and appropriate. Sometimes one answer is clearly better than another, and a good *Q/A* model should be able to discern which answers are better. While examining this problem, we assume we are working with a system of cooperative and honest intentionality. Furthermore, we restrict ourselves to the domain of story understanding in which question answering is used to demonstrate comprehension. These assumptions provide a useful basis for a first pass at the problem. Given this orientation, we assume the best answers are those that convey the most relevant information in the most efficient way.

One of the stories that SAM understands is the Leone's story:

> John went to New York by bus. On the bus he talked to an old lady. When he left the bus, he thanked the driver. He took the subway to Leone's. On the subway his pocket was picked. He got off the train and entered Leone's. He had some lasagna. When the check came, he discovered he culdn't pay. The manamgement told him he would have to wash dishes. When he left, he caught a bus to New Haven.

After SAM has read this story, SAM answers:

Q: Why did John wash dishes at Leone's?
A: Because he had no money.

This is not a very good answer, for it does not convey any information that the questioner could not have figured out for himself. A patron washing dishes in a restaurant is so stereotypic that being unable to pay the check is an immediate inference. Knowing that John could not pay the check, we find it obvious[1] that John did not have any (or enough) money. So anyone who knows that John washed dishes at Leone's must also know by inference that John probably did not have any money. In particular, the person asking Q1 must know this.

A much better answer would be "John couldn't pay the check because his pocket was picked." This answer conveys a lot of information. By inference it tells us that John had no money and therefore the management of the restaurant made him wash dishes. It communicates an entire causal chain, which starts at the pickpocketing and ends with John's washing dishes. And because part of the causal chain (John's having no money and not being able to pay) is easily inferred, this answer has communicated information very efficiently.

Answer-Selection Rule #1:
An answer that conveys information
by inference is preferable to one that
spells out such inferences explicitly.

In this chapter we present an answer-selection model that compares a number of possible answers to a question and selects one as the best. This model has been implemented in a computer program (ASP). After describing ASP, we

---

[1]These inferences are "immediate" and "obvious" in the sense that people have no trouble making them. The actual processes that produce them are far from trivial or obvious.

discuss some of the weaknesses inherent in the answer-selection model. From there we consider alternative approaches, including strategies for knowledge-state assessment and stronger structures for memory representation.

9.1   ANSWER-SELECTION MODEL

One approach to characterizing the best answer is to design a procedure that receives as input a set of possible answers to a question, and returns the best answer from that given set. To make this choice, such a procedure will have to characterize the answers it examines along various dimensions and execute comparisons of answers.

In trying to design such an answer selection procedure, we are forced to ask what elements of an answer are important. Then we must formalize those characteristics that intuitively seem to contribute to the strength or weakness of an answer. The model we are about to describe represents a first attempt in this direction. This model will not always pick the best answer from any set of possible answers, but enough was learned from it to progress beyond the notion of answer selection.

9.1-1   Definitions

Data Context.   The data context (DC) is the story representation to which a question refers.

Independent of Data Context.   Answers to questions can be characterized as being independent of data context (IDC) if they are answers one might reasonably guess without having read any story in connection with the question. These are answers people come up with when asked an artificial question out of the blue.

Q: Why did John see a doctor?
A: John was sick. (IDC)

Q: Why did John fall asleep?
A: John was tired. (IDC)

Explicitly Dependent.   Answers that are derived from the data context by being explicitly present in the data context are explicitly dependent (ED) on the data context.

Implicitly Dependent.   Answers derived from the data context by applying inference processes to the data context are Implicitly Dependent (ID) on the data context.

Examples:

EX1: One morning John noticed that his dog was having trouble walking. That afternoon he took it to the vet.

> *Q:* Why did John take his dog to the vet?
> *A:* It was sick or injured. (IDC)
> *A:* It was having trouble walking. (ED)
> *A:* He wanted to make it well. (ID)

EX2: One day John broke his mainspring of his watch. The dentist who lived next door fixes old watches for a hobby. So John took his watch to the dentist.

> *Q:* Why did John take his watch to the dentist?
> *A:* He had broken the mainspring. (ED)
> *A:* The dentist fixes old watches. (ED)
> *A:* He wanted to get his watch fixed. (ID)

EX3: One day John broke the mainspring of his watch. The dentist who lived next door fixes old watches for a hobby. So John called the dentist.

> *Q:* Why did John call the dentist?
> *A:* He wanted to make an appointment. (IDC)
> *A:* He had broken the mainspring of his watch. (ED)
> *A:* The dentist fixes old watches. (ED)
> *A:* He wanted to get his watch fixed. (ID)

EX4: One day John broke the mainspring of his watch. He took it to the jeweler's to see if they would buy it.

> *Q:* Why did John take his watch to the jeweler's?
> *A:* It was broken. (IDC, ED)
> *A:* He had broken the mainspring. (ED)
> *A:* He wanted to see if they would buy it. (ED)

EX5: While walking home, John realized he didn't have his umbrella with him. He remembered last havint it at the restaurant he went to for lunch. John walked over to the restaurant.

> *Q:* Why did John go to the restaurant?
> *A:* He wanted to get something to eat. (IDC)
> *A:* He wanted to find his umbrella. (ID)
> *A:* He last had his umbrella at the restaurant. (ED)

EX6: John got three Fs on his report card. He decided not to show it to his parents.

Q: Why didn't John want to show his report card to his parents?
A: His grades weren't good enough. (IDC)
A: John was afraid they would be angry. (ID)
A: John had gotten three Fs. (ED)

EX7: John was on the side of a highway when a large truck skidded off the road. At the scene of the accident John noticed an oil slick covering the pavement. When he saw a taxi approaching the spot at high speed, he waved his arms frantically, trying to signal the driver.

Q: Why was John waving at the taxi?
A: John wanted a ride. (IDC)
A: John wanted to prevent it from skidding off the road. (ID)
A: John wanted to stop it. (IDC)
A: John was trying to signal the driver. (ED)

9.1-2 More Definitions

The preceding definitions characterize single answers in relation to the text to which they refer. The following definitions characterize answers in terms of their conceptual content and relationships to other answers.

Causal Antecedent. Given two answers, *A1* and *A2,* A1 is said to be a causal antecedent of *A2* if and only if it makes sense to say *"A2 because A1."*

Intentional Consequent. Given two answers, *A1* and *A2, A2* is said to be an intentional consequent of *A1* if and only if:

1. *A2* is of the form "X wanted to . . . C1 . . ."
2. *A1* is of the form "X . . . C2 . . ."
3. It makes sense to say
   "X . . . C2 . . . in order to . . . C1 . . . ."

Plan Component. Given two answers, *A1* and *A2, A2* is the plan component of *A1* if and only if:
1. *A1* is of the form "X wanted . . . C1 . . ."
          or "X needed . . . C1 . . ."
2. It makes sense to say
       ". . . A1 . . . and X knew that . . . A2 . . ."
3. X is not the actor of *A2*.

Consistent. Two answers are said to be Consistent if and only if each can readily be inferred from the other in the given data context. For example, in

EX5, John's wanting to find his umbrella and John's wanting to get something to eat are not consistent answers. But in EX3, John's watch being broken and John's wanting to get his watch fixed are consistent answers.

Motive Oriented.   An answer, *A1,* is said to be motive oriented if and only if:
1. *A1* is not of the form "X wanted . . ." and
2. *A1* describes an activity or state that strictly precedes the activity or state of the question concept in time.

9.1-3 Selection Rules

The following rules are to be applied in succession. At the end of Rule 3, a tentative answer (TA) has been picked. The tentative answer may be changed by Rules 4–6. The tentative answer becomes the final answer only after the application of RULE 6 is completed.

Rule 1:   An IDC is the preferred answer only if there are no EDs or IDs.

Illustration:
If we are told in a story that John always eats lasagna at Italian restaurants, and must then answer "Why did John order lasagna at Leone's?" an IDC answer is "Because he wanted to eat lasagna." A much better response it the ED answer "Because he always has lasagna at Italian restaurants."

Rule 2:   An ID is preferred over an ED only when the question has at least one IDC and the ID is not consistent with the IDCs.

Illustration:
In EX5, we have *A1:*   Because he wanted to find his umbrella.
             A2:   Because he last had his umbrella at the restaurant.
             A3:   Because he wanted to get something to eat.
A3 is an IDC, *A1* is an ID, and *A2* is an ED. *A1* is preferred because *A1* and *A3* are not consistent.

Rule 3:   Given a choice of EDs, first eliminate those that are also IDCs (these are the least interesting answers). Next test to see whether there are any motive-oriented EDs. Eliminate these. If there is still a choice, report to Rule 3a.

Illustration:
In Ex 3, we have ED1:   Because he had broken the mainspring of his watch.

ED2: Because the dentist fixes old watches.
Because ED1 is motive oriented, ED2 is the preferred answer.

Rule 3a: Given a choice of EDs, first eliminate those that are also IDCs. Next test each ED by removing its explicit concept from the data context. The ED in question is the best answer if:

1. The revised data context makes no sense, or
2. The revised data context generates an ID that is not consistent with the ED in question.

Illustration:
In EX4, we have ED1: Because he had broken the mainspring.
ED2: Because he wanted to see if they would buy it.
The revised DC with respect to ED1 is: John took his watch to the jeweler's to see if they would buy it.
This generates *A1:* Because it was broken. (IDC)
A2: To see if they would buy it. (ED)
Neither (1) nor (2) of the test holds here.
The revised DC with respect to ED2 is: One day John broke the mainspring of his watch. He took it to the jeweler's.
This generates *A1:* Because it was broken. (IDC) (ED)
A2: Because he broke the mainspring. (ED)
A3: Because he wanted it fixed. (ID)
Here A3 is not consistent with ED2; (2) holds in this case, and so we choose ED2 as the answer.

Another Illustration:
In EX2, we have ED1: Because he had broken the mainspring.
ED2: Because the dentist fixes old watches.
The revised DC with respect to ED1 is: The dentist next door fixes old watches as a hobby. John took his watch to the dentist.
This generates *A1:* Because he had broken it. (ID)
A2: Because he wanted it fixed. (ID)
Neither (1) nor (2) holds here.
The revised DC with respect to ED2 is: One day John broke the mainspring of his watch. John took his watch to the dentist.
Because this DC makes no sense (Why take a watch to a dentist?), (1) holds in this case, and so we take ED2 as our answer.

Note on Rules 4–6. In the application of Rules 4–6, we do not consider IDCs as possible replacements for the TA.

Rule 4: If the TA is the causal antecedent of another answer, replace the TA with the other answer.

Illustration:

In EX6 we have   *A1:*   John had gotten three Fs on it.

                     A2:   John was afraid they would be angry.

A1 is the TA by the time Rule 4 is applied. *A1* is a causal antecedent of *A2,* because it makes sense to say "John was afraid that they would be angry because he had gotten three Fs on it. So *A2* replaces A1 on the TA.

Rule 5:   If another answer is the intentional consequent of the TA, replace the TA with the other answer.

Illustration:

In EX7 we have   *A1:*   John was trying to signal the driver.

                     A2:   John wanted to prevent him from skidding off the road.

A1 is the TA. *A2* is an intentional consequent of *A1,* because it makes sense to say "John was trying to signal the driver in order to prevent him from skidding off the road." So *A2* replaces *A1* as the TA.

Rule 6:   If another answer is a plan component of the TA, replace the TA with the other answer.

Illustration:

In EX3 we have   *A1:*   John wanted to get his watch fixed.

                     A2:   The dentist fixes old watches.

A1 is the TA. *A2* is a plan component of *A1,* because it makes sense to say "John wanted to get his watch fixed and he knew that the dentist fixes old watches." So *A2* replaces *A1* as the TA.

9.1-4   Implementing the Model

The answer selection program (ASP) that implements this answer selection model is not a fully automatic system. It is an interactive program that falls back on the user whenever an answer must be characterized according to the given definitions. For example, if the program needs to determine whether a given answer is motive oriented, it asks the user whether the state or activity of the question precedes the question concept in time. It then categorizes the answer according to the response given by the user.

This interactive approach was adopted to avoid constructing an actual language processing system. ASP does not understand the data context, the question, or the answers in any conceptual sense. It categorizes answers by querying the user and applies the selection rules without any understanding. A fully automatic implementation of the answer selection model would require tremendous amounts of world knowledge in order to recognize valid causal relationships, reasonable human motives, and common inferences. The point of ASP is to identify what are important characterizations competing answers to a question, not to solve all the problems of computational inference.

9.1-5 ASP Output

The next few pages contain three interactive sessions with ASP, these illustrate how the program asks the user for information in order to apply the answer selection rules.

*ST1
(ONE MORNING JOHN NOTICES THAT HIS DOG WAS HAVING TROUBLE WALKING. THAT AFTERNOON HE TOOK IT TO THE VET)
*

*Q1
(WHY DID JOHN TAKE HIS DOG TO THE VET?)
*

*A1
(IT WAS SICK OR INJURED)
*

*A2
(IT WAS HAVING TROUBLE WALKING)
*

*A3
(HE WANTED TO MAKE IT WELL)
*

*

*(ASP)
SET !A TO THE LIST OF POINTERS
*(SETQ !A @ (A1 A2 A3))

NOW ASSIGN THE CATEGORY TYPES FOR EACH ANSWER IN !A
A1 HAS CATEGORIES: *(IDC)
A2 HAS CATEGORIES: *(ED)
A3 HAS CATEGORIES: *(ID)

(RULE 1 EXECUTED)

GIVEN THE DATA CONTEXT, CAN ONE OF "HE WANTED TO MAKE IT WELL" AND "IT WAS SICK OR INJURED" BE INFERRED FROM THE OTHER? (TYPE YES OR NO) *YES

(RULE 2 EXECUTED: NO ID IS PREFERRED OVER THE EDS)

THE TA IS: "IT WAS HAVING TROUBLE WALKING"

DOES IT MAKE SENSE TO SAY HE WANTED TO MAKE IT WELL BECAUSE IT WAS HAVING TROUBLE WALKING? (TYPE YES OR NO) *YES

(RULE 4 HAS BEEN EXECUTED)

THE TA IS NOW: "HE WANTED TO MAKE IT WELL"

(RULE 5 HAS BEEN EXECUTED)

THE TA IS NOW: "HE WANTED TO MAKE IT WELL"

DOES IT MAKE SENSE TO SAY HE WANTED TO MAKE IT WELL AND HE KNEW THAT IT WAS HAVING TROUBLE WALKING? (TYPE YES OR NO) *YES

(RULE 6 HAS BEEN EXECUTED)

THE BEST ANSWER IS "BECAUSE IT WAS HAVING TROUBLE WALKING"

---

*ST2
(ONE DAY JOHN BROKE THE MAINSPRING OF HIS WATCH. THE DENTIST WHO LIVED NEXT DOOR FIXES OLD WATHCES AS A HOBBY. SO JOHN TOOK HIS WATCH TO THE DENTIST)
*

*Q2
(WHY DID JOHN TAKE HIS WATCH TO THE DENTIST?)
*

*A4
(HE HAD BROKEN THE MAINSPRING)
*

*A5
(THE DENTIST FIXES OLD WATCHES)
*

*A6
(HE WANTED IT FIXED)
*

*

*(ASP)

SET !A TO THE LIST OF POINTERS
*(SETQ !A @ (A4 A5 A6))

NOW ASSIGN THE CATEGORY TYPES FOR EACH ANSWER IN !A
A4 HAS CATEGORIES: *(ED)

A5 HAS CATEGORIES: *(ED)
A6 HAS CATEGORIES: *(ID)

(RULE 1 EXECUTED)

(RULE 2 EXECUTED: NO ID IS PREFERRED OVER THE EDS)

(THERE IS A CHOICE OF EDS: RULE 3 WILL BE EXECUTED)

(IDCS ARE ELIMINATED FROM THE EDS)
(THERE IS STILL A CHOICE OF EDS)

DOES THE STATE OR ACTIVITY OF "THE DENTIST FIXES OLD WATCHES" STRICTLY PRECEDE THE STATE OR ACTIVITY OF THE QUESTION STATEMENT IN TIME? (TYPE YES OR NO) *NO

DOES THE STATE OR ACTIVITY OF "HE HAD BROKEN THE MAIN-SPRING" STRICTLY PRECEDE THE STATE OR ACTIVITY OF THE QUESTION STATEMENT IN TIME? (TYPE YES OR NO) *YES

(MOTIVE ORIENTED EDS HAVE BEEN ELIMINATED)
(THERE IS STILL A CHOCIE OF EDS: RULE 3A WILL BE EXECUTED)

REVISE THE DATA CONTEXT BY REMOVING THE STATEMENT CORRESPONDING TO "THE DENTIST FIXES OLD WATCHES"

DOES THE REVISED DATA CONTEXT STILL MAKE SENSE?

(TYPE YES OR NO) *NO

(RULE 3A HAS BEEN EXECUTED)

THE TA IS: "THE DENTIST FIXES OLD WATCHES"

DOES IT MAKE SENSE TO SAY HE WANTED IT FIXED BECAUSE THE DENTIST FIXES OLD WATCHES? (TYPE YES OR NO) *NO

DOES IT MAKE SENSE TO SAY HE WANTED IT FIXED BECAUSE THE DENTIST FIXES OLD WATCHES? (TYPE YES OR NO) *NO

DOES IT MAKE SENSE TO SAY HE HAD BROKEN THE MAINSPRING BECAUSE THE DENTIST FIXES OLD WATCHES? (TYPE YES OR NO) *NO

(RULE 4 HAS BEEN EXECUTED)

THE TA IS NOW: "THE DENTIST FIXES OLD WATCHES"

(RULE 5 HAS BEEN EXECUTED)

THE TA IS NOW: "THE DENTIST FIXES OLD WATCHES"

(RULE 6 HAS BEEN EXECUTED)

THE BEST ANSWER IS "BECAUSE THE DENTIST FIXES OLD WATCHES"

---

*ST7
(JOHN WAS ON THE SIDE OF A HIGHWAY WHEN A LARGE TRUCK
SKIDDED OFF THE ROAD AT THE SCENE OF THE ACCIDENT JOHN NO-
TICED AN OIL SLICK COVERING THE PAVEMENT WHEN HE SAW A TAXI
APPROACHING THE SPOT AT HIGH SPEED HE WAVED HIS ARMS FRAN-
FICALLY TRYING TO SIGNAL THE DRIVER)
*

*Q7
(WHY WAS JOHN WAVING AT THE TAXI?)
*

*A20
(JOHN WANTED A RIDE)
*

*A21
(JOHN WANTED TO PREVENT IT FROM SKIDDING OFF THE ROAD)
*

*A22
(JOHN WANTED TO STOP IT)
*

*A23
(JOHN WAS TRYING TO SIGNAL THE DRIVER)
*

*

*(ASP)

SET !A TO THE LIST OF POINTERS
*(SETQ !A @ (A20 A21 A22 A23))

NOW ASSIGN THE CATEGORY TYPES FOR EACH ANSWER IN !A
A20 HAS CATEGORIES: *(IDC)
A21 HAS CATEGORIES: *(ID)
A22 HAS CATEGORIES: *(IDC)
A23 HAS CATEGORIES: *(ED)

(RULE 1 EXECUTED)

GIVEN THE DATA CONTEXT, CAN ONE OF "JOHN WANTED TO PREVENT IT FROM SKIDDING OFF THE ROAD" AND "JOHN WANTED TO STOP IT" BE INFERRED FROM THE OTHER (TYPE YES OR NO) *YES

GIVEN THE DATA CONTEXT, CAN ONE OF "JOHN WANTED TO PREVENT IT FROM SKIDDING OFF THE ROAD" AND "JOHN WANTED A RIDE" BE INFERRED FROM THE OTHER? (TYPE YES OR NO) *NO

THE TA IS: "JOHN WANTED TO PREVENT IT FROM SKIDDING OFF THE ROAD"

DOES IT MAKE SENSE TO SAY JOHN WAS TRYING TO SIGNAL THE DRIVER BECAUSE JOHN WANTED TO PREVENT IT FROM SKIDDING OFF THE ROAD? (TYPE YES OR NO) *YES

(RULE 4 HAS BEEN EXECUTED)

THE TA IS NOW: "JOHN WAS TRYING TO SIGNAL THE DRIVER"

DOES IT MAKE SENSE TO SAY JOHN WAS TRYING TO SIGNAL THE DRIVER IN ORDER TO PREVENT IT FROM SKIDDING OFF THE ROAD? (TYPE YES OR NO) *YES

(RULE 5 HAS BEEN EXECUTED)

THE TA IS NOW: "JOHN WANTED TO PREVENT IT FROM SKIDDING OFF THE ROAD"

(RULE 6 HAS BEEN EXECUTED)

THE BEST ANSWER IS "BECAUSE JOHN WANTED TO PREVENT IT FROM SKIDDING OFF THE ROAD"

9.2 GOING BEYOND ANSWER SELECTION

There are many problems with the answer selection model described in the preceding section. It is easy to come up with examples in which the model fails to find the best answer. By examining cases where the model fails, we can see what is missing and better understand what is needed.

9.2-1   What Is Wrong with the Answer Selection Model?

One fault derives from the fact that the model is not sensitive to preceding dialogue. Each question and set of answers are considered in absolute isolation of a conversational context. Suppose the model decides that the best answer to

> *Q1:* Why did John take his watch to the dentist?

is

> *A1:* He knew that the dentist fixes watches for a hobby.

Although this might be quite reasonable if *Q1* is the first question in a dialogue, it seems rather odd when *Q1* is preceded by an exchange which establishes that John knew the dentist fixes watches for a hobby.

> *Q2:* Did John know that the dentist fixes watches for a hobby?
> *A2:* Yes.
> *Q3:* Why did John take his watch to the dentist?
> *A3:* He knew the dentist fixes watches for a hobby.

A more natural dialogue would not contain repetitive information:

> *Q4:* Did John know that the dentist fixes watches for a hobby?
> *A4:* Yes.
> *Q5:* Why did John take his watch to the dentist?
> *A5:* He liked the dentist better than the jeweler.

If a question answering system is not sensitive to preceding dialogue in some way, it cannot avoid needlessly repetitive exchanges. The basic problem seems to revolve around a very simple principle:

Answer-Selection Rule #2:
A good answer does not tell the
questioner something he already knows.

The answer selection model described in the last section has no sense of what the questioner knows or does not know. In the above examples, the previous dialogue provides information about what the questioner knows because can we assume that answers to previous questions are incorporated into the questioner's knowledge state. But does this mean that we have to formulate a system of knowledge state modeling before we can address problems in answer selection? It seems that some principles of retrieval can be identified without knowing what form a knowledge state model must assume.

When an answer to a question is dependent on information conveyed in previous dialogue, we cannot talk about the retrieval processes that arrive at that answer without reference to a knowledge state model of some sort. But knowledge state assessment is also important on the more immediate level of single questions and answers. When someone asks a question, they are telling you something about what is in their knowledge state. One has to know something in order to ask a question in the first place.

The answer selection model outlined in Section 9.1 does not examine questions with this in mind. In fact, the answer selection model hardly looks at the question at all. All of the selection rules are concerned with relationships between competing answers and relationships between answers and the data context. The only time the model looks at the question is when the answers are initially categorized as IDC, ID, or ED answers. The identification of IDC answers involves the question, for IDC answers could reasonably be offered in response to a question out of the blue, without reference to any story. At some point in its processing, the model should examine the question for information about what the questioner knows in order to find the most appropriate answer.

If knowledge about what the questioner knows and does not know can be useful in forming an answer to a question, and if the question itself provides some information about what the questioner knows and does not know, there must be times when examining the question for such information is necessary in finding the best answer. In QUALM the notion of knowledge state assessment was mentioned, though not examined very deeply (see subsection 4.1-3). The answer selection problem illustrates how some questions require more attention to knowledge state assessment.

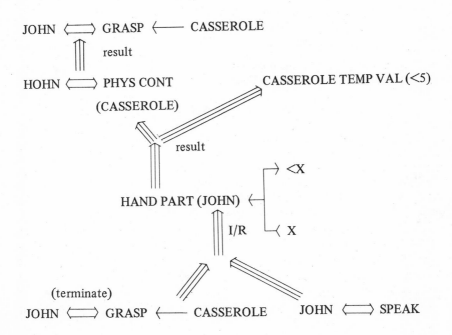

Consider the following story:

John forgot the pot holders when he removed the casserole from the oven. When he picked it up, he yelled and dropped it on the floor.

In the causal chain representation of this story, both John's yelling and his dropping the casserole share the same causal antecedent of John's being burned:

If the retrieval mechanism for why-questions were designed to pick up the immediate causal antecedent of a question concept, both

Q4: Why did John yell?

and

Q5: Why did John drop the casserole?

would be answered with "Because he got burned." But something interesting happens when, after reading the story, some people are asked Q4 and others are asked Q5. In an informal experiment, 11 people read this story; five were asked *Q4,* and six were asked *Q5.* The responses were:

Q4: Why did John yell?
A4a: He burned his hand.
A4b: He had burned his hands on the hot casserole.
A4c: He hurt his hand picking up the hot casserole.
A4d: The hot casserole burned him.
A4e: Because he burned his hand.

Q5: Why did John drop the casserole?
A5a: Because it was too hot to hold.
A5b: It was hot.
A5c: He burned his hand because it was hot.
A5d: Because it was hot.
A5e: Because it was hot.
A5f: It was hot.

In all the answers to *Q4,* a reference is made to the physical state change that John underwent. Everyone says that John got hurt or burned. Some of the answers indicate that the casserole was responsible for it, but many of them simply say that John was burned or that John's hand was burned, without referencing the casserole at all. The answers to *Q5* are somewhat different. Not all of the answers to *Q5* mentioned that John was hurt or burned. But they all explain that the casserole was hot. If one wanted to conceptualize what the questioner knew after getting an answer to *A4,* the conceptualization would involve a negative physical state change initiating the reason for John's yelling:

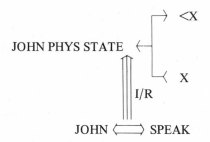

The conceptualization describing what the questioner would know after hearing an answer to *Q5* would entail John's picking up the casserole; his physical contact with the casserole, combined with the temperature of the casserole, resulting in John's getting burnt; and this initiating the reason for his dropping the casserole:

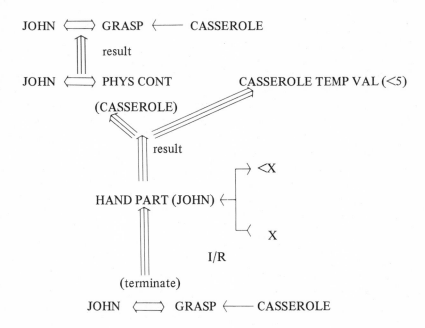

Some of the answers do not explicitly contain all of this. *A5c* is the only answer that describes John's being burned. But answers to *Q5* leave the questioner with more information than answers to *Q4*, because the questioner starts out having more information in *Q5*. The differences in answers are attributable to the differences in what the questioner knows at the time the question is asked. These differences are implicit in the questions.

Q4 indicates that the questioner knows John yelled. *Q5* indicates that the questioner knows John had picked up a casserole (in order to drop something, you have to have picked it up to begin with) and that John subsequently dropped the casserole.

The knowledge state corresponding to *Q4* is:

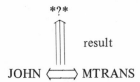

The knowledge state corresponding to *Q5* is:

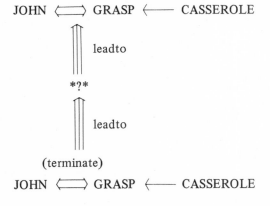

When a question asks about a single conceptualization, adequate answers can be found by looking for a single causal antecedent. But when a question asks about a causal chain, a good answer will allow the questioner to construct the missing parts of the chain. This distinction is a major one from a processing point of view. Some questions ask about causal antecedents of single concepts, while others ask about an entire causal chain. The process that returns a single antecedent is bound to be less involved than one that must deal with missing parts in a causal chain. To see exactly how much more involved, consider what happens when people answer questions of the second variety.

One way to make sure the questioner can fill in a causal chain is to spell it all out for him. So one answer to *Q5* would be "Because John got burned from holding the hot casserole." This answer explicitly describes John's being in contact with the casserole, the casserole's being hot, and John's getting burned as a result. But in answering *A5* nobody really does this. The answers to *Q5* mention some parts of the chain and not others. The questioner is relied upon to fill in the missing parts by inference.

One inference the questioner of *Q5* is expected to make is that John is in physical contact with the casserole. This is a very low-level inference, which is immediate from John's picking up the casserole. (The inference is immediate in the sense that people find it obvious — not in the sense that we have a good model of how it is done.) Many of the answers to *Q5* simply state that the casserole was hot. From this the questioner is expected to construct a chain that includes John's being in contact with the casserole and consequently getting burned.

When an answer must provide the questioner with enough information to complete a causal chain, the formation of that answer must use knowledge about what kinds of inferences can readily be made. People who answer *Q5* with "It (the casserole) was hot" are assuming that anyone who knows

1. John picked up the casserole.
2. The casserole was hot.
3. John dropped the casserole.

can infer that

1. John was in physical contact with the casserole.
2. John got burned.

This knowledge about inferences affects the retrieval processes that select an answer. How is this knowledge incorporated in the retrieval heuristics? There are at least two possible approaches:

1. Possible answers could be generated and tested by a simulation program, which would endeavor to simulate the questioner and see whether a complete causal chain could be constructed on the basis of the proposed answer. This simulation might be achieved by implementing a causal-chain-filling program that uses general rules of inference of the sort proposed by Chuck Rieger (1975a).

2. The memory representation and retrieval heuristics could be designed in some way which would enable the memory search to identify a good answer from which a chain could be constructed without simulating the construction itself.

Before discussing which of these approaches seems more promising, we review some of the important observations made thus far:

[1]. A question must be examined to find out what the questioner does and does not know. This amounts to a form of MLOC assessment.

[2]. A question can be asking about either a single conceptualization or an incomplete causal chain. Knowledge state assessment based on the original question determines which case holds.

[3]. A question that asks about a single concept can be answered by describing a direct causal antecedent.

[4]. A question that asks about an incomplete causal chain should be answered by supplying only those parts of the chain that the questioner needs to complete the entire chain.

We have suggested two ways that an answer may be constructed to fill in an incomplete causal chain. The first method is a generation and test approach in which one bases memory retrieval on a simulation of the questioner's processing proposed answers. The second method is to incorporate rules of knowledge state assessment within the retrieval heuristics. Although principles of question-based knowledge state assessment and causal chain generation must be incorporated in the memory search in some way, it seems that this knowledge could be internalized in terms of the search techniques and memory representation alone. That is, a method of the second sort that encodes these principles on the level of memory representation and straightforward retrieval heuristics would be a much more effective model. In the next section we see how this can be done.

9.2-2   A Retrieval Rule Incorporating MLOC Assessment

In this section we look at one way a retrieval heuristic can incorporate principles of knowledge state assessment and causal chain generation. With such heuristics the best answer to a why-question can be found without considering competing answers. These retrieval heuristics must start with a question concept, analyze the question concept as it resides in the story representation, determine whether the question is asking about a single conceptualization or a causal chain, and, in the case of an incomplete causal chain, find concepts that enable the questioner to construct the entire chain.

KSA[2] Rule 1: Terminating acts.   This rule applies to Causal Antecedent questions that ask about the termination of a conceptual act or activity. For example:

Q1: Why did John drop the casserole?
Q2: Why did John stop playing golf?
Q3: Why did John blow out the candle?

When a question asks about a termination, an immediate knowledge state assessment can be made. The questioner must know that the activity terminated was occurring over some interval of time preceding its termination. The person asking *Q1* must know that John had picked up a casserole. To ask *Q2,* you have to know that John had been playing golf, and *Q3* presupposes that the candle was burning.

---

[2]KSA = Knowledge State Assessment.

Because these knowledge state assessments give the questioner knowledge of acts preceding the question concept, the question indicates that the first and last acts of a causal chain are known: The question is asking about what went on in the middle of that chain. So questions of this sort fall into the chain completion category.

The retrieval heuristic for KSA Rule 1 does not work for all questions that ask about terminating acts. But before we can further specify the questions for which this rule is intended, we must first refine our memory representation. Until now, our system of causal chains has functioned quite nicely with a very small number of rather general causal links (result, enable, reason, etc.) Here it becomes necessary to refine the notion of a result link. In the casserole story, grasping the casserole is a continual act. John's physical contact with the casserole is maintained continuously over the interval of time during which he is grasping the casserole. As soon as John ceases to grasp the casserole, physical contact terminates. This relationship is a sort of simultaneous causality. In a paper that identifies 28 types of causal relationships, Rieger (1975b) calls this relational link, in which a resultant is continually in effect over an interval of time, a continuous-causality link. We call it a continuous-result link. This same type of link connects John's being in physical contact with the casserole and John's getting burned. As long as John is touching the casserole, he is being burned by it. Now we are ready to describe which questions our rule is intended for.

KSA Rule 1 applies to situations in which:

1. The question concept describes a terminating act.

2. Both the question concept and its corresponding initialization exist in the causal chain representation of the story.

3. The initializing act has a causal consequent connected to it by a continuous-result link.

This rule therefore applies to *Q5* when it is asked in the context of the casserole story. John's dropping the casserole is the termination of a GRASP act. Both John's GRASPing the casserole and his terminating the GRASP are present in the causal chain representation. Finally, the act of John's GRASPing the casserole has a causal consequent of John's being in physical contact with the casserole that is connected by a continuous-result link.

The retrieval heuristic for this situation is based on the following intuitions: When a conceptual act is ongoing over a period of time, it is very often the case that a causal chain is simultaneously maintained by the continuous act as long as the act persists. When this simultaneous chain leads to an undesirable state change, the initial act that maintains the chain is sometimes terminated in order to avoid the undesired state. The claim behind KSA Rule 1 is that when the three situational criteria of the rule are satisfied, the continuous act was terminated in order to avoid an undesired state change.

This is clearly the case in the casserole story. To see why the constraint concerning a continuous-result link is necessary, consider the following story:

> John was shopping in a grocery store. Just as he was taking a steak from the meat cooler, he noticed the ceiling begin to collapse in front of him. John dropped his basket and ran.

In this case John picks up a steak, is frightened by an impending disaster, drops the basket, and runs away. There are no continuous-result links in the causal chain representation for this story. Furthermore, one understands that John dropped the basket either because he was frightened or because he could run better without it. No one who understands this story would imagine that John dropped the basket because he thought it would stop the ceiling from collapsing. The shopping script assures us that the story representation will contain the act of John's picking up a basket. So the first two criteria of KSA Rule 1 are satisfied. The absence of a causal chain continuously dependent on John's grasping the basket is what tells us not to assume that the basket was dropped in order to avoid the collapsing ceiling.

Knowing that the three criteria for KSA Rule 1 specify a situation in which the act is terminated to avoid some state, we still have the problem of deciding which concepts in the story representation should be returned for an answer. The answer should communicate enough information for the questioner to construct the causal chain. In the event that the causal chain has more than one or two intermediate concepts, a good answer will probably not spell out everything that is there. Some things can be left for the questioner to infer.

The problem is one of finding rules that can be applied to the memory representation to identify which concepts in the causal chain have to be mentioned. By looking at the answers people gave to *Q4* and *Q5*, we see one immediate difference in retrieval. Some of the answers to *Q4* (Why did John yell?) specified the immediate causal antecedent:

A4a: He burned his hand.
A4e: Because he burned his hand.

It is interesting that when an answer to *Q4* provides more information than this, no gaps are left in the causal chain. People do not tend to answer *Q4* with an explanation like "Because the casserole he was holding was hot." That answer would require the questioner to infer that John was in physical contact with the casserole and that the casserole burned him. All of the answers to *Q4* mention John's being burned or hurt, the casserole being hot, and John's being in contact with the casserole.

A4b: He burned his hands on the hot casserole.
A4c: He hurt his hand picking up the hot casserole.
A4d: The hot casserole burned him.

In A4d, physical contact with the casserole is not explicitly mentioned, but it is implicitly present in the conceptual definition of "to burn" that is being used here. This sense of the word requires an $object_1$ that is probably hot to come into contact with or close proximity to another $object_2$. This state change then results in a negative physical-state change to $object_2$.

No one in our informal experiment answered $Q4$ with "Because the casserole was hot." This answer would require the questioner to piece together the casserole's being hot with John's yelling by making the inferences that John had touched the casserole and had been burned. Intuitively it seems that one could connect those concepts with the right inferences, but apparently this is reaching too far. A good answer should not make the questioner work too hard to make sense of it. The answers received in response to $Q4$ illustrate a general principle:

Answer-Selection Rule #3:
When a question asks about a single conceptualization
(as opposed to a causal chain), good answers do not
require the questioner to infer the missing parts of an
incomplete causal chain.

This principle leads us to a general rule about memory retrieval:

Retrieval Heuristic:

When a question indicates that the questioner has knowledge of only a single conceptualization, the answer should specify an immediate causal antecedent (in the case of a cooperative intentionality) or a complete causal chain leading up to the question concept (in the case of a more loquacious intentionality).

So questions about single concepts do not require retrieval heuristics that incorporate knowledge about what the questioner can infer. But we cannot avoid that problem when a question indicates that the questioner is trying to complete a causal chain. $Q5$ (Why did John drop the casserole?) is such a question. The answers received in response to Q5 all require the questioner to make some inference or inferences.

A5a: Because it was too hot to hold.

This answer says that John dropped the casserole because the casserole was hot enough to make holding it result in some undesirable state. The answer does not specify this state, the questioner must infer that the undesirable state that results from holding a hot object is a negative physical state of being burned. The answer is also constructed in such a way that it does not tell the questioner John was holding the casserole. So this answer requires the questioner to infer that John was in physical contact with the casserole, and that he was burned by the casserole. With these inferences and with the concepts conveyed in the answer, the causal chain — starting with John's picking up the casserole and ending with his dropping it — is completed.

A5c: He was burned because it was hot.

This answer says that John dropped the casserole because he had burned his hand and that this was caused by the casserole's being hot. To complete the chain this time, the questioner must infer that John was in physical contact with the casserole. Everything else in the chain is given.

The four other responses simply described the casserole as being hot. This answer requires the questioner to infer that John was in physical contact with the casserole and that this resulted in John's being burned which in turn was responsible for John's dropping the casserole.

Although there are differences in these responses, they all have some things in common: (1) they all explain that the casserole was hot; and (2) none of them explains that John was in physical contact with the casserole. Intuitively some of this makes sense: knowing that someone has picked up an object produces an immediate low-level inference that they must be in contact with that object, unless we were specifically told that an intermediate device of some sort (tongs, gloves, a dust pan) was used. If John picks up the casserole, we all expect him to be holding it for some period of time immediately following the act of picking it up. The part that is a little less intuitive is that everyone describes the casserole as being hot. It appears that people are expected to infer that John was burned from knowing that he was holding a hot casserole. But why are people not expected to infer that the casserole was hot from knowing that John was holding the casserole and that he was burned? Why don't people consistently mention John's getting burned instead of the casserole being hot? There are many possible explanations:

1. It is easier to infer state changes that static properties. (Getting burned is a state change; being hot is a property.)

2. It is easier to infer concepts that are simple linear pieces of a causal chain than to infer concepts that are causally concurrent in a causal chain. (Getting burned has one causal antecedent and one causal consequent; the casserole being hot is simultaneously coupled with physical contact to cause John's getting burned.)

3. It is harder to infer concepts that have fewer causal links typing them to the chain. (The casserole being hot is the only concept joined to the chain by a single link — a continuous-result link; all the others have both a causal antecedent and a causal consequent.

There is even a fourth possibility, which is not apparent from the causal-chain representation as we have described it. Concepts may be chosen on the basis of information stored with each causal link. During the understanding process when the causal chain is being generated, each causal link is generated from some knowledge source. Some causalities are recognized by scripts, some by plans, while perhaps others are derived from low-level inference mechanisms of the sort proposed by Rieger (1975a). It might be useful to differentiate links in terms of different structures within these knowledge sources.

We have actually done this already in the SAM system, when the script applier tags interference/resolution pairs. Those tags provide additional information about what sort of general structure within a script was responsible for recognizing the causal relationships in chains beginning with interferences and ending in resolutions. All such chains are found in branches that leave the default path of the script. These tags are used in answering why-questions that ask about script resolutions. It may very well be that tagging interference/resolution pairs is simply one particular case of an extensive system of processing tags that need to be incorporated in story representations. It will be easier to investigate this possibility when a system is designed that has access to both scripts and plans. When stories require different kinds of knowledge sources, it may be critical to have a story representation that easily reflects which knowlege sources were used to understand causalities.

If such information were incorporated in the representation for the casserole story, it might look like this:

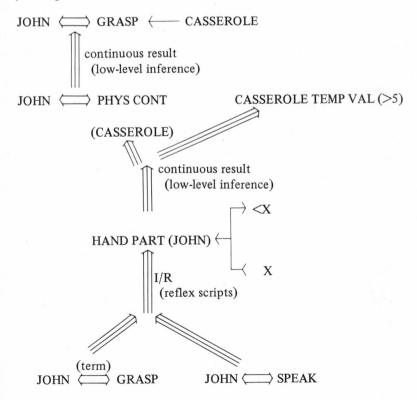

Although it is very difficult at this time to guess which of the possible rules underlie retrieval, it seems plausible that rules of this general nature can succeed. The idea of tagging causal links according to the knowledge sources responsible for them is a particularly promising approach. In fact, there is an example of memory retrieval falling under the control of KSA Rule 1 that seems to indicate a strong need for such tags. Consider a new story:

> John was playing golf one day when he pulled a muscle. He stopped playing, went home, and called the doctor.

The story representation for this looks like:

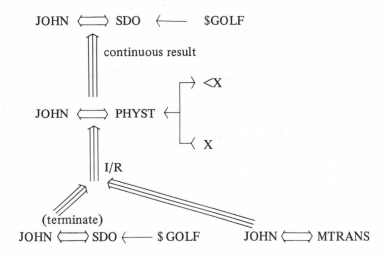

Now suppose that we ask the question

Q6: Why did John stop playing golf?

This question in the context of the golf story satisfies the criteria of KSA Rule 1. The question asks about a termination; the story representation contains both the termination concept and its corresponding initialization (John playing golf); and the initializing concept has a causal consequent that is connected to it by a continuous result link. But the answers that people give in response to *Q6* differ in an interesting way from those given for *Q5*. Of five people who were asked to answer *Q6* after reading the golf story, the responses given were:

A6a: Because he was hurt.
A6b: It hurt to play.

A6c: Because his muscle hurt.

A6d: He was worried it might get worse.

A6e: It was painful for him to play, and he didn't want it to get worse.

What is interesting about these responses in contrast to those given for *Q5* is that two of these answers (*A6b* and *A6e*) refer to the fact that John was playing golf. None of the answers to *Q5* mention John's grasping the casserole. Yet *Q6* indicates that the questioner knew John was playing golf, just as *Q5* indicated that the questioner knew John had picked up the casserole. So why tell the questioner something he already knows when answering *Q6?* The reason is fairly simple: Although the questioner knows that John was playing golf, he does not have any information about what playing golf is causally related to. If we give an answer like *A6a,* which simply states that John was hurt, it is harder to infer that playing golf was responsible for the injury. It is not *too* difficult to infer this; otherwise people would not give answers that require that causal inference (like *A6a,* A6c, and *A6d*). But it is harder to infer that playing golf results in being hurt than to infer that picking up a casserole results in being in physical contact with the casserole. It is harder because playing golf only occasionally results in being hurt, whereas picking up an object always results in inferred contact with the object.

The story representation can reflect these fuzzy probabilities by including knowledge-source tags on its causal links. If knowledge-source tags were placed in the representation for the golf story, the link between playing golf and getting hurt would be attributed to an interference in the golfing script. The link from getting hurt to stopping would derive from a resolution in the golfing script, and the link from getting hurt to calling the doctor would derive from some plan or script concerned with maintaining good health. A retrieval heuristic that examined knowledge-source tags could be designed to return causal antecedents of script interferences but to ignore causal antecedents of low-level inferences. Such an instruction would account for the fact that some people mentioned playing golf, whereas no one mentioned picking up the casserole.

9.3 LOOKING INSIDE MBUILDS

In the last section we developed a rule that incorporated knowledge state assessment. The rule looked for structural aspects of a particular causal chain structure: (1) the initiation and termination of an act; and (2) a continuous-result link emanating from the initiation of that act. Each of these features is a structural aspect of causal chain representation.

In trying to develop a set of such structural retrieval rules, a very striking phenomenon reveals itself. Most answers to why-questions describe motivations, goals, desires, or mental states.

Q1: Why did John take his watch to the dentist?
A1: He wanted to get it fixed.

Q2: Why didn't John show his parents his report card?
A2: He was afraid they would be angry.

Q3: Why was John waving at the taxi?
A3: He wanted to prevent it from skidding off the road.

Q4: Why did John yell?
A4: He burned his hand.

All of these answers describe aspects of mental states. There is a difficulty in retrieving concepts of mental activity because causal chains do not provide much structure for such information. Consider the watch story:

One day John broke the mainspring of his watch. His neighbor, a dentist, fixes watches for a hobby. John took his watch to the dentist.

In understanding this story, one makes roughly the following inferences about John's mental processes:

1. John liked his watch when it ran.
2. John's watch being broken makes John unhappy.
3. John didn't break his watch on purpose.
4. John wanted to get his watch fixed.
5. John knew that the dentist fixes watches for a hobby.
6. John thought that the dentist must get pleasure from fixing watches.
7. John thought that the dentist might fix his watch for the pleasure of it.

To see that each of these inferences is made, consider variations of the story that contradict each of these inferences. For example, to see that the second inference is valid, consider this variation:

One day John broke the mainspring of his watch. John was very pleased by this. His neighbor, a dentist, fixes old watches for a hobby. John took his watch over to the dentist.

Here the contradiction forces us to think that: (1) John is strange; or (2) John had been waiting for an excuse to visit his neighbor; or (3) John has some sort of plan that we do not know about yet. None of these inferences was made in the context of the original story.

The problem with causal chains is that they cannot capture all of the inferences we would like to make in a story like this. The causal chain representation for the watch story looks like this:

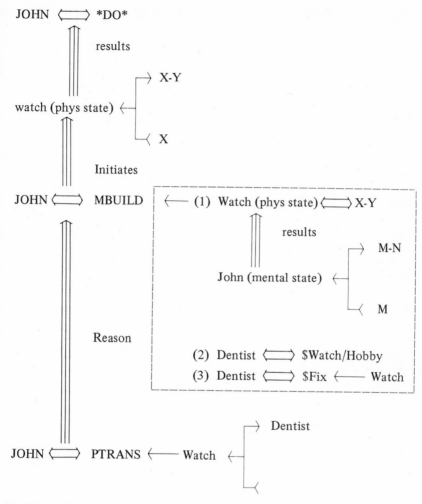

All of the inferences about John's mental state belong inside John's MBUILD process. Although the causal chain provides a place for all of the inferences about John's goals, desires, and mental states (within the MBUILD conceptualization), it does not specify how this information should appear. The problem we are faced with is what form these inferences inside John's MBUILD should assume.

These mental-activity inferences are related to one another by various kinds of causalities and mental strategies. Taking the watch to the dentist is a subgoal of wanting to get it fixed. The generation of this subgoal relied on knowing the dentist fixes watches for a hobby. The strategy for getting the dentist to fix his watch is to inform him that the watch is broken. This strategy is expected to work because the dentist presumably enjoys fixing watches. John's ultimate goal (to get the watch fixed) resulted from the watch being broken, the broken watch displeasing John, and John seeing the revival of his watch as something that will alleviate his displeasure.

All of this should be present in the memory representation. But what kinds of links express these relationships? What is missing is a rigid structure for what goes on inside an MBUILD. If inferences about John's mental state were organized according to a fixed set of structural laws concerning mental processes, then retrieval rules based on this structure could be developed for retrieving information about goals and motives.

9.3-1 Plan-Based Retrieval Heuristics

Some problems are solved by invoking reliable scripts, but others require cognitive processing beyond script selection. Although it is clear that people often invoke scripts for restaurants or food preparation in response to their hunger states, a script cannot be invoked when you find out your wife is conspiring with your best friend to murder you. If we are going to answer questions about why people do the things they do, we must understand the planning processes that are relied upon when there is no apparent script for a given situation, or when a choice must be made from a variety of applicable scripts.

Suppose we were answering questions about the following story:

> John needed to finish his article for the magazine by Friday. He figured he had to work at least 20 hours a day to get it done, and even then it would be close to the wire. Every time he became sleepy that week he felt angry and anxious. But he finished it on time. He came down with the flu right after the deadline and was very thankful to have gotten it then.

If we want to answer the questions:

> *Q1:* Why did John get angry when he became sleepy?
> *Q2:* Why was John thankful when he got the flu?

we must first understand that anger is not a common reaction to the daily need for sleep. In the same way we must realize that people do not normally experience relief when they get the flu. These questions cannot be answered without accessing information from the story that makes these causalities valid. Either the story representation or additional world knowledge must indicate that these causalities are not standard, but need to be accounted for by special circumstances.

The answers to both of these questions must make some reference to John's overriding goal of making the deadline. His anger can only be understood as a response to goal interference. Needing to sleep meant taking time away from his work. This constituted an interference in his plan for making the deadline. Anger is an understandable reaction to goal interference. So an answer to *Q1* must reference his threatened goal or the plan he invoked to achieve that goal:

He was afraid he wouldn't make the deadline.
(references goal)

He needed to work almost continuously.
(references goal plan)

Similarly, answers to *Q2* must account for John's mental state in terms of his previous anxiety. The flu does not normally cause feelings of gratitude. But if we understand that the consequences of having the flu would have been much more serious had it struck a few days earlier, then we can understand that John is grateful for the delay of a few days:

If he had gotten the flu earlier, he would have missed his deadline.
(references alternative course of events and consequent goal failure)

The causal relationships between goals, goal interferences, plans, and mental state changes cannot be represesented on the level of causal chains. Causal chains encode chronologies of physical events. When physical events are interpreted in terms of motivations and intentionality, we are concerned with another level of understanding, which is founded on rules about people's desires and the plans they invoke to satisfy them. If we want to know why John was angry about becoming sleepy or why he was thankful to get the flu when he did, we must look inside John's head and understand what he was doing in terms of goals and plans. Where does this level of understanding belong in a story representation?

Although all of this information can appropriately be placed inside John's MBUILDs, it may not necessary to be quite so graphic about it. To put all of the planning information inside John's MBUILDs would mean placing inside the MBUILD act a copy of the top-level causal chain that would appear within a syntax for internal MBUILDing. An alternative representation could avoid copying the causal chain acts by overlaying a system of plan-oriented links on the original causal chain. This new level of linkages would connect acts in terms of goal/subgoal relationships, goal/subgoal interference relationships, and other links that are not appropriate for causal chain syntax. This latter approach is the representational system adopted by PAM.

9.3-2   Retrieval Heuristics in PAM

PAM builds a causal chain of events just as SAM does, but final story representations generated by PAM also include pointers from conceptual acts to various planning structures, such as goals, plans, subgoals, and goal interferences. This additional structure in the story representation is examined by the retrieval heuristics whenever a why-question is asked.

The only why-questions that have been implemented for PAM are those that retain their initial conceptual categorization (Causal Antecedent or Goal Orientation) after interpretation is completed. For example, "Why did John kill the dragon?" has the conceptualization representing "John killed the dragon" as its underlying question concept, and is understood to be a Causal Antecedent question.

The first task of the memory search is to find the question concept in the story representation. This is done by a straightforward matching search. Once the underlying question concept is found in the causal chain, its immediate causal antecedents are extracted from the causal chain of events. Each of these antecedents is then checked to see whether it is tagged as an act that instantiates some plan. Any act that is tagged as being part of a plan instantiation will have a pointer to the immediate goal motivating that plan. If a plan instantiation is found, its immediate goal is returned as the conceptual answer. If the question type is Goal Orientation, the answer is expected to be found under the goal of a plan instantiation. If the question type is Causal Antecedent, there is one more place to look: When none of the direct antecedents yields a goal through plan instantiation, the same list of antecedents is searched for a concept that was motivated by a state. If one is found, its causal motivation is returned as the conceptual answer.

In the dragon story, questions are answered in terms of both immediate goals and motivating states:

> John loved Mary but she didn't want to marry him. One day, a dragon stole Mary from the castle. John got on top of his horse and killed the dragon. Mary agreed to marry him. They lived happily ever after.

Why did John get on his horse?
Because he wanted to be near Mary.
   (immediate goal)

Why did Mary agree to marry John?
Because she was indebted to him.
   (motivating state)

Why did John kill the dragon?
Because he wanted Mary to not die.
   (immediate goal)

The heuristics described above rely on four plan-oriented links, which identify acts according to their relationships in terms of planned behavior:

CAUSEDBY — points to all direct causal antecedents
PLANINSTANTIATE — tags a conceptualization that instantiates a plan
FORGOAL — points to the goal behind a plan instantiation
MLEADTO[3] — connects a motivation to a conceptualization.

---

[3]The MLEADTO link used here is not the same as the LEADTO link that acts as an unspecified causal link in causal-chain syntax.

This system of plan-based retrieval is a mere beginning. It is far from what we need to answer questions like "Why was John thankful when he got the flu?" Part of the difficulty in specifying a more complete set of retrieval heuristics is that we do not know exactly what story representations should look like in many cases. A complete theory of predictive understanding mechanisms based on plans is still under development. We need to process a wider range of plan-based stories before we can identify crucial problems in retrieval and propose a complete set of retrieval heuristics for stories understood with plans.

9.4   CONCLUDING REMARKS

In this chapter, we have outlined the complications involved in choosing a best answer, and we have described various approaches to the problem. From our meanderings, we emerge with two basic conclusions:

[1]. Some form of knowledge state assessment is needed. A capacity for knowledge state assessment can be implicitly encoded in the retrieval heuristics (9.2.2). But a comprehensive theory of knowledge state assessment will be needed regardless of how its rules manifest themselves in a Q/A system. In Chapter 11 we look at some of the difficulties involved in building an explicit model of the questioner's knowledge state.

[2]. Our memory representation must be strongly structured in the area of human motivations, goals, plans, and reasoning. Causal Antecedent and Goal-Orientation questions often ask about human behavior. These questions rely on a thorough understanding of why people do the things they do.

In this chapter, we have seen how critical it is for the story representation to encode information about structures internal to MBUILDs. In general, the Q/A task is very adept at detecting weaknesses in memory representations. In Chapter 10 we see how Q/A problems have motivated a system of representational primitives.

10 Conceptual Primitives for Physical Objects

When we discover a class of questions that is particularly difficult to handle, it is probably because the memory representation is weak or inadequate. Some questions have proved to be difficult because our memory representations do not deal with physical objects very satisfactorily. Conceptual Dependency is a very action-oriented representation; its primitives are all primitive acts.

In this chapter, a system of seven Object Primitives is proposed. When nouns are represented by decomposition into these primitives, we are able to see conceptual similarities and differences between objects in the same way that the primitive acts of Conceptual Dependency reflect conceptual similarities and differences between verbs. For example, a faucet and an underground spring are conceptually similar because they are both objects that commonly "produce" water. The representation for these two concepts should reflect this similarity:

S1: John drank from the faucet.
Q1: What did John drink?
A1: Water.

S2: John filled his canteen at the spring.
Q2: What did John get at the spring?
A2: Water.

When we hear *S1*, we infer that water came out of the faucet. A similar inference is made for *S2* about water coming out of the spring. Conceptual descriptions of objects should encode the knowledge needed for inferences of this sort. Furthermore, the organization of this knowledge should be structured so that the same inference mechansim that produces *A1* will also produce *A2*. If inferences about different objects rely on different mechanisms for each object, we do not have a very viable theory of inference. Processes of inference should depend on conceptual descriptions of objects, but not on specific objects themselves. The Object-Primitive descriptions for a faucet and a spring make it possible for a single inference mechanism to work in both cases. Object-Primitive decompositions provide a representational system for encoding knowledge about objects needed for natural language processing.

10.0 INTRODUCTION

Many inferences rely on knowledge about physical objects and a mundane understanding of physical causality. For example, if John is drinking coffee in the back of a car, and the coffee spills when the car hits a bump, we should infer that the coffee spilled because the car hit the bump. But if we were told instead that the coffee spilled when the car radio went dead, we would not want to infer that the car radio going dead was responsible for the coffee spilling. These inferences cannot be made on the basis of scripts. If we put into a riding-in-the-car script all of the possible events that would result in liquid spilling from an open container, the script would contain too much information to be workable. Even if all that information were successfully incorporated in a car script, it would have to be duplicated for a train script, and then a bus script, and so on.

People have a mundane knowledge of physical causality, which they use in their inferencing processes. Knowledge about when liquids can spill must be general, and not tied to all the specific situations in which liquids can spill (in cars, trains, boats, airplanes, etc.). To build a natural language processing system, we must develop a knowledge base incorporating this mundane knowledge of the physical world.

One general inference mechansim should be able to recognize that a full coffee cup can spill during a bumpy car ride for the same reasons that can cause a full glass of water to spill in a dining car when the train pulls out. But a general rule of this sort requires a representational system that recognizes how cars are similar to trains and how full glasses of water are similar to full coffee cups. A conceptual representation for objects is required for very fundamental recognition processes.

Yorick Wilks (1976) points out a critical problem in the current formulation of script application that illustrates the recognition problem nicely. Wilks refers to a paper by Eugene Charniak (1975a) in which Charniak's formulation for a supermarket frame (script) includes references to entities like "basket." For example the script contains an act describing the shopper obtaining a basket. Wilks asks (quite rightly) how such a surface representation can be implemented in an understanding system in which we must recognize the shopper getting a box, carrier-bag, push cart, plastic sack, or any number of other possible carrying devices? How will the system understand that these various lexical items refer to objects that should match the notion of a "basket" in the supermarket script? This criticism is just and deserving of attention. Wilks could have been talking about SAM's restaurant script as well. But Wilks goes on to cite this failing as a weakness inherent in the notion of scripts, when, in fact, this failing merely indicates that we do not have an adequate representation for physical objects. At the end of this chapter, we return to this problem of script application with a solution based on a new representational system.

The representational system we propose is designed to facilitate inference processes. For example, in understanding "John went to the store and got some milk," it is important to infer that the milk is in a milk container. No one hearing that sentence imagines John cupping a small quantity of milk in his hands. But, "John went into a fancy restaurant and got some milk" should be understood to mean that John ordered some milk and received it in a glass. People make inferences of this sort as soon as they hear these sentences. If these inferences were not made, then the following stories would not be bothersome:

S3: John went to the store and got some milk. But the glass was very full and he spilled it on the floor.

S4: John went into a fancy restaurant and got some milk. But the container was partially open, and so he asked for another one.

In *S3,* the reference to a very full glass that spills does not make sense. Stores do not supply milk in open glasses. In *S4,* the same sort of confusion arises. We expect John to be served milk in a glass. When we hear that it came in a container, we are forced to conclude that the restaurant must be more like a cafeteria than the term "fancy restaurant" suggests.

10.1 OBJECT PRIMITIVES

In the same way that a set of primitive acts has been developed in Conceptual Dependency for the conceptual representation of acts, a set of Primitive Objects is used to represent physical objects. We propose seven primitives for representing physical objects. Just as a verb is conceptually represented by a decomposition into primitive acts, a noun is conceptually represented by a decomposition into Object Primitives. When two objects are conceptually similar in some ways and different in others, their Object Primitive decomposition should reflect those similarities and differences. Object Primitive decomposition is very reminiscent of decomposition into primitive acts, but with one exception. When an object is decomposed into an Object Primitive description, it is usually described in terms of simultaneous and parallel Object Primitives. This is somewhat different from the primitive decomposition of actions, in which each verb receives only one "top-level" primitive act in its decomposition.[1] The primitives proposed here are designed to encode prototypical information about objects. They reflect normal

---

[1]For example, "give" is usually a top-level ATRANS with an instrumental PTRANS. Multiple-object primitives are not embedded within a single hierarchical structure.

expectations that people have about familiar objects. But "normality" is a property that changes with context. While milk is normally found in a milk container in a store, it is normally found in a glass when being served at a restaurant. Therefore, Object Primitives rely to some extent on contingent descriptions. That is, part of the information in an Object Primitive decomposition may be applicable at some times and not at others. For example, an Object Primitive description of milk will encode the expectation that a shopper in a grocery store will find milk in a milk container, whereas a restaurant patron expects to find milk in a glass.

10.1-1 SETTING

When an object is big enough to hold a person, it is often called a place. From a conceptual viewpoint, what is important about a place are the activities that are predictably associated with it. Places like dining cars and grocery stores are characterized by the scripts associated with them. When a place has associated scripts, it is represented by the Object Primitive SETTING. SETTINGs can be associated with other SETTINGs as well as with scripts. For example, a dining car is a SETTING that invokes the related SETTING of a passenger train. Once we hear that John is in a dining car, we immediately infer that John is in a passenger (coach) train. If we hear a subsequent reference to "the train," there is no confusion about what train:

John was sitting in a dining car. The train pulled out.

When the second sentence references a train, there is no ambiguity about what kind of train. We do not wonder whether it is freight train, a toy train, a subway train, or a train of thought. We have already been told (by implicit inference) that John is on a passenger train. The Object Primitive SETTING describes objects in terms of their associated scripts and other SETTINGs:[2]

> [Washing Machine
>   (a SETTING with
>   <Scripts = $Washing Machine>
>   <Settings = Home, Laundry>)]
>
> [Dining car
>   (a SETTING with
>   <Scripts = $Restaurant, $Preparefood>
>   <Settings = Passenger Train>)]

---

[2]It is sometimes useful to describe a SETTING in terms of a single conceptual act. In these cases the slot name "Acts" is used. For example, a sandwich has a SETTING description with Act = INGEST. In subsection 10.2-3 we see an example of how associated acts are used.

[Classroom
    (a SETTING with
    <Scripts = $Teaching>
    <Settings = School>)]

[Pen
    (a SETTING with
    <Scripts = $Pen>)]

A SETTING need not be a place; it is either a place with situational scripts or an object with instrumental scripts. When a SETTING is a place (e.g., a dining car or classroom), the associated scripts describe activities that take place within those SETTINGs. But when a SETTING is not a place in the sense of being occupied by people (e.g., a washing machine or pen), then the associated scripts describe the instrumental or functional aspects of that object. Because the normal use of an object can be described in terms of a script, there is no problem encoding such information under the primitive SETTING. SETTINGs do not distinguish between places where scripts take place and objects that are the primary prop of a script. The scripts themselves make this distinction. A situational script describes an activity that commonly occurs in a fixed situation, whereas an instrumental script describes an activity that can occur in various situations but that requires a specific prop for its execution. Hence, the restaurant script depends on a restaurant locale, but the pen script relies on only the presence of a pen.

10.1-2 GESTALT

Many objects are characterized as being something greater than the sum of their parts. Trains, stereos, universities, kitchens — all evoke images of many components that may interrelate and interact in any number of ways. The Object Primitive that is designed to capture these clustering effects is a GESTALT. All GESTALT objects are described by their Parts. A place setting is a GESTALT object whose Parts include a plate, knife, fork, spoon, glass, napkin, placemat, and so forth. But a place setting is more than just the set of those elements. It is a particular configuration of those elements. If a plate is balanced on an upside-down glass, we would hesitate to recognize that as part of a place setting. Similarly, a train is thought to be a linear configuration of cars usually headed by the engine; it is not a set of cars piled on top of each other.

[Freight Train
    (a GESTALT with
    <Parts = Engine Car, Freight Cars, Caboose)
    <Configuration = linear string of engine,
                        freight cars, & caboose>)]

[Place Setting
  (a GESTALT with
   < Parts = Plate, Glass, Bowl, Silverware, Napkin>
   <Configuration = Radial configuration with plate at center, silverware at
             right on top of napkin, glass at one o'clock, bowl at
             eleven o'clock>)]

10.1-3 RELATIONAL

In addition to objects that are described by their components or parts, many objects are described by the relationships they normally assume with other objects. Containers (rooms, bottles, shopping carts, etc.) are described by a capacity for containment. Supporting objects (tables, chairs, plates, etc.) are described by their ability to support other things. Hinges support doors, bulletin boards hold papers, and blackboards can be covered with chalk. The Object Primitive that encodes prototypical relationships between objects is a RELATIONAL object.

All RELATIONAL objects have a Relationlink that specifies the relation that the object normally assumes. The Relationlink value for a table will be "on-top-of," while a bottle takes the Relationlink value "inside-of." Each RELATIONAL object includes constraints for the relations specified under its Relationlink. For example, a piano bench of the variety that opens up has two Relationlinks: on-top-of and inside-of. But different constraints operate on the objects that assume these relations. Something that goes inside the piano bench must not exceed certain dimensional constraints. A final aspect to RELATIONAL objects is the possibility of instrumental objects that enable certain relationships. For example, a bulletin board maintains a "stuck-to" relationship with papers, but only if a thumbtack is used.

[Table
  (a RELATIONAL with
   <Relationlink = On-top-of>)]

[Blackboard
  (a RELATIONAL with
   <Relationlink = Stuck-to>
   <Constraints = Chalk>)]

[Bulletin Board
  (a RELATIONAL with
   <Relationlink = Stuck-to>
   <Constraints = Paper>
   <Instruments = Thumbtack>)]

One aspect of RELATIONAL objects that may seem to be a natural part of these descriptions is the notion of specific defaults. For example, an egg carton is a RELATIONAL object with a very strong tendency to harbor eggs. The idea of default objects of this sort is a very strong one that enables a large class of inferences. If John fills his lighter, it is standard to infer that the lighter was filled with lighter fluid. If a pen leaks, it is expected to leak ink. When the tank of a car is full, it should be full of gasoline. This characteristic is not restricted to RELATIONAL objects, however. A faucet is expected to produce water, and a radio commonly emits music or verbal communication. The ideas of production and consumption among objects motivate the next two Object Primitives.

10.1-4 SOURCE and CONSUMER

A SOURCE is an object that is characterized by its tendency to produce other things. Sugar bowls are SOURCEs of sugar, egg cartons are SOURCEs of eggs, and faucets are SOURCEs of water. A CONSUMER is an object that tends to consume other things. A drain consumes liquids and a slot machine consumes coins. Of course a slot machine can also be a SOURCE of coins, but it tends to be more of a CONSUMER.

A SOURCE is related to the objects it produces by an Output link, while CONSUMERs have corresponding Input links. In addition to these descriptors, some SOURCEs and CONSUMERs require Activation scripts and/or Deactivation scripts. For example, a radio and a light fixture are both SOURCES that need to be activated and deactivated.

[Wine Bottle
   (a SOURCE with
   <Output = Wine>
   <Activation = $Pour>)]

[Book
   (a SOURCE with
   <Output = MObject>
   <Activation = $Read>)]

[Mailbox
   (a CONSUMER with
   <Input = Letters>)]

[Ice-Cube Tray
   (a SOURCE with
   <Output = Ice Cubes>)
   (a CONSUMER with
   <Input = Water>)]

[Sponge
   (a SOURCE with
   <Output = Liquids>
   <Activation = $Squeeze>)

```
        (a CONSUMER with
        <Input = Liquids>
        <Activation = $Wipe>)]

    [Pipe
        (a SOURCE with
        <Output = Smoke>
        <Activate = $Smoke>)
        (a CONSUMER with
        <Input = Tobacco>
        <Activation = $Smoke>)]
```

Object Primitives can be used to encode conceptual senses of some verbs and adjectives, as well as nouns. For example, "to empty" something means to use it as a SOURCE. "To fill" something means to use it as a CONSUMER. So if John empties an ice-cube tray, we infer from the SOURCE description of an ice-cube tray that he got ice from it. If John fills an ice-cube tray, we infer from the CONSUMER description of an ice-cube tray that he put water in it.

When objects are described as SOURCEs and CONSUMERs, their descriptions are necessarily based on egocentric experience. That is, the most common experience of these objects must dominate their conceptual description. For example, most people experience a wine bottle as a SOURCE of wine. But it is conceivable that a wine bottle might be more properly conceptualized as a CONSUMER. Someone who works in a winery and fills the bottles but never drinks wine will conceptualize a wine bottle as more of a CONSUMER than a SOURCE. Most people share a tremendous amount of episodic knowledge. Because the inferences made in natural language processing are derived from this realm of generally shared and common experience, the knowledge representations used in natural language processing must reflect this body of common episodic knowledge.

This egocentric bias in conceptual perception has significant impact on all of our inferencing mechanisms. A teenager often views his father as a SOURCE of money. He can think of his father as someone who produces money, with little consideration for the reality of earning a living and providing for a family. A person who does not smoke but has to clean up after someone who does will perceive ashtrays as a SOURCE of dirt. A person who smokes but does not clean up will perceive an ashtray as a CONSUMER. Environmentalists try to convince people that the earth is not an endless SOURCE of resources and that it may not be very bright to think of the ocean as a CONSUMER of all our wastes. People conceptualize the world according to their immediate experience of it and therefore operate with something less than a global view of things. A garbage can is a CONSUMER of garbage because objects that make it to the garbage can do not have to be dealt with anymore. The fact that garbage does not mysteriously disappear from the cosmos is an intellectual awareness that lacks the immediacy of episodic knowledge.

10.1-5 SEPARATOR and CONNECTOR

In causal chain theory, states and acts alternate; states very often enable acts, and acts result in state changes (Schank, 1973a). A state is often conceptually significant because of the acts it enables or disenables. The last two Primitive Objects are designed to represent objects in terms of states that enable and disenable conceptual acts.

A SEPARATOR disconnects two regions or spatial locations with respect to a primitive act. SEPARATORs disenable specific acts. A CONNECTOR joins two regions or spatial locations with respect to a primitive act. CONNECTORs enable specific acts. Objects must assume a fixed state when being described in terms of SEPARATORs and CONNECTORs. For example, an open window is a CONNECTOR with respect to MTRANSing and PTRANSing between the inner and outer regions bounded by the window. A closed window is still a CONNECTOR with respect to visual MTRANSing, but it is a SEPARATOR with respect to auditory MTRANSing and all PTRANSing. An open window and a closed window are two conceptually distinct objects. It must be understood that an open window can be transformed into a closed window, and vice-versa, but the conceptual representation of a window is ambiguous unless we know whether the window is open or closed.

A closed window and an open window are conceptually distinct objects because of the different inferences that apply to each. If a window is open, we want to infer that air passes through it and that physical objects (of appropriate dimensions) can be PTRANSed through it. But if a window is closed, none of this should be assumed. Conceptual descriptions of objects should distinguish objects in terms of valid inferences about those objects.

[Window (closed)
    (a SEPARATOR with
    <Disenabled = PTRANS,
                  MTRANS $\xleftarrow{\text{I}}$ SPEAK>)
    (a CONNECTOR with
    <Enabled = MTRANS   ATTEND $\xleftarrow{\text{I}}$ EYES>)]

[Window (open)
    (a CONNECTOR with
    <Enabled = MTRANS, PTRANS>)]

[Road
    (a CONNECTOR with
    <Enabled = $Drive, $Bicycle, $Walk>)]

[Cut (open)
    (a CONNECTOR with   → outside (hum0)
    <Enabled = PTRANS ←—— Blood ←
                                  ⟨ inside (hum0)

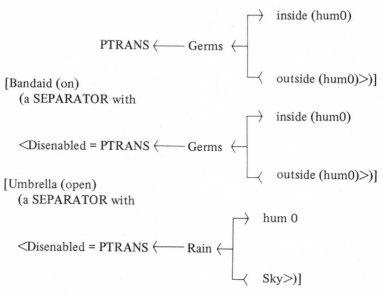

It is important to describe SEPARATORs and CONNECTORs in terms of enabled and disenabled acts. For example, a dog leash might be thought of as a CONNECTOR that fixes some locational proximity on the dog. But this is not a very useful representation in terms of potential inferences. A dog leash (when on the dog) is actually SEPARATOR that disenables the dog from PTRANSing itself outside a fixed radius.

10.2 APPLICATIONS FOR OBJECT PRIMITIVES

A representational system must be judged in terms of the processes that it facilitates. Although Object Primitives were motivated by problems in question answering, there appear to be many areas in which they can be used. Four such applications are discussed: state descriptions, script application, finding answers for where-questions, and general inference mechanisms. A brief description of a problem and an outline of the solution is presented in each of these four areas. But first we look at a computer program that uses Object Primitives in order to understand.

10.2-1 COIL

COIL is a natural language processing program that implements Object Primitive descriptions in its memory representations. When COIL hears that John went into the kitchen and got some milk, a memory representation is generated that includes John getting a milk container full of milk out of a refrigerator. Had COIL heard that John went into a restaurant and got some milk, the memory representation would have involved someone serving John a glass filled with milk. COIL implements the locational specification heuristic described in subsection 10.2-4 in order to answer certain where-questions. Inference mechanisms like the demon found in subsection 10.2-5 are used by COIL during the understanding process to generate causal connections. For example, one of the inference rules used by COIL is designed to recognize that if a depleted SOURCE object is thrown away, it is thrown away because it was depleted.

Here is a sample story and *Q/A* session with COIL. COIL periodically flips between story understanding and question answering:

> John picked up a newspaper. He went from the hall into the kitchen and got some milk.
>
> *Q:* Where did John come from?
> *A:* THE HALL
>
> *Q:* Where did the milk come from?
> *A:* THE REFRIGERATOR

But the milk carton was empty, and so he threw it out.

> *Q:* Where did the milk carton go to?
> *A:* THE GARBAGE BAG
>
> *Q:* Why did John throw the milk carton away?
> *A:* BECAUSE THE MILK CARTON WAS EMPTY

He turned on the light and radio. Then he listened to music and read.

> *Q:* Where did the music come from?
> *A:* THE RADIO
>
> *Q:* What did John read?
> *A:* THE NEWSPAPER
>
> *Q:* Why did John turn on the light?
> *A:* SO HE COULD READ THE NEWSPAPER
>
> *Q:* Why did John turn on the radio?
> *A:* SO HE COULD HEAR THE MUSIC

How Object Primitives Were Used.

JOHN PICKED UP A NEWSPAPER'.
> An expectation is aroused that John may read the newspaper. This is done by activating the Associated Scripts under the SETTING description of a newspaper.

HE WENT FROM THE HALL INTO THE KITCHEN . . .
> An expectation is aroused that John may prepare food. This is done by activating the Associated Scripts under the SETTING description of a kitchen.

The context of a kitchen is established from which we could derive the inference that John is in a house. This context is established by activating the Associated SETTINGs found in the SETTING description of a kitchen.

. . . AND GOT SOME MILK.

There was a milk carton with milk in it. This inference is made on the basis of the OutputFrom link for milk (this link is contingent on the SETTING kitchen).

There was a refrigerator. This inference is made on the basis of the Defaultlocation link for a milk carton (this link is contingent on the SETTING kitchen).

John moved the milk carton from inside the refrigerator. This is the conceptual representation for "getting some milk," given the last two inferences and the RELATIONAL description of a refrigerator.

BUT THE MILK CARTON WAS EMPTY . . .

There is no milk in the milk carton. The conceptual representation for the milk carton previously included a SOURCE description with Output = milk. This SOURCE description is now removed from this particular instantiation of a milk carton.

. . . SO HE THREW IT OUT.

There was a garbage bag. This is derived from the GESTALT description of a kitchen.

John threw the milk carton into the garbage bag. "Throwing something out" invokes a demon that searches for an object with an appropriate CONSUMER description. GESTALT parts of the current SETTINGs are examined. When the garbage bag is found to satisfy the requirements of the demon, it is incorporated into the conceptual representation for "Throwing it out."

John threw the milk carton away because it was empty. When the conceptual representation for throwing the milk carton away is generated, a demon is triggered that tries to account for why things get thrown away. When this demon sees that the milk carton is not realizing its prototypical SOURCE description, it concludes that this is why it is being disposed of.

HE TURNED ON THE LIGHT AND RADIO.

There was a light fixture that began to emit light after John switched it on. This is represented by instantiating the SOURCE description for the light fixture.

There was a radio that began to produce either music or some other verbal communication after John switched it on. This is represented by instantiating the SOURCE description of the radio.

THEN HE LISTENED TO MUSIC AND READ.

The music came from the radio. This inference is immediate from the SOURCE description of the radio.

John's listening to music was enabled by the radio's being on. This inference is made by a demon that examines SOURCE descriptions to account for enabling conditions underlying conceptual acts of ATTENDing.

John's reading was enabled by the light's being on. This inference is made by the same demon that connected the radio being on with listening to music.

John read the newspaper. This is an instantiation of the reading script. The inference is made on the basis of the original expectation aroused at the beginning of the story, when John picked up the newspaper.

10.2-2 State Descriptions

Many states are conceptually significant in terms of inferences. It is perfectly reasonable to hear:

S1: John opened the bottle and poured the wine.

But it is much more difficult to understand:

S2: John recorked the bottle and poured the wine.

S1 suggests that John poured the wine from the bottle he opened. It is impossible for John to pour wine from a bottle that he just stopped up; so *S2* forces us to assume that John poured wine from some other bottle.

Being open and being closed are important states because they direct inference processes about enabled and disenabled acts. *S1* sets up an enabling condition for moving liquid from the interior of the bottle, and *S2* disenables movement. *S1* makes sense because we can make a causal connection between opening a bottle and pouring its contents: John opened the bottle so he could pour the wine. *S2* makes less sense because no such causality can be inferred: It is not clear how corking a bottle relates to pouring wine.

A conceptual representation for states should make it easy to recognize the causal relationships between states and acts. It is not enough to tag a memory token with the descriptor "Open" or "Closed" because these state descriptors mean different things for different objects. Open doors, open coats, open umbrellas, and open electrical switches all carry inferences that are specific to those objects. By using the Object Primitives CONNECTOR and SEPARATOR, the acts enabled and disenabled by these states are immediately apparent in the conceptual representation for these objects.

CONNECTORs and SEPARATORs can be used to describe the states "open" and "closed." SOURCEs and CONSUMERs can be used to describe other states, such as on, off, full, and empty. When a radio is off, it is not realizing its SOURCE description. When it is on, it is. When a wine bottle is empty, it is not realizing its SOURCE description. When it is full, it is. When a garbage disposal is on, it is realizing its CONSUMER description.

Other miscellaneous states can also be described in terms of Object Primitive descriptions. When the sun is "up," it is realizing its SOURCE description with Output = light and heat. When John has his sunglasses "on," they are acting as a SEPARATOR that disenables the PTRANS of light from the sun to John's eyes. When the telephone is "broken," it is not realizing its SETTING description with the associated telephone script.

These state descriptions are useful because they specify in what way the state of a particular object relates to potential actions. Any representation of states that does not lend itself to object-specific inferences is a weak representation. Object Primitives provide a method for state representation when the conceptual meaning of a given state varies over different objects that can assume that state.

10.2-3 Script Application

In the beginning of this chapter, we alluded to a criticism of scripts voiced by Yorick Wilks (1976). The problem involved a representational weakness in scripts when a script should recognize that some objects could be appropriately substituted for other objects. For example, if John goes into a grocery store and puts items in a cardboard box or plastic bag, the script applier should be able to recognize that these are acceptable alternatives for a shopping cart or shopping basket. If John goes into the grocery store and proceeds to put items in the pockets of his coat, the script applier should realize that John is not acting in accordance with the shopping script. Other memory processes should take over at this point to deduce that John is probably up to something.

If the script applier used Object Primitive descriptions, there would be no difficulty in this recognition process. An object that can be used appropriately in the script is one that has the following features in its Object Primitive description:

(a SETTING with
    <Acts = HUM $\Longleftrightarrow$ PTRANS $\longleftarrow$ OBJ $\xleftarrow{\text{I}}$ GRASP

    HUM $\Longleftrightarrow$ PTRANS $\longleftarrow$ OBJ $\xleftarrow{\text{I}}$ PROPEL³>)

(a RELATIONAL with
<Relationlink = Inside-of>)
    (a CONNECTOR with
    <Enabled = MTRANS $\xleftarrow{\text{I}}$ ATTEND $\Longleftrightarrow$ EYES>)

---

³The Act specifiers described here have incomplete instrument fillers. The fully expanded representations would describe PTRANSes that correspond to pushing, pulling (PROPELs), or carrying (GRASP). In these conceptualizations, OBJ is a self-reference to the thing being described.

These Object Primitive descriptions specify a container that can be carried, pushed, or pulled and that does not obscure or hide its contents. Any appropriate substitute for a shopping basket (a pushcart, box, carrier-bag, plastic sack, etc.) will meet these specifications. Inappropriate objects like pockets, book shelves, dump trucks, plates, or hollowed-out books will fail to meet these descriptive constraints.

OK Things:
pushcart
box (if open)
crate
carrier-bag
plastic sack
basket

Not OK Things:
pocket (fails the CONNECTOR specification)
book shelf (fails the SETTING specification)
dump truck (fails the SETTING specification)
plate (fails the RELATIONAL specification)
hollowed-out book (fails the CONNECTOR specification)

If a script applier encodes descriptions of objects in terms of Object Primitives and can check Object Primitive decompositions of the objects mentioned in input sentences, there will be no recognition problem when appropriate substitutions for prototypical objects can be made.

10.2-4   Locational Specification

Upon hearing the sentences:

John was sitting in a dining car. When the train pulled out, the soup spilled.

the answers people give to:

Q1: Where was the soup?

generally reference one of two places:

A1: In a bowl.
A2: On the table.

What is remarkable about this are all the answers that are not given:

A3: On a plate.
A4: On a floor.
A5: In the train.

Although "In the train" is a feasible answer to *Q1* "On a plate," is a very strange answer. But what retrieval mechanism is responsible for recognizing that *A1* and *A2* are slightly better and more natural answers than *A3–5?* The memory representation that is generated in the course of reading the two sentences must include some relational description that places the soup inside the train. This representation should connect the soup and the train by a series of relational links specifying a path of objects that begins with the soup and ends with the train. If we generate a memory representation that uses the relational links On-top-of and Inside-of, the path between soup and train would look something like:

soup (inside-of)
bowl (on-top-of)
plate (on-top-of)
tablecloth (on-top-of)
table (on-top-of)
floor (inside-of)
dining car (inside-of)
train

Given this path of objects and relational connections, how does a retrieval heuristic know that "in a bowl" and "on the table" are good answers, but that "on a plate" is not? One could argue that "on a plate" is not a good answer because the soup does not rest directly on a plate. But this is not a satisfactory explanation, for the same reasoning could be used to argue that "on the table" is not a good answer (the soup does not rest directly on the table either).

If an Object Primitive decomposition is used in constructing the path from the soup to the train,[4] the answers "In a bowl" and "On a table" can readily be preferred. A path construction using Object Primitives begins with the soup and goes to the next contingent object of contact (the bowl), but then recognizes that the bowl and plate are conceptually grouped together as parts of the GESTALT object place setting. The place setting is recognized as part of the table setting, and the table setting would then be linked to the table by an on-top-of link. If a Part-of link were used to indicate membership in a GESTALT description, the path from soup to train would look like this:

soup (inside-of)
bowl (part-of)
place setting (part-of)
table setting (on-top-of)
table (part-of)
dining area (part-of)
dining car (part-of)
train

---

[4]The actual construction of this path is described in subsection 10.2-5.

This memory representation connecting the soup to the train lends itself to a very simple heuristic for answering questions about locational specification: When a path of locational descriptions must be searched for an answer, skip over those objects connected by part-of links. The two objects in the above path that are not connected by part-of links are precisely the bowl and the table.

The above heuristic will not work in all cases in which a choice must be made in answering a locational specification question. A complete heuristic will have to rank preferences over all of the possible relational links that may occur in a path. But the point to be made here is that a strong memory representation will result in simple retrieval heuristics. When people conceptualize the soup in the dining car, they tend to clump together the bowl and the plate. Because this conceptual clumping affects answers to questions, the memory representation should reflect clumping phenomona of this sort. The notion of a GESTALT object can be used to clump objects appropriately. If further information were required (as would be the case if we asked "what was directly under the bowl?"), a memory search on the conceptual notion of a place setting could be conducted to find out that the bowl was on top of a plate. But the memory representation should not make this information predominant. We should be able to see where the plate fits in if needed, but the concept of a plate should not be as readily available as the concepts of a bowl and table.

10.2-5 Inference Mechanisms

After reading:

John was sitting in a dining car. When the train pulled out, the soup spilled.
it is natural to answer:

Q1: Why did the soup spill?
A1: Because the train moved.

The causal connection between the train moving and the soup spilling must have been established at the time the two sentences were understood. If these causal connections were not immediately made at the time of understanding, it would not bother us to hear:

John was sitting in a dining car. When the train pulled out, the salt shaker exploded.

This last sentence should bother us to the extent that we cannot account for the salt shaker exploding. It was reasonable for the train's movement to cause the soup to spill, but it is less agreeable that the salt shaker exploded because the train moved. The causal mechanisms that try to tie conceptualizations together into causal chains cannot establish a sufficient causal link to account for the salt shaker exploding.

In this section, we see how Object Primitives can be used in the implementation of an inference mechanism that will recognize that the train pulling out caused the soup to spill.

A Demon

When something spills, we know that a substance of some sort has been propelled from the inside of a container to the outside. Furthermore, something must have happened to cause this occurrence, because substances do not normally behave in such a manner without provocation. We do not know exactly what happened, but whatever it was, it entailed movement on the part of the container. To paraphrase the Conceptual Dependency representation of spilling, some unidentified force either PROPELled or PTRANSed a container, which resulted in a substance PROPELling itself from inside of that container. To differentiate spilling from pouring, we will assume that the unidentified force is an unknown natural force. Because natural forces do not embody intentionality, we know that the act was not intended by anyone.

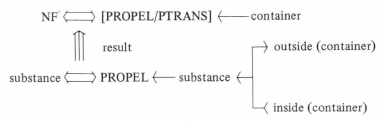

In our example we ultimately want to identify the unknown force as being the train. Once the train is known to be the force at the head of the spilling conceptualization, it will be simple to answer why the soup spilled. The identification of the train relies on a capacity for recognizing the transitivity of PTRANS over containment relations.

If John puts a shirt in his suitcase and takes the suitcase to New York, we should infer that the shirt went to New York as well. But containment is not the only relation that can carry a PTRANS. On-top-of relations are also susceptible, as well as various adhesive relationships. A mechanism that recognizes when PTRANS carries across objects is essential in establishing the causal antecedent for our spilled soup. We return to this transitivity problem shortly, after a brief description of the inference mechanism.

The actual mechanism is a demon (Charniak, 1972; Selfridge, 1959), which is created whenever we describe an unknown natural force as PROPELling or PTRANSing an object. The purpose of the demon is to identify the unknown natural force whenever possible.

The Spilling Demon:

1. is CREATED whenever we describe:
   NF $\Longleftrightarrow$ [PROPEL/PTRANS] $\longleftarrow$ Object$_1$
2. is ACTIVATED whenever if finds[5]
   X $\Longleftrightarrow$ [PROPEL/PTRANS] $\longleftarrow$ Object$_2$
3. Once the demon is activated, it then TESTS to see whether Object$_1$ *depends* on Object$_2$
4. If the test succeeds, then the demon ACTS by creating a result link and identifying the previously unknown force:

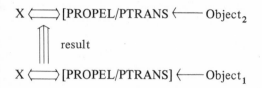

In the spilled-soup problem, the conceptualization for the soup spilling creates the spilling demon (Object$_1$ = unspecified container), and the train pulling out activates it (Object$_2$ = X = train).

There are two points to be made about this mechanism. First, it does not make inferences about the PROPELling and TRANSing of dependent objects until it has to. If no mention is made of the knife on the table, then no conceptualization involving that knife is generated. But should an unexplained movement of the knife arise, either in subsequent text or during question answering, then this mechanism would be invoked. So this is essentially a retroactive mechanism that is summoned only when needed. It is very different from a "forward-inferencing" device, which would go into action whenever any object got moved to see what other objects must have been moved as a consequence. A forward-inferencing device would immediately generate conceptualizations for the movement of every object inferred to be on the train, as soon as it heard that the train moved. Incidents like spilling are especially suited to retroactive processing because we do not want to generate hypotheses about everything that might possibly spill in response to any movement of any object.

The second point concerns the test part of the demon. The test does not specify a particular relationship between Object$_1$ and Object$_2$. It merely indicates some vague notion of dependence. This is intended to keep the spilling demon

---

[5] "Finding" means:
   1. Search previous conceptualizations.
      If this is not successful, go on to
   2. Create triggers under PROPEL and PTRANS so that a subsequently created PROPEL or PTRANS will activate the demon.

sufficiently general so that it can account for a variety of causal chains. If we had specified an "Inside-of" relation, we would have had to create another demon with an "On-top-of" test to take care of cases like:

When John bumped into the table, the vase spilled.

Because both demons would be identical except for their tests, it makes more sense to consolidate them into one mechanism and leave the testing relation a little vague. To clarify the test, we could think of the dependence relation as being either "On-top-of" or "Inside-of." In the next section we assign a workable meaning to the general notion of dependence that is appropriate for this inference mechanism.

From Soup to Trains

In the last subsection, we outlined roughly what sort of causal mechanism is needed to understand that the train moving caused the soup to spill. But we have merely outlined the process. Now we ask precisely how such a device can be implemented. In particular, we decide what is meant by the nebulous dependency relation between objects.

In our example, we want to establish that the soup is in some sense dependent on the train. But how can this connection be made? In permanent memory there will be associative links connecting objects. For example, it is not unreasonable to have a link connecting a dining car to a train. But we cannot expect to find in memory a direct associative link connecting soup and trains. To get from soup to the train, we must construct a path of connecting links. In subsection 10.2-4, we discussed what that path might look like, but now we must specify how that path can be constructed. The computation that creates a path must be carefully constrained by context so that the proper connection can be made without constructing every possible associative path between soup and trains. It will not help to establish a path that envisions cases of soup being shipped in a freight train.

Before we can describe the mechanism that creates a path, we must know a little more about the associative links that exist between objects in permanent memory. In subsection 10.1-4, we saw how a wine bottle is described as a SOURCE with Output = wine. This description of a wine bottle effectively encodes an associative link from wine bottles to wine; if we examine the conceptual description of a wine bottle, we get to wine. But there should also be a link that will allow us to get from wine to wine bottles; the conceptual description of wine should lead us to a wine bottle in most contexts. In the same way, the GESTALT description of a table setting will take us to plates, but there should also be an associative link from plates to table settings. And the RELATIONAL description of a bulletin board will take us to thumbtacks, but another link is needed to get from thumbtacks to a bulletin board. Before inserting reciprocal links in memory, two restrictions must be observed.

1. Some associative links should operate in one direction only. For example, it is reasonable that a link should exist from dining cars to restaurants, because a dining car can easily be recognized as a type of restaurant. But it is not so clear that a link should exist from restaurants to dining cars. If asked to enumerate all the different kinds of restaurants, dining cars may not get included as an example.

2. Associative links may be present in some contexts but not in others. For example, in the context of eating at a table, it is reasonable that there should be a link from plates to table settings. But in the context of washing dishes, it is less likely that a plate will be perceived as part of a table setting. The organization of associative memory should be sensitive to context.

The first restriction prevents us from postulating associative links arbitrarily whenever a need for one seems to arise. The second restriction forces us to design contingencies in conceptual memory. In the same way that the context of a story sets priorities on word senses for the parser, the context of a story controls descriptions of objects in conceptual memory so that associative links between objects are contingent upon context.

There are four kinds of contingent links that can exist between objects outside of their Object Primitive descriptions. The type of link used in any given case is determined by the object being pointed to. The four links are:

1. Outputfrom (points to a SOURCE)
2. Inputto (points to a CONSUMER)
3. Partof (points to a GESTALT)
4. Defaultlocation (points to a RELATIONAL).

The conceptual definition of a prototypical object in memory may include one or more of these associative links, along with default or contingent values. A contingency in these cases is always described by either a SETTING or a script.

For example, the conceptual definition for soup describes a food that is Outputfrom a bowl during the eating script, and Outputfrom a can while in the SETTING of a kitchen or supermarket. It also has a Defaultlocation inside a pot during the prepare-food script. A bowl is described as a RELATIONAL object with Locationlink = Inside-of, and as a SOURCE object during the eating script with Output = food. It is also partof a place setting during the eating script, and it has a defaultlocation inside a cabinet when in the SETTING of a kitchen. In addition to the soup, conceptual descriptions for a place setting, table setting, table, dining area, dining car, train, and passenger train are also needed to establish a path from the soup to the train. In the following descriptions, the Configurations of GESTALT objects and some contingent links have been omitted because they are not crucial to the problem at hand.[6]

---

[6]In these descriptions "$" is used to denote a script. Contingent specifiers that are not preceded by a "$" are SETTINGs. The contingent links that do not appear specify scripts or SETTINGs that would not be active in the context of the spilled-soup problem. A few irrelevant links have been included, but not all.

[Soup
 <OUTPUTFROM   =   (a Bowl during $Eating)
                =   (a Can during Kitchen
                    during Supermarket)>]

[Bowl
   (a RELATIONAL with
   <Locationlink = Inside-of>)
   (a SOURCE during $Eating)
   <PARTOF = (a Place Setting during $Eating)>
   <DEFAULTLOCATION = (a Cabinet during Kitchen)>]

[Place Setting
   (a GESTALT with
   <Parts = Glass, Plate, Bowl, etc.>)
   <PARTOF = (a TableSetting)>]

[TableSetting
   (a GESTALT with
   <Parts = a PlaceSettings, TableCloth, etc.>)
   <DEFAULTLOCATION = (a table)>]

[Table
   (a RELATIONAL with
   <Locationlink = On-top-of>)
   <PARTOF = (a DiningArea during $Restaurant)>
   <DEFAULTLOCATION = (a Floor)>]

[Dining Area
   (a GESTALT with
   <Parts = (Tables, Chairs)>)
   (a SETTING with
   <Scripts = $Eating>)
   <PARTOF = (a Restaurant during $Restaurant)
          = (a House during House)>]

[DiningCar
   (a SETTING with
   <Scripts = ($Eating, $Restaurant)>
   <Settings = Passenger Train>)
   (a GESTALT with
   <Parts = (Kitchen, Dining Area, . . .)>)
   <PARTOF = (a Train during PassengerTrain)>]

[Train
   (a GESTALT with
   <Parts   =   (EngineCar, DiningCar, CoachCar, . . .
               during PassengerTrain)

$\qquad$ = (EngineCar, FreightCar, . . .
$\qquad \qquad$ during FreightTrain)
$\qquad$ = (EngineCar, CommuterCar, . . .
$\qquad \qquad$ during CommuterTrain)>)]

[Passenger Train
$\quad$ (a SETTING with
$\quad$ <Scripts = ($Train, $Trip)>]

These conceptual descriptions are used by our inference mechanism to construct a path from the soup to the train. Remember the original problem:

John was sitting in a dining car. When the train pulled out, the soup spilled.

As soon as the first sentence is parsed, the scripts associated with a dining car are triggered. These are the eating and restaurant scripts, which are found under the SETTING description of a dining car. The current context is set with the SETTING of a dining car and any other SETTINGs that are found under the SETTING description of the dining car. In this way, the current context picks up the SETTING of a passenger train in addition to the dining car SETTING. The conceptual parse of the second sentence produces two conceptualizations corresponding to (1) the train moving, and (2) the soup spilling:

(1) Train ⟺ PROPEL ⟵ Train

(2) NF$_1$ ⟺ [PROPEL/PTRANS ⟵ X$_2$

$\qquad \qquad$ result

$\qquad \qquad \qquad \qquad \qquad \qquad$ → Outside (X$_2$)

Soup ⟺ PROPEL ⟵ Soup ⟵

$\qquad \qquad \qquad \qquad \qquad \qquad$ ⟵ Inside (X$_2$)

When the causal antecedent of the second conceptualization is generated (NF$_1$ ⟺ [PROPEL/PTRANS] ⟵ X$_2$) the spilling demon described in subsection 10.2-4 is created. The spilling demon then searches the previous conceptualizations to see whether it can find something of the form:

$\qquad$ X ⟺ [PROPEL/PTRANS] ⟵ Y

When it finds that the conceptualization for the train's pulling itself satisfies this description, the spilling demon is triggered. It must then test to see whether the soup is "dependent" on the train. Now we can define what we mean by "dependent." For one object to be dependent on another in the sense that this demon requires, we must be able to construct a path of associative links between the two objects.

To begin the path, we start with the soup. Looking at the conceptual representation for soup, we see that there are two Outputfrom links from soup. One is contingent on the eating script, and the other is contingent upon the kitchen and supermarket SETTINGs. In the processing of our two sentences, a dining car was mentioned, thus adding the SETTING of a dining car to the immediate context. This SETTING in turn triggered the eating and restaurant scripts. So the only associative link from soup that exists in the context of our story is the link pointing to a bowl. We therefore infer that the soup comes from a bowl.

Soup (Outputfrom during $Restaurant) Bowl

Now we examine the conceptual representation for a bowl and find that it has an associative link contingent on the eating script. This link compels us to infer that the bowl is part of a place setting.

Bowl (Partof during $eating) Place Setting

The conceptual definition of a place setting gives us an associative link to a table setting. This is a default link that operates in any context.

PlaceSetting (Partof) TableSetting

The conceptual representation for a table setting specifies a default location on top of a table.

TableSetting (Defaultlocation) Table

Now when we look at the conceptual definition for a table, we see that there are two paths that could be followed. A table is part of a dining area during the restaurant script, but it also has a default location on a floor.

Table (Partof during $Restaurant) DiningArea
Table (Defaultlocation) Floor

If we follow the path out from a dining area, we get to a restaurant by a contingent Partof link. If we follow the path out from a floor, we get to a general room by a Partof link. Neither of these brances takes us to a train. In fact, both branches terminate at the concepts restaurant and room. In the current context, no associative links for either restaurants or rooms exist. But this does not mean that a connecting path does not exist. We have constructed a path starting from soup and followed it out as far as it will go. Now we must start from the conceptual representation for a train and see whether a path starting from a train will cross any of the concepts in the path generated from the soup.

When we went from the soup, we followed associative links between objects: Partof, Defaultlocation, Outputfrom, Inputto (the Inputto link did not arise in this example). Starting from the other direction, we follow only those links that are internal to an Object-Primitive description.

When we examine the conceptual representation for a train, we see that it is a GESTALT object whose parts are contingent on the particular type of train. The type of train we are dealing with is encoded under a SETTING constraint. In our current context, we are working within the SETTING of a passenger train. This SETTING tells us that the parts of the train are an engine car, a dining car, a coach car, perhaps a club car, and whatever other cars belong in a passenger train. So each of these parts begins a path leading from the concept of a train.

Train (with Parts during PassengerTrain)
    Engine, DiningCar, CoachCar, Clubcar, etc.

Now we must examine the conceptual representations for the engine car, the dining car, the coach car, and so forth. Each of these will be GESTALT objects with various parts. So if we assume that there are five parts to a passenger train and each of these has 10 parts of its own, then there would be 50 distinct paths starting with the train. The search from this end is growing exponentially, but it stops at the second node expansion. One of the parts of the dining car will be a dining area, and this node intersects with the path that was generated starting from the soup.

DiningCar (with a Part) DiningArea

The path is therefore completed; the spilling demon decides that the soup is "dependent" on the train; and the demon acts by placing the train as the actor in the causal antecedent for the spilled soup. The path just constructed also tells us that the container from which the soup spilled was a bowl.

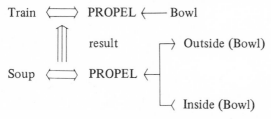

The path constructing mechanism used by this inference mechanism is reminiscent of the intersection searches that Quillian (1968) proposed in his semantic networks. But the use of a conceptual representation for objects and the notion of context-sensitive associations reduce the number of false leads dramatically.

In the path propagation originating from the soup, there are no multiple paths until the fifth generation of links. At that point the search leads to a dining area and to a floor. The search in this direction would then have two paths to follow in the sixth generation, both of which would terminate at the sixth generation. Coming from the other direction, the paths propagate exponentially, but it takes only two generations to make the intersection. In this heuristic, path propagation is always worse coming down than going up. The path generated from the bottom follows associative links that are tightly constrained by context. The path from the top is also constrained by context, but it will fan out whenever the parts of a GESTALT have to be traced, as was the case here.

One of the difficulties in implementing intersection searches is how to know when to quit and conclude there is no path. Quillian's formulation of an intersection search never specified how the search would know to give up. In our Object Primitive-based heuristic, it is feasible that paths generated from the bottom will terminate by themselves (as was the case here), and that path generation from the top could be effectively stopped after a fixed number of nodes had been touched or a fixed number of generations had been propagated.

By using associative networks that vary according to contextual constraints, the search space in an associative memory is greatly diminished. A search through associative links that is sensitive to context can be tightly directed and therefore avoid examining concepts completely irrelevant to the situation at hand. When someone is in a dining car and soup spills, there is no need for memory to be concerned with crates of soup in a freight car or cans of soup in a supermarket.

10.3 CONCLUSIONS

The system of Object Primitives presented here can be exploited in a variety of ways to handle many issues in knowledge representation. We have seen a few concrete applications of Object Primitives in the tasks of text understanding and question answering. Now we step back for a moment and look at Object Primitives from a more global viewpoint.

10.3-1 Theories of Human Memory

The literature of cognitive psychology is filled with theories of human memory. Information is not stored in memory in isolated bits and pieces; there appears to be a cohesive structure that connects everything according to some overall organization. Three "types" of memory are commonly recognized within the AI paradigm: semantic, episodic, and associative. Endel Tulving (1972) proposed a distinction between semantic and episodic memory. The work of Quillian (1968) is usually described as a model of semantic memory. The knowledge structures of scripts and plans (Schank & Abelson, 1977) are models of episodic memory. John Anderson and Gordon Bower (Anderson & Bower, 1973) have proposed a computational model of associative memory. As researchers in natural language processing, the key question we must ask when evaluating a theory of human memory is:

How can a proposed model of human memory
be used by processes
that understand and generate language?

This question defines a process model approach to the problem of understanding human memory organization.

In our formulation of Object Primitives, we are proposing an organizational structure of associative links, as well as a representational system. There are two fundamental differences between our model and the memory models of Quillian and of Anderson and Bower: (1) the use of contextually dynamic memory organization, and (2) primitive decomposition in the underlying representation. In the next two sections, we discuss the advantages of these features in terms of cognitive process models.

10.3-2   Contextually Dynamic Memory

Object-Primitive descriptions can be connected by contingent links that are sensitive to context. That is, an associative link may exist in one context, but not in another. In the context of a restaurant, there is an associative link between milk and drinking glasses. In the context of a store, milk is linked to a milk container. In the context of a dairy barn, milk is linked to cows. This means that the structural organization of memory is a dynamic system that alters itself as context changes.

From a processing point of view, contextual constraints are used to control searching strategies. The path generation described in subsection 10.2-5 exemplifies contextual control. The basic method is an intersection search (Quillian, 1968), but with one critical innovation. Intersection searches tend to grow exponentially and cover ground that should never be touched. In a sufficiently limited knowledge domain, this may not be an issue. But for a large knowledge base (as is needed for natural language processing), an exponential search strategy is not a feasible processing technique. Contextual constraints of the sort outlined in subsection 10.2-5 dictate a tightly controlled direction, which effectively renders the search blind to paths that cannot possibly work in the current context (e.g., finding soup being shipped in a freight train for the soup/train problem). Contextual control has been the key to a number of problems in parsing (Riesbeck, 1975; Riesbeck & Schank, 1976) an in inferencing (Schank & Abelson, 1977). It is therefore not surprising that contextually sensitive memory links should also be advantageous to theories of cognitive process.

The question "Where was the soup?" opened up an entire strategy for ex-amining associative links in memory. Locational Specification questions can tell us about the comparative strengths of associations in memory. Grice (1975) has hypothesized a set of conversational postulates that contain some basic rules of thumb. One of them is "Do not state the obvious." Although this is undeniably good advice, he offered no hints as to how one should go about determining the relative obviousness of things in any given situation. Here we have a representa-tional system that can reflect some relative strengths within associative links. A Partof association is a very strong link because it is usually independent of content and is therefore likely to be a very obvious association. A stereo set is expected to have speakers, an amplifier, and turntable or tapedeck no matter where it is found — in a home, store, or recreation center. A Defaultlocation link is more likely to be contingent on the current context and therefore less obvious in the sense of general associations. We can predict milk to be in a glass, a milk container, or a cow. But these predictions are dependent on SETTINGs like restaurants, stores, and dairy farms. Outputfrom and Inputto links are likely to be more obvious because they are less sensitive to context. Ice-cube trays are typically filled with water or ice, no matter where they are.

We have already seen how the relative strengths of these links can be exploited in memory retrieval. The locational-specification heuristic in subsection 10.2-4 is based on a preference for Output from and Defaultlocation links over Partof links. If we hypothesize that Outputfrom and Defaultlocation links are "less obvious" than Partof links, this would account for the naturalness of "In a bowl" and "On a table" as answers to "Where was the soup?" It seems promising that many memory phenomena may be explainable in terms of a model that is very fluid in its sensitivity to context. Although the specific links proposed here are totally intuitive and not supported by any psychological data, a model for asso-ciative memory constructed in terms of Object Primitives could readily accom-modate psychological data.

10.3-3 Primitive Decomposition — Why Do It?

When initially confronted with primitive decomposition as a theory of cognitive processing, a common reaction is "Why do all that work? — it seems like so much trouble." This impression results from a certain nearsightedness. When one be-gins to hypothesize specific mechanisms of inference and recognition, the advan-tages of a conceptual representation become apparent. But without this wider view of the processes we would like to account for, decomposition may indeed seem to be more trouble than it is worth.

There is one inference mechanism in COIL that is responsible for recognizing the enabling causality between the light being on and John reading. This same mechanism is responsible for establishing that the radio being on enables John's listening to music. The same mechanism could also find the enablement between a flashlight being on and John seeing, a car running and John smelling gas, and so on. The generality of this inference mechanism relies on the use of primitive descriptions of objects and acts. It looks for SOURCE objects and ATTEND acts.

Consider what would be needed if we did not have a level of conceptual description using primitives. Say that we tried to manipulate purely lexical entities like "light," "car," "radio," and so on. In this case, we would need a specific enablement-inference mechanism for each pair of words that can be related by enablement. This means that each time we add a new word to our vocabulary, we have to add a set of inference mechansims to cover that word. The number of inference mechanisms needed will grow linearly with the size of our vocabulary. This has a disastrous implication for theories of learning: The more words you know, the harder it is to learn a new one.

The semantic system proposed by Katz and Fodor (1964) is an example of an essentially lexical representational system. In their representation a dictionary definition for a word is a case-frame description with semantic markers constraining the entities that can appropriately fill a case slot. Case frames specify grammatical cases like "subject" and "object." Semantic markers are lexical descriptions like "higher animal," "physical object," "large," and aesthetic object." Projection rules are then responsible for checking semantic markers and making sure that words are being combined "legally."

There are a number of differences between the Katz and Fodor model of semantic representation and the representational system being proposed here.

1. Semantic markers are oriented toward finding legal word combinations, not toward representing the meaning of a sentence. Semantic markers have no way of recognizing that "John sold the book to Mary" and "Mary bought the book from John" are almost identical in meaning.

2. Semantic markers do not encode knowledge about concepts. There are no conceptual prototypes in the theory of semantic markers. A "ball" will have alternative definitions, such as "for the purpose of social dancing" or "having globular shape". These are standard dictionary descriptions that are necessarily circular and cannot reflect conceptual knowledge.

3. Semantic markers do not encode general knowledge about the world. A semantic-marker theory will find "The mouse chased the cat" just as acceptable as "The cat chased the mouse."

4. No theoretical structure is offered to describe what semantic markers exist or whether there is a taxonomy of markers. "Pretty" would be defined to modify things that are (Inanimate V ~ (Male)). The sense of "addled" that means "rotten" would have to take the marker (Egg). Conceptual features (inanimate, male, etc.) are being confused with associative links between words ("addled eggs").

5. Semantic markers were conceived for the task of determining whether a single isolated sentence is "grammatically acceptable" or potentially ambiguous. This task has little to do with the cognitive processes that understand and generate

memory representations for text. For example, there are no systems of inference based on semantic markers.

The major challenge facing a theory of natural language processing is the problem of inferences. When are what inferences made? Where do they come from? How are they used? We need a strong theory of human inference that operates on the level of conceptual manipulation. Any theory that is formalized in terms of lexical maniplulations is doomed to failure in a system with a large (the size of an adult human) vocabulary.

If we use primitive decomposition, we need only one inference mechansim for recognizing valid enablement causalities between SOURCEs and ATTENDs. We can add new words to the system, and the original inference mechanism will automatically extend to the concepts underlying these new words. The amount of work involved in learning a new word stays constant: All we need to do is to add a conceptual entry to the conceptual dictionaries for the parser and the generator. We do not need to add new inference mechanisms to make more inferences.

In the soup/train problem, we saw an example of an inference mechanism that operates on the level of conceptual representation: the spilling demon (see subsection 10.2-5). This one mechanism suffices to understand how soup can spill in a train, how coffee can spill in a car, how a vase can spill if someone walks into the table it is sitting on, how a bucket can spill if it is dropped, and innumerable other spilling situations. It would be impossible to achieve this sort of generality if we could not recognize conceptual entities like RELATIONAL objects, PROPEL, and PTRANS.

In the long run, primitive decomposition is a very effective and efficient way to encode information. If information is not manipulated on a conceptual level, the processes that must be devised will be extremely specific and nonextendible when the knowledge base is increased. Primitive decomposition provides a very powerful representational system because the processes that recognize and manipulate primitive descriptions will be general and extendible.

The use of Object Primitives in natural language processing is an area that deserves further attention. A number of interesting theoretical problems became apparent in the course of writing COIL. But an exploration of Object Primitives and their use in general inference mechanisms requires another book. The notion of Object Primitives was introduced here mainly to illustrate how easily one can move from problems in question answering to problems of memory representation. When question answering heuristics become terribly complicated, it may be that the memory representation is inadequate. When we tried to develop heuristics to answer "Where was the soup?" is was apparent that this answer could not be derived from our original memory representation. In this way, the question answering task provides a concrete criterion for judging the strengths and weaknesses of memory representations.

11 More Problems

11.0 PREFACE

In the last few chapters, we have examined problems in memory representation and retrieval heuristics, which are central issues in designing a question-answering model. In this chapter, we turn to some issues that are somewhat more peripheral. There are a number of lesser problems that must eventually be handled by any theory of question answering that claims to be complete. A few of these are outlined here.

11.1 CONSISTENCY CHECKS

There are different ways that questions can fail to make sense.

Q1: Why did John hit Mary?
A1a: Who's John?
A1b: But John *did* hit Mary.

**A question fails to make sense
whenever the processing of that question
breaks down for some reason.**

Processing failures can occur at different stages within the overall process model. If a question asks about John and the system does not know who John is, the interpretive processing of the question will break down during the internalization of the initial parse: No memory token for a human named John will be found. If a question asks why John hit Mary and the system does not know that John hit Mary, the processing will break down during the memory search: No answer key will be found for the question concept.

When people cannot answer a question because it does not make sense to them, they can identify what is wrong and respond accordingly. *A1a* and *A1b* are answers that respond to processing failures. These responses are generated by consistency-check routines.

Consistency checks are procedures embedded throughout the process model that generate appropriate responses whenever processing breaks down. There are consistency checks for interpretive breakdowns and failures within the memory search. Most consistency checks are passive and are triggered only when a question-answering process fails. For example, a causal-antecedent consistency check is passive, for it is triggered only if the matching search fails to find an answer key. This passive process would be responsible for objecting to "Why did John hit Mary?" when John had not hit Mary. But some consistency checks must be actively implemented. For example, an active consistency check for Expectational questions must be triggered whenever the question concept for an Expectational question is found in memory. "Why didn't John hit Mary?" makes no sense if John did hit Mary.

In the computer-program implementation of QUALM for SAM and PAM, priority was given to the successful processing of questions that make sense. Therefore no consistency-check heuristics have been implemented in QUALM. The design of consistency-check procedures is a problem whose solutions will naturally be derived from the processes designed to handle sensible questions. That is, if we understand how to answer all of the reasonable questions that can be asked of a story, then the additional processing needed for intelligent responses to unreasonable questions will be obvious and easy to add.

11.2   MODELING KNOWLEDGE STATES

In Chapter 9, we discussed retrieval-heuristic-based strategies for knowledge state assessment in question answering. But we limited our observations to what can be inferred from a single isolated question. In an actual question-answering dialogue, people keep track of the information communicated. People are not content to loop indefinitely:

Q: Who hit Mary?
A: John.
Q: Who hit Mary?
A: I just told you — John.

The impatience people experience when they are asked the same question twice is a by-produce of processes that build and check models of other people's knowledge states.

In coherent question-answering dialogues, questions are not answered in isolation. Answers to questions are produced in accordance with what has and has not been said before. In the question-answering dialogues that occur in courtrooms between a lawyer and a witness, the continuity of the questions asked and answers given in so tight that it is possible to see where the examination is heading; after a certain point we can predict what will be asked next (at least in dramatized courtroom dialogues). In the context of answering questions about stories, the continuity of a question-answering dialogue is not so important. Questions about stories are asked only for the purpose of demonstrating comprehension. The communication is therefore somewhat artificial (because the questioner knows the answers). But even in this situation we can feel disturbed by a lack of continuity:

John took a bus to New York. Then he took the subway to Leone's. He had lasagna. He took the bus back to New Haven.

Q1: How did John go to New Haven?
A1: By bus.

Q2: What did he eat?
A2: John ate lasagna.

Q3: Did John eat?
A3: Yes.

Q4: How did John go to New York?
A4: John went to New York by bus.

Q5: Did John go back to New Haven?
A5: Yes.

Q6: Where did John go?
A6: New York.

This dialogue seems to be lacking direction. The questioner appears to be totally ignorant of the answers given. People would not normally ask a question like "Did John eat?" immediately after hearing "John ate lasagna." The same questions could have been asked in a much more reasonably organized dialogue:

Q6: Where did John go?
A6: New York.

Q4: How did John go to New York?
A4: John went to New York by bus.

Q3: Did John eat?
A3: Yes.

Q2: What did he eat?
A2: John ate lasagna.

Q5: Did John go back to New Haven?
A5: Yes.

Q1: How did John go to New Haven?
A1: By bus.

The lack of continuity in the first dialogue and the apparent continuity of the second are due to a process of knowledge-state assessment. Whenever people answer questions, they try to keep track of what the questioner knows. That is, the answerer maintains a model of the questioner's knowledge state. Whenever a question is answered, the information communicated in that answer is incorporated into this model. If the questioner asks a question that violates our assessment of his knowledge state, we get impatient and wonder what is wrong.

Knowledge state assessment makes the difference between a system that mindlessly answers any question it hears and one that has some sense of when a question is or is not reasonable. Underlying all *Q/A* dialogues is an implicit principle:

> **Questions are asked to draw attention to**
> **gaps in the questioner's knowledge state;**
> **questions are answered to fill those gaps.**

This principle applies to all *Q/A* dialogues, including the more artificial ones in which the person answering must do so as though he were really supplying the questioner with missing information.

Some task domains that involve question-answering capabilities rely on a very sophisticated capacity for knowledge-state assessment. For example, a system that answers (or asks) questions in a teaching situation must have a very accurate sense of what the student does and does not know in order to be effective (Collins, 1976). A system that answers questions in the context of technical-information retrieval will be more effective if it knows how sophisticated the questioner's knowledge state is. When a question is answered on a level that is either too far above or below the questioner's level of competence, the answer will fail to communicate information.

In many cases inferences about someone's knowledge state are made on the basis of what that person has said. If you ask me whether all Lebesgue-integrable functions are Riemann-integrable, I will assume from your question that you know something about integration theory. More inferences are made on the basis of what I have said to you. For example, if I tell you that not all Lebesgue-integrable functions are Riemann-integrable, I might reasonably expect you to remember that and to know it from then on. So alterations of knowledge state models can be made anytime anybody says anything in a *Q/A* dialogue.

In QUALM we proposed that a last MLOC update (LMU) be maintained as a minimal processing technique for knowledge state assessment (see subsection

4.1-3). The LMU is a simple device for maintaining conversational continuity, and it is an intuitively valid idea because people must surely remember the conceptual content of their last statement. It is invalid insofar as it stops short of seriously modeling a memory representation for conversations. People must have memory structures of conversation that are maintained for at least some period of time. But precisely what this memory representation looks like and how it is related to the problem of knowledge state assessment is very difficult to say.

Knowledge state assessment is closely related to theories of conversation, overall memory organization, and issues of short-term versus long-term memory. Even very simple minded notions of knowledge state models run into severe difficulties in terms of representation and overwriting. For example, suppose we wanted to create a short-term knowledge state model for a given conversation. We won't even worry about integrating the information in this short-term memory structure into a more permanent memory structure. The simplest structure we can propose is a list of concepts. Suppose that every time a concept is communicated to Mary by John, John adds that concept to his knowledge state list model for Mary. Even in this short-term memory model, we run into problems of updating. Consider the following dialogue:

Mary: Does Susan live in New York?
John: No.
Mary: Where does she live?
John: She lives in Washington.

The following entries must be made in John's MLOC model for Mary:

1. Susan does not live in New York.
2. Susan lives in Washington.

We have a duplication of information here. If Mary knows that Susan lives in Washington, it is useless to maintain a conceptualization that encodes the fact that Mary knows Susan does not live in New York. But this reduction is possible only if a memory process of some sort determines that living in New York and living in Washington are mutually exclusive possibilities.

Suppose that we could update the list model to eliminate redundancies. Then we would have a knowledge state model that encodes the knowledge Mary acquired in the course of the conversation, but no trace is present in this model of Mary's previous knowledge states. After this dialogue, John should be able to conclude that Mary did not know where Susan lived before he told her (unless he has some reason to believe she has been deceiving him). Her first question indicated that Mary had some reason to believe that Susan might live in New York. If this is important to John or if it is surprising to him, he is likely to remember that Mary thought Susan lived in New York. A knowledge state model that records only those concepts communicated by the person maintaining the model, and that eliminates redundant communications, will not be adequate for representing previous knowledge states that can be inferred from a question. This raises another issue.

Should a complete running history of Mary's knowledge states be maintained? If not, how much information about previous knowledge states should be kept? Which information? What is really going on here is much more complicated than keeping lists. John is likely to remember that Mary thought Susan lived in New York only if this fact is significantly or unexpected. To determine whether a given piece of information is significant or unexpected, a lot of memory interaction must be taking place with John's long-term memory in order to pick out inconsistencies and surprises. Much more has to be known about overall memory structures and integrative processes before problems of this magnitude can be tackled in a serious manner.

11.3 CONVERSATION THEORY

Question-answering dialogues are a form of conversation. There are rules of conversational structure that are used to arrive at correct interpretations and appropriate responses. The conversational continuity rules described in Chapter 4 deal with very simple phenomena in conversation. To get some idea of how much more complicated conversational structure can be, let's look at an example of nested question-answering dialogue:

Mary: Do you know anyone who can referee some papers before August?
John: Is Bill Sand going to be around this summer?
Mary: Who?
John: Don't you know the members of the editorial board?
Mary: Yes, but that name isn't familiar.
John: I think he just joined. He's a new member.
Mary: No, I don't think he is.
John: Then we can't ask him.

In this conversation Mary disagrees with John about Bill Sand's being a member of the editorial board. John seems to give in to her opinion about the matter, and says something that indicates they should not ask anyone outside of the editorial board to referee papers. The critical juncture in this conversation occurs when John says "I think he just joined. He's a new member," at which point Mary says "No, I don't think he is." Conversational continuity forces us to interpret Mary's statement as a reply to John. Mary seems to be saying that she does not think there is a new member of the editorial board named Bill Sand. John's final reply, "Then we can't ask him," is also interpreted in terms of the preceding reply. John seems to be saying that if the person he is thinking of is not a member of the editorial board, then they cannot ask him to referee papers.

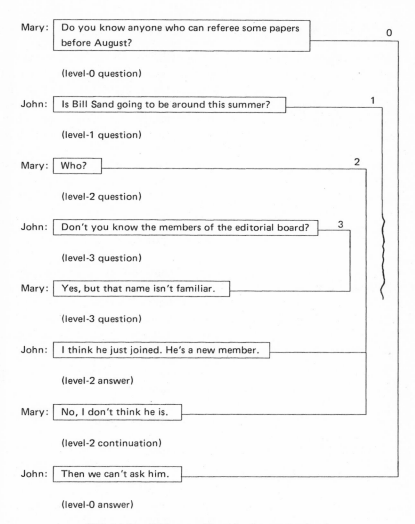

FIG. 11.1. Dialogue without level-recovery signal.

The conversation makes sense as it stands, and there does not seem to be any confusion about what is being said. But now look what happends when one small alteration is made:

Mary: Do you know anyone who can referee some papers before August?
John: Is Bill Sand going to be around this summer?
Mary: Who?

John: Don't you know the members of the editorial board?
Mary: Yes, but that name isn't familiar.
John: I think he just joined. He's a new member.
Mary: Oh yes, now I know who you mean. No, I don't think he is.
John: Then we can't ask him.

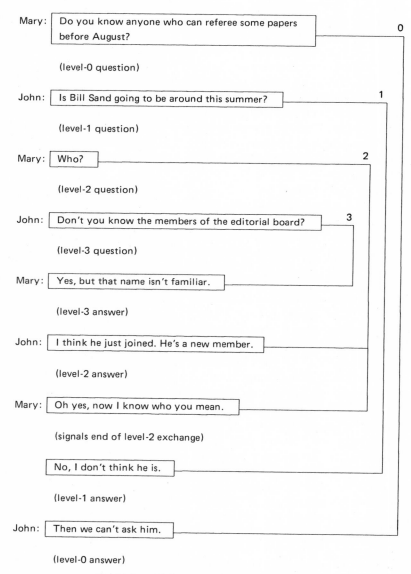

Fig. 11.2.   Dialogue with level-recovery signal.

The only change is an addition to Mary's last statement, "Oh yes, now I know who you mean." This declaration acts as a signal to tell John that she is resuming a suspended exchange. Without this signal, her next statement, "No, I don't think he is," is interpreted as a response to John's "I think he just joined. He's a new member." But with the added signal, "Oh yes, now I know who you mean," "No, I don't think he is" is interpreted as a reply to the earlier suspended question, "Is Bill Sand going to be around this summer?" The signal is critical here because the nesting of processes is three deep. People can recover from one level without signals to establish a return to the next, but when more than one level has to be recovered, clues must be supplied to help the transitions.

Without a theory of conversational structures, it is impossible to recognize when a question-answering exchange is being dropped, suspended, or resumed. Questions and answers are merely units of communication within larger conversational exchanges. These exchanges are themselves subject to structural laws of combination, which include nesting phenomena. Complete conceptual processing for question-answering dialogue must be sensitive to these larger units of conversational structure.

11.4 WHAT EVERY LAWYER SHOULD KNOW

In a sophisticated model of memory representation, a story representation will evolve over time and be subject to various interference and blocking factors. Bartlett's famous experiments with "The War of the Ghosts" (1932) investigated some of the ways in which memory representations deteriorate and change over time. Factors other than time can also affect memory.

In a study by Elizabeth Loftus (1975), subjects were shown a movie of a sports car driving down a country road. After the movie the subjects were asked a series of questions. One group was asked, "How fast was the car going down the country road?" The other group was asked, "How fast was the car going when it passed the barn driving down the country road?" (No barn appeared in the film.) One week later, subjects were again asked questions about the movie, but without a second viewing. One of the questions at this subsequent session was "Did you see a barn?" Only 2.7% of the first group answered yes, but 17.3% of the second group answered yes.

This suggests that memory representations or retrieval mechanisms can be altered by the questions that access them. In areas where a memory representation is weak or uncertain, concepts presupposed in a question can be incorporated into the memory representation. This incorporation could occur either by revising the story representation or by setting up detours for retrieval mechanisms. Presuppositions must be checked against the story representation and, in the event that no contradiction is found, new information could be added to the story representation or short circuits could be set up to a more recent and slightly altered story representation generated at the time of a question-answering dialogue.

11.5 GENERAL Q/A

QUALM has been implemented in the task domain of answering questions about stories. But the strategies of conceptual categorization, inferential analysis, and elaboration options are also needed for a theory of general Q/A. All of the specific interpretive rules and content specification options outlined in this thesis are applicable to general Q/A. For example:

Q1: Do you want a drink?
A1: No thanks, I have to drive home.

A1 results from an application of the Correction/Explanation option. The elaboration in *A1* answers the Expectational question "Why don't you want a drink?"

Conversational scripts are knowledge structures for specific conversational contexts. If a Q/A dialogue is embedded in a sufficiently stereotypic conversational context, these knowledge structures will guide the interpretive processing of a question. For example, a stockbroker talking to a client will understand:

Q2: When did you sell?

to be a question about the selling price, not the time of the transaction. Stereotypic situations and relationships often provide specific predictions about what a question really means.

Theories of inference and of knowledge state assessment will enable inferential analysis to understand what a questioner is really asking when a Q/A dialogue occurs in the context of nonstereotypic goal-oriented behavior. For example, if John and Mary are camping out and are about to cook dinner, the following exchange could occur:

John: Will you go down to the river?
Mary: I think there's enough here.

Knowledge of general goals and plans is needed to understand that *Q3* is asking, "Will you go down to the river (to get some water [for dinner])?" Then *A3* can be understood — "I think there's enough (water) here (for dinner)." If Mary did not know that John wants water, that he wants it for dinner, and that the river is where you go to get water, then she could not have responded as she did.

The inferences needed to understand questions in general goal-oriented situations are identical with those needed to comprehend text when a story describes goal-oriented behavior. If we heard:

John needed to go down to the river before he could start dinner.

we would have to use the knowledge of scripts and plans to understand how going to the river can be causally related to preparing dinner. In the context of camping out, water exists in rivers, you frequently need water to prepare food, if you do not have something you need you must get it, and if something you need exists elsewhere you can go there to get it. This knowledge needed to understand causal connections in general text is identical with the knowledge needed to carry on general *Q/A* dialogues.

12 Perspective and Conclusions

12.0 PREFACE

The theory of question answering proposed by QUALM is essentially one of natural language processing. This natural language perspective distinguishes QUALM from many other question-answering systems that are motivated by information retrieval or automatic theorem proving. Many systems that attempt to answer questions phrased in natural language have been designed in two pieces: (1) a memory retrieval system, and (2) a natural language interface. Very often the interface problem is considered secondary to the retrieval system, and the two subsystems are designed as if they were theoretically independent of each other.

The question-answering system based on QUALM can likewise be decomposed into memory retrieval (QUALM per se) and natural language interface (parsing and generation). But in QUALM, this division distinguishes language-dependent cognitive processes from those that are purely conceptual and independent of language. The theory of QUALM extends theories of cognitive processing that originated with the study of conceptual memory (Schank, 1975a), parsing (Riesbeck, 1975), and generation (Goldman, 1975). QUALM therefore rests on a foundation of ideas in conceptual information processing. This orientation constitutes a fundamental departure from information retrieval and other viewpoints in which natural language processing is treated as merely a "front end" for question-answering systems.

12.1 OTHER Q/A SYSTEMS

A number of question-answering systems have been designed over the last 20 years. We do not attempt to review here all of the research in computational question answering. But it might be useful to compare QUALM with some of the more recent question-answering systems in order to clarify comparative strengths and weaknesses. The reader who is not familiar with the systems discussed here should refer to the references cited for a complete description of these research efforts.

12.1-1 Winograd (SHRDLU)

SHRDLU (Winograd, 1972) was well publicized as the first computer program to understand English. The program's world knowledge was limited to a blocks world; SHRDLU simulated robotic manipulation of blocks on a table top. It could respond to requests (Please put the red pyramid on the blue block) and inquiries (Where is the red pyramid?).

From a theoretical viewpoint, Winograd presented SHRDLU as a program based on "procedural representation of knowledge" (Winograd, 1975). Winograd maintains that the knowledge needed for a natural language processing system can be represented as procedures within that system. In SHRDLU, the understanding of "Please pick up the block" consists of executing a procedure that simulates picking up the block. This approach to knowledge representation is strongly dependent on the task domain Winograd chose for SHRDLU.

In a performative domain (like the blocks world), procedural representation may seem appropriate. But when language is understood in nonperformative contexts, procedural representations fail to make sense. Story understanding is one context in which procedural understanding is not adequate. Suppose that a story understanding system hears that John loved Mary but Mary did not want to marry him. What procedure is the understanding system supposed to execute to indicate that it understood? The knowledge needed to manipulate blocks does not extend to domains in which knowledge about human motives and intentionality is needed.

The question-answering techniques used by SHRDLU are also limited by the task domain of the system. For example, when SHRDLU answers a why- or how-question, it consults a goal stack that was generated as a history of the system's manipulations. Why-questions are answered by finding the question concept in the goal stack and pushing the stack; how-questions are answered by finding the question concept and popping the stack. Although this heuristic works in any domain where we are interested in purely procedural manipulations, it does not work in domains where some goals are more significant than others, and when goals are not the only causal antecedents for events.

Why did John wash dishes at Leone's?

is a question with answers that describe causal antecedents but not goals:

He couldn't pay the check.
He had no money.
He was pickpocketed.

Even when a goal-oriented answer is appropriate, some answers derived from a goal tree are poor because they do not take into account inferences that the questioner can make for himself:

Why did John get on his horse?
So he could ride it.

This is an exasperating answer that would result from simply pushing the goal stack. Some selection heuristic is needed to produce a better answer:

Why did John get on his horse?
So he could be close to Mary.

SHRDLU was a very impressive system, for it was the first interactive computer program that responded to English input. But the theories of memory representation underlying SHRDLU have not been extended beyond its original task domain. The crucial role of knowledge representation in natural language processing has become widely recognized in recent years. But at the time SHRDLU was written, most researchers were still sorting out the real issues in natural language processing.

12.1-2 Woods (LSNLIS)

LSNLIS (Woods, Kaplan, & Nash-Webber, 1972) was a prototype natural language query system designed for accessing a large data base of technical information about the moon rock samples collected during the Apollo 11 mission. The parser for LSNLIS is an augmented transition network that maps English questions into a parse tree. Semantic processing then translates the syntactic parse tree into a semantic meaning representation. The semantic representation for a question is actually a program expression that is directly executed for memory retrieval.

The memory representations and semantic processes used in LSNLIS were largely adequate for the technical data the system was designed to access. But there are weaknesses in the system's retrieval heuristics and semantic interpretation (Nash-Webber, 1976). For example, in order to answer:

Do all breccias contain lanthanum?

LSNLIS successively enumerates the breccias and tests each one to see whether it contains lanthanum. If all of them do, the answer is yes. But if the data base were organized to include information like:

All samples contain every element.
Breccias are samples.
Lanthanum is an element.

then a deduction process would be able to answer yes without testing each breccia sample. This problem of how to use a deductive process instead of a generate and test strategy is typical of question answering issues when a task domain involves technical descriptive information.

The question-answering techniques developed for QUALM were not designed for technical information retrieval. It appears that technical information must be handled differently from essentially conceptual information. For example, in a technical domain it is appropriate to be concerned with deductive processes (where "deduction" describes the generation of predicates that must be correct). But in nontechnical domains, processes of inference (where "inference" describes the generation of assumptions that may be wrong) are more useful than deductive processes. We have seen how answers to questions can be correct and still be terrible answers (see Chapters 1, 4, 7, 10). Purely deductive processes that are sensitive only to the truth values of propositions cannot evaluate whether a correct answer is also an appropriate one. The question-answering problems that arise in a system like LSNLIS have very little in common with problems that arise in the context of story understanding. It is therefore useful to differentiate technical information processing from conceptual information processing.

It is too early at this stage to predict how technical and conceptual processing strategies relate to each other and precisely where the boundaries of their knowledge domains lie. A rough distinction may be made in terms of the following test: If the information encoded in a system is the sort that a single person (with a good memory) could be expected to remember, then the information is conceptual. Otherwise, it is technical. Using this guideline, stories from a weekly news magazine would belong in a conceptual information processing system, while the results of 13,000 chemical analyses belong in a technical information processing system.

12.1-3 Waltz (PLANES)

The PLANES system (Waltz, 1977) is another query system that accesses a large data base of technical information. The data base for PLANES contains information about naval aircraft maintenance and flight data. It appears to be similar to LSNLIS except that the initial parse bypasses a syntactic parse tree representation in favor of a paraphrase expression of canonical phrases. This paraphrase is then fed back to the user for confirmation before an interpretive phase maps the paraphrase into a formal query language expression, which is directly executed for memory retrieval.

Both LSNLIS and PLANES are examples of systems aimed at practical implementation in a relatively narrow knowledge domain. Design issues that would be critical for a more general system are not encountered when the task domain is sufficiently restricted. For example, relatively few words and virtually no sentences in the PLANES world are ambiguous. This simplifies parsing strategies and removes any need for inferential analysis or knowledge-based interpretation of the sort found in QUALM. The whole issue of context-sensitive interpretation can be ignored when a system is designed to operate in one context only.

PLANES claims to be a data-independent system. This means that the language front end of the system would not have to be substantially altered to accommodate an extended data base or a new record-based data base that is suitably constrained. (The primary alterations would be the addition of new vocabulary.) On the other hand, the data-accessing programs in PLANES would have to be substantially modified for a new data base with retrieval functions specific to that data base. The generality of PLANES is therefore defined by the type of data it accesses.

Although it is difficult to make direct comparisons between strategies for conceptual-information processing and those for technical-information processing, there might be a comparison in terms of relative generality. If we draw a parallel between data bases and individual stories, then a story-understanding system that has to alter its question-answering techniques for each new story is analogous to a data-base query system that has to alter its question-answering techniques for each new data base.

QUALM has been implemented to function with story-understanding systems that process stories according to theories of script and plan application. QUALM can answer questions about any story that has been understood in terms of scripts and plans. This means that new scripts can be added to SAM to increase its knowledge base, and QUALM will be able to answer questions about stories using these new scripts without any modifications.

Because scripts and plans describe general knowledge structures, any process that relies on general properties of scripts and plans will not be affected by the addition of new scripts and plans. QUALM is designed for memory representations generated by script- and plan-based story understanding systems. This gives QUALM a very powerful generality in the context of story understanding. Scripts and plans describe an extensive amount of knowledge used in text comprehension. Insofar as we can predict what scripts and plans look like in general, QUALM can be confidently applied to stories using new scripts and plans regardless of their specific knowledge content.

When a script-based retrieval technique (see Chapter 6) is required, a new script necessitates a modification to QUALM. But even then this modification is general in the sense that it will accommodate any story understood by that script. Although script- and plan-specific modifications may be required, at no time should we make a story-specific modification to QUALM.

The PLANES system has been implemented with only one data base, and it does not try to substantiate claims about its generality. QUALM was originally implemented when SAM had three scripts in its data base. SAM is currently running with a total of 24 scripts, and no changes to QUALM have been necessary for stories based on these new scripts.

12.1-4   Scragg (LUIGI)

LUIGI (Scragg, 1975) simulates stereotypic food preparation routines within the setting of a kitchen in order to answer questions like these:

What utensils would I need if I toasted bread?
How do you make cookies?

When LUIGI receives a question, it accesses the appropriate routine (toasting bread or making cookies) and simulates the process specified. When the simulation has provided the appropriate information, the question is answered.

The theory of knowledge representation underlying LUIGI is a theory of what Scragg calls rote-oriented knowledge. From all his descriptions, rote-oriented knowledge appears to be identical with our formulation of scripts. The basic difference between LUIGI and QUALM is that LUIGI answers questions about rote-oriented procedures (scriptal activities) as a general information system, while QUALM answers questions about stories. That is, LUIGI will answer general questions about its knowledge domain; QUALM expects questions to be about some story that has been processed. LUIGI is not a story-understanding system, but Scragg has suggested that rote-oriented knowledge could be used for inferencing during story understanding in the same way that SAM applies scripts during understanding to generate inferences (Scragg, 1975).

The simulation processing that LUIGI implements corresponds to the proposed processing of Judgmental questions in QUALM. Judgmental questions require the questioner to make a projection about what is likely to happen on the basis of general world knowledge. What we would call a projected script instantiation, Scragg calls a process simulation. Although Scragg has described the details of processing Judgmental questions more completely than we have. QUALM covers more ground that LUIGI in terms of an overall theory. QUALM is a more comprehensive theory of question answering, because LUIGI handles only 2 of the 13 conceptual question categories that QUALM processes (Judgmental and Instrumental Procedural). Because of this task limitation, Scragg has not developed any processing theory that corresponds to QUALM's conceptual categorization, inferential analysis, or content specification.

12.1-5   Bobrow (GUS)

GUS (Bobrow et al., 1977) is an interactive dialogue program designed to assume the role of a travel agent in a goal-oriented conversation with a client. GUS is composed of interactive modules: a morphological analyzer, syntactic analyzer, the frame reasoner, and the language generator. The frame-reasoner component of the system has received the focus of research efforts in GUS. The notion of a frame in GUS is consistent with Minsky's (1975) general formulation of frames as prototypical template structures that can be instantiated to represent specific instances of events or entities.

GUS uses its system of travel-related frames to direct dialogue and instantiate memory representations for what it is told. For example, a date frame contains slots that can be filled specifying the month, day, year, and weekday. Other frames used by the system include person, city, placestay, timerange, flight and tripspecification frames. When GUS initiates a dialogue with a client, the system asks questions in an attempt to instantiate all of its frames with information provided by the client or inferred by the system. One type of inference made by GUS is generated by default assignments for certain frame fillers. For example, the "homeport" slot in the tripspecification frame is never requested by GUS. This slot is automatically filled with a default assignment of Palo Alto (GUS is based in Palo Alto) unless the client specifies otherwise.

GUS is concerned with question answering from a perspective slightly different than QUALM's. GUS is concerned with asking questions and understanding answers, whereas QUALM is concerned with understanding questions and producing answers. Despite this difference in perspective, the notion of a knowledge-specific frame system of the type used by GUS corresponds to conversational scripts in QUALM's inferential analysis (see Chapter 4).

In QUALM these predictive knowledge structures for specific conversational contexts were proposed as interpretive mechanisms for contextual understanding. In GUS these same knowledge structures are proposed as control structures that can drive dialogue by using the notion of procedural attachment (Winograd, 1975; Bobrow & Winograd, 1977). GUS is concerned with implementing one specific conversational frame system, while QUALM is interested in characterizing conversational scripts as a general knowledge structure that can organize contextual knowledge for question-answering dialogues in a variety of contexts.

The design for frame-driven dialogues proposed by GUS appears to be a promising start for mixed-initiative conversation programs. GUS is still in its developmental stages. The strengths and weaknesses of its final implementation should be an instructive contribution toward a theory of conversational dialogue.

12.2 SUMMARY

The computational model of question answering proposed by QUALM is a theory of conceptual information processing based on models of human-memory organization. It has been developed from the perspective of natural-language processing in conjunction with story-understanding systems. In the design of QUALM, the following claims about question answering have been made:

1. The processes that are specific to question answering are independent of language. This means that QUALM can operate with a parser or generator for any language without modifications to QUALM.

2. Questions can be understood on many levels of conceptual interpretation.

3. The level of detail inherent in a question can be determined at the time of

memory search; at this time, retrieval heuristics can answer the question on a level of detail appropriate to the question.

4. It is more useful to describe answers in terms of their appropriateness than of their truth value alone. (An answer may be technically correct and still be a terrible answer.)

5. Retrieval heuristics and memory representations are two sides of the same coin. The question-answering task provides concrete criteria for judging the strength of a memory representation.

6. In the context of story understanding, some questions can be answered only by accessing expectations aroused at the time the story was initially read. These expectations can be reconstructed by integrating general world knowledge with the story representation.

7. A strong taxonomy of inference based on a process model of memory will have to be developed before any general claims can be made about which inferences are made at the time of (story) understanding and which inferences are made at the time of question answering.

The ideas behind QUALM span a wide range of research areas within the field of natural language processing. To formulate a theory of question answering, we have been forced to confront problems in memory representation, parsing, conceptual inference, memory retrieval, knowledge structures in memory, knowledge state assessment, conversational rules and generation. There are few areas within natural language processing that are not directly related to question answering in some way. Q/A is also a natural task criterion for any language processing system that claims to understand text, or for any knowledge-based system that claims to be knowledgeable.

Q/A is therefore at the center of natural language processing, both in terms of the natural language theory needed for question answering and in terms of the natural language systems that can be tested by question-answering tasks. A complete theory of natural language processing must account for question-answering phenomena. Conversely, a theory of question answering cannot be developed in isolation of natural language processing issues. Most of the research in computational question answering has treated question answering as an information retrieval problem that requires natural language processing only as a front end interface. QUALM is a theory of question answering that is founded on and extends theories of natural language and conceptual information processing.

References

Anderson, J. R., & Bower, J. G. *Human associative memory.* New York: Wiley, 1973.

Bartlett, R. *Remembering: A study in experimental and social psychology.* London: Cambridge University Press, 1932.

Bobrow, D. G., Kaplan, R., Kay, M., Norman, D., Thompson, H., & Winograd, T. GUS, a frame-driven dialog system. *Artificial Intelligence,* April 1977, *8* (2).

Bobrow, D. G., & Winograd, T. An overview of KRL, a knowledge representation language. *Cognitive Science,* 1977, *1,* 3—46.

Bower, G. H. *Comprehending and recalling stories.* Div. 3 Presidential Address, American Psychological Association, Washington, September, 6, 1976.

Bransford, J. D., & Franks, J. J. The abstraction of linguistic ideas. *Cognitive Psychology,* 1971, *2,* 331—350.

Carbonell, J. *Ideological belief system simulation.* New Haven: Department of Computer Science, Yale University, 1977.

Charniak, E. *Towards a model of children's story comprehension.* Unpublished master's thesis (AITR-266), M.I.T., 1972.

Charniak, E. Organization and inference in a frame-like system of common knowledge. *Proceedings from Theoretical Issues in Natural Language Processing,* Cambridge, Mass., 1975. (a)

Charniak, E. A partial taxonomy of knowledge about actions. *Proceedings of the Fourth International Joint Conference on Artificial Intelligence,* Tbilisi, USSR, 1975. (b)

Collins, A. Processes in acquiring knowledge. In J. R. Anderson, R. J. Spiro, & W. E. Montague (Eds.), *Schooling and the acquisition of knowledge.* Hillsdale, N.J.: Lawrence Erlbaum Associates, 1976.

Cullingford, R. E. An approach to the representation of mundane world knowledge: The generation and management of situational scripts. *American Journal of Computational Linguistics,* 1975. (Microfiche No. 44)

Cullingford, R. E. The uses of world knowledge in text understanding. *Proceedings of the Sixth International Conference on Computational Linguistics,* Ottawa, Canada, 1976.

Cullingford, R. E. *Script application: Computer understanding of newspaper stories* (Research Rep. No. 116). Department of Computer Science, Yale University, 1978.

DeJong, G. F. *Skimming newspaper stories by computer* (Research Rep. No. 104). New Haven: Department of Computer Science, Yale University, 1977.

Feigenbaum, E. A. The simulation of verbal learning behavior. In E. A. Feigenbaum & J. A. Feldman (Eds.), *Computers and thought*. New York: McGraw-Hill, 1963.

Goldman, N. M. Conceptual generation. In R. C. Shank (Ed.), *Conceptual information processing*. Amsterdam: North-Holland, 1975.

Grice, H. P. In D. A. Norman & D. E. Rumelhart (Eds.), *Explorations in cognition*. San Francisco: Freeman, 1975.

Katz, J., & Fodor, J. The structure of a semantic theory. In J. Katz & J. Fodor (Eds.), *The structure of language*. Englewood Cliffs, N.J.: Prentice-Hall, 1964.

Lehnert, W. Human and computational question answering. *Cognitive Science*, 1977, *1*(1), 47–63.

Loftus, E. F. Leading questions and the eyewitness report. *Cognitive Psychology*, 1975, *7*, 560–572.

Minsky, M. A framework for representing knowledge. In P. H. Winston (Ed.), *The psychology of computer vision*. New York: McGraw-Hill, 1975.

Nash-Webber, B. *Semantic interpretation revisited* (A.I. Report No. 48). Boston: Bolt Beranek and Newman, 1976.

Norman, D. *Memory, knowledge, and the answering of questions*. San Diego: Center for Human Information Processing, University of California, 1972. (Memo CHIP-25)

Quillian, M. R. Semantic memory. In M. Minsky (Ed.), *Semantic information processing*. Cambridge, Mass.: M.I.T. Press, 1968.

Rieger, C. Conceptual memory. In R. C. Schank (Ed.), *Conceptual information processing*. Amsterdam: North-Holland, 1975. (a)

Rieger, C. The commonsense algorithm as a basis for computer models of human memory, inference, belief and contextual language comprehension. *Proceedings from Theoretical Issues in Natural Language Processing*, Cambridge, Mass., 1975. (b)

Riesbeck, C. Conceptual analysis. In R. C. Schank (Ed.), *Conceptual information processing*. Amsterdam: North-Holland, 1975.

Riesbeck, C. & Schank, R. *Comprehension by computer: Expectation-based analysis of sentences in context* (Research Rep. No. 78). New Haven: Department of Computer Science, Yale University, 1976.

Schank, R. C. Conceptual dependency: A theory of natural language understanding. *Cognitive Psychology*, 1972, *3*(4), 552–631.

Schank, R. C. *Causality and reasoning* (Tech. Rep. No. 1). Castagnola, Switzerland: Istituto per gli Studi Semantici e Cognitivi, 1973. (a)

Schank, R. C. Identification of conceptualizations underlying natural language. In R. C. Schank & K. M. Colby (Eds.), *Computer models of thought and language*. San Francisco: Freeman, 1973. (b)

Schank, R. C. Adverbs and belief. *Lingua*, 1974, *33*(1), 45–67. (a)

Schank, R. C. *Understanding paragraphs* (Tech. Rep. No. 6). Castagnola, Switzerland: Istituto per gli Studi Semantic e Cognitivi, 1974. (b)

Schank, R. C. *Conceptual information processing*. Amsterdam: North-Holland, 1975. (a)

Schank, R. C. The structure of episodes in memory. In D. G. Bobrow & A. Collins (Eds.), *Representation and understanding: Studies in cognitive science*. New York: Academic Press, 1975. (b)

Schank, R. C., & Abelson, R. P. Scripts, plans, and knowledge. *Proceedings of the Fourth International Joint Conference on Artificial Intelligence*, Tbilisi, USSR, 1975.

Schank, R. C., & Abelson, R. P. *Scripts, plans, goals and understanding*. Hillsdale, N.J.: Lawrence Erlbaum Associates, 1977.

Schank, R. C., & Colby, K. M. *Computer models of thought and language*. San Francisco: Freeman, 1973.

Schank, R. C., & Yale A. I. Project. *SAM – A story understander* (Research Rep. No. 43). New Haven: Department of Computer Science, Yale University, 1975.

Scragg, G. W. Answering questions about processes. In D. A. Norman & D. E. Rumelhart (Eds.), *Explorations in cognition.* San Francisco: Freeman, 1975.

Selfridge, O. Pandemonium: A paradigm for learning. In D. V. Blake & A. M. Uttley (Eds.), *Proceedings of the Symposium on Mechanisation of Thought Processes.* London: H. M. Stationary Office, 1959.

Shortliffe, E. H. *MYCIN: A rule-based computer program for advising physicians regarding antimicrobial therapy selection.* Stanford, Cal.: Stanford Artificial Intelligence Laboratory, Stanford University, 1974. (Memo-AIM251)

Tulving, E. Episodic and semantic memory. In E. Tulving & W. Donaldson (Eds.), *Organization of memory.* New York: Academic Press, 1972.

Waltz, D. *An English language question answering system for a large relational data base.* Urbana, Ill.: Coordinated Science Library, University of Illinois, 1977. (Submitted to the Communications of the ACM)

Wilensky, R. Using plans to understand natural language. *Proceedings of the Annual Conference of the ACM,* Houston, Texas, 1976.

Wilks, Y. *De minimis, or the archaeology of frames.* Edinburgh, Scotland: Department of Artificial Intelligence, University of Edinburgh, 1976.

Winograd, T. *Understanding natural language.* New York: Academic Press, 1972.

Winograd, T. Frame representations and the declarative-procedural controversy. In D. G. Bobrow & A. Collins (Eds.), *Representation and understanding.* New York: Academic Press, 1975.

Woods, W. A., Kaplan, R. M., & Nash-Webber, B. The lunar sciences natural language information system: Final report. BBN Report No. 2378, Bolt Beranek and Newman, Inc. Cambridge, Mass., June 1972.

Author Index

Subject Index

DATE DUE

AUG 05 1983			